Opening the World of Learning™

A COMPREHENSIVE EARLY LITERACY PROGRAM

Teacher's Guide
Unit 2 Friends

Judy Schickedanz, Ph.D.
David Dickinson, Ed.D.

in collaboration with
Charlotte-Mecklenburg Schools

PEARSON EARLY LEARNING
Pearson Learning Group

T 41562

C0-AKC-795

The following people have contributed to the development of this product:

Art and Design: Stephen Barth, Sherri Hieber-Day, David Mager, Judy Mahoney, Elbaliz Mendez, Jim O'Shea, Dan Trush, Jennifer Visco, Heather Wendt Kemp

Editorial: Diane Arnell, Danielle Camaleri, Teri Crawford Jones, Jaime Dritt, Deborah Eaton, Mary Lou Mackin, Susan Poskanzer

Marketing: Diane Bradley, Laura Egan

Production/Manufacturing: Karen Edmonds, Nathan Kinney, Jennifer McCormack

Publishing Operations: Carolyn Coyle, Richetta Lobban

Photographs: All photography © Pearson Education Inc. (PEI) unless otherwise specifically noted.

3: © Ariel Skelley/Corbis. 5: *t.l.* Judy Schickedanz; *r.* Nancy Pearce/Charlotte-Mecklenburg Schools; *b.l.* Stephen Vedder, MTS, Boston College; 19, 26, 32, 33, 38, 39, 45, 48, 63, 64, 70, 71, 76, 77, 84, 95, 102, 103, 111, 116, 117, 122, 123, 141, 145, 152, 156: *b.* © Steve Gorton/DK Images.

Acknowledgments

In grateful acknowledgment to Alice Klein, Ph.D., and Prentice Starkey, Ph.D., who have selected activities from the Pre-K Mathematics Curriculum for use in *Opening the World of Learning*™. The Pre-K Mathematics Curriculum is scientifically-research based, and was developed and field-tested over eight years. Math Activity Aids previously published in PRE-K MATHEMATICS CURRICULUM by Klein, Starkey, and Ramirez, copyright © 2002 by Pearson Education, Inc.

Contributing Writers: Annmarie Blaney, Molly Collins, Cynthia Hoisington, Ann B. Morse, Danielle J. Pazos

"Clap Your Hands" Copyright © 1948 by Ruth Crawford Seeger. Used by permission.

The Little Red Hen (Makes a Pizza) retold by Philemon Sturges. Illustrated by Amy Walrod. Text © 1999 Philemon Sturges. Illustrations © 1999 Amy Walrod. Published by the Penguin Group.

A Letter to Amy by Ezra Jack Keats. © 1968 Ezra Jack Keats. Published by the Penguin Group.

Matthew and Tilly by Rebecca C. Jones. Illustrated by Beth Peck. Text © 1991 Rebecca C. Jones. Illustrations © 1991 Beth Peck. Published by the Penguin Group.

Dandelion by Don Freeman. © 1964 Don Freeman. Published by the Penguin Group.

Hooray, a Piñata! by Elisa Kleven. © 1996 Elisa Kleven. Published by the Penguin Group.

Use of the trademarks and copyrights listed below implies no relationship, sponsorship, endorsement, sale, or promotion on the part of Pearson Education.

DUPLO™ is a trademark of the LEGO Group.

KAPLA© is copyrighted by Kapla World.

Lauri® is a registered trademark of Learning for All Ages.

ISBN 1-57212-748-1

Printed in the United States of America

2 3 4 5 6 7 8 9 10   08 07 06 05 04

Opening the World of Learning™ is a trademark of Pearson Education, Inc.

Pearson Early Learning

Pearson Learning Group

1-800-321-3106
www.pearsonlearning.com
www.pearsonearlylearning.com

CONTENTS

To preschoolers, friendship means playing together. ▶

UNIT 2 Introduction

LC-P
Pa16
2005
prek
bg
V.2

A Comprehensive Program

Opening the World of Learning™ (**OWL**) is a comprehensive early literacy program designed for use with preschoolers. Teachers of young children have long known preschoolers are eager learners. Recent research has made abundantly clear that, for many children, these years hold the key to children's later academic success and social adjustment. *OWL* works to tap the learning capacities of all children during these critical early years.

Skills-Based Learning

OWL offers teachers the detailed guidance required to implement a comprehensive preschool program. The research-based activities contained in the Teacher's Guides foster children's learning in all content areas. The activities also build the personal and social skills required to function well in a classroom community and to establish positive relationships with peers and adults. *OWL* builds these early academic and social skills by

- enabling teachers to use strategies consistent with current research to teach all of the concepts and skills associated with oral language and literacy, including those that use and systematically support "learning code," such as alphabet knowledge, early writing, and phonemic awareness.

- supporting language skills throughout the day, as teachers are helped to identify and reinforce vocabulary and to strengthen conversation skills.

- building children's mathematical knowledge across the full range of concepts and skills identified by research as a foundation to later mathematical competence, including number concepts, basic computation, geometry, and measurement.

- addressing standards in a variety of content areas.

- providing a range of opportunities for children to develop the social skills required in a variety of settings.

- offering activities that help children become aware of their feelings and those of others.

- encouraging the practice of social skills and skills helpful for regulating behavior in the face of strong emotions.

- supporting children's sense of competence, curiosity, and creativity through experiences that involve creative exploration, discovery, and imaginative play.

- providing children with many opportunities to experience success, as a consequence of individual effort and through guided practice in contexts where adults provide necessary scaffolding.

Effective teaching of young children is a highly complex activity, and teachers in most settings have far too little time to plan curriculum, think carefully about the intricacies of instruction, and gather and construct materials. *Opening the World of Learning*™ provides teachers with richly interconnected sets of experiences that appeal to children and ensure learning of the academic, personal, and interpersonal skills essential for school success.

Meet the Authors

Judy Schickedanz is a Professor of Literacy/Language and Cultural Studies in the School of Education at Boston University. She received her Ph.D. at the University of Illinois at Urbana-Champaign. She served as director of the Laboratory Preschool and coordinator of the early childhood program at Boston University. She has worked with a wide range of preschool programs. Dr. Schickedanz served as past president of the Literacy Development in Young Children Special Interest Group of the International Reading Association (IRA). She also served as a member of the Teaching Resources Team for NAEYC's accreditation standards revision in 2004. Dr. Schickedanz is the senior author of several books, including *Much More Than the ABCs, Understanding Children and Adolescents,* and *Writing in the Preschool: Orchestrating Meaning and Marks.*

David Dickinson is a Professor of Language and Literacy at the Lynch School of Education, Boston College. He received his doctoral training at Harvard's Graduate School of Education after working as an elementary school teacher in the Philadelphia area for five years. For twenty years he has studied language and early literacy development among low-income populations and developed and studied varied approaches to helping preschool teachers more effectively support children's language and literacy growth. He has served on many national advisory panels, including serving as a commissioner to NAEYC helping it to revise its program accreditation standards. Dr. Dickinson is the author of numerous research articles and book chapters and has edited or co-edited four books: *The Handbook of Early Literacy Research* (Volumes 1 and 2), *Beginning Literacy With Language,* and *Bridges to Literacy.*

The **Charlotte-Mecklenburg Schools,** Charlotte, North Carolina, are pioneers in the implementation of a literacy-based curriculum designed to lay the foundation for early school success. They continue to participate in the scientific research and assist in creating the professional development materials for *Opening the World of Learning™.*

Charlotte-Mecklenburg Schools

UNIT 2 Overview

Theme: Friends

In Unit 2, children will be talking about friendship, how to be a good friend, and ways to resolve conflicts with friends. Through the Story Time books, children will hear about the importance of being who you are, helping friends, enjoying special times together, and getting along. In addition to listening to stories, children will learn to identify rhyming words and beginning letters and sounds in words, as they build vocabulary and comprehension skills. They will also participate in a variety of music, poetry, math, science, and art activities.

Theme Concepts

- A friend is someone we like and want to spend time with. Friends like to do things together. They enjoy each other's company.
- We can have more than one good friend, and we might like to do some things with one friend and other things with other friends.
- Friends usually share with and help one another.
- Friends may have arguments and get mad at one another. Usually, friends work out their problems and continue to be friends.
- We can make new friends and also keep old friends.

UNIT SKILLS

Language and Literacy
- Engages in conversation and uses language to enter into play situations and to develop relationships
- Tells a personal narrative
- Uses language to resolve conflicts
- Follows two-step directions, and builds up to multiple-step directions
- Listens to/attends to several turns in a conversation
- Responds to verbal cues from a partner in dramatic play
- Identifies different kinds of texts
- Recognizes own name; names all the letters in own name; writes own name, using good approximations of letters needed
- Names the main characters when asked, "Who is in this story?"; recalls some main events when asked, "What happens in this story?"
- Uses own experiences to understand story events and expository text and characters' feelings and motivations
- Recites songs, rhymes, and poems
- Links characters' basic emotions to their actions

- Finds words with the same beginning sound; segments the beginning sounds in words
- Substitutes sounds to create new words

Social Studies
- Demonstrates an emerging awareness and respect for culture and ethnicity, and for abilities
- Becomes aware of the roles, responsibilities, and services provided by community workers
- Discusses the various kinds of work people do
- Discusses and dramatizes wants and needs, and develops understanding of their relationship to producing/consuming and buying/selling

Science
- Observes, explores, and asks questions about materials and objects in the environment; displays familiarity with the properties and behaviors of many kinds of materials
- Demonstrates and explains the safe and proper use of tools, equipment, and materials
- Makes comparisons among objects

Mathematics
- Counts accurately up to ten objects in a set using one-to-one correspondence
- Begins adding and subtracting to solve multi-step story problems using concrete objects

- Uses one-to-one correspondence to equally divide a set of objects
- Indicates the position of objects or people in a line (first, second, third) and refers to the order of steps in a process (first, second, third)
- Sorts objects into subgroups by attributes

Social and Emotional Development
- Follows rules and routines
- Initiates interaction with other children
- Interacts with other children by cooperating, helping, sharing, and expressing interest
- Begins to recognize and express own emotions using words rather than actions

The Arts
- Sings and listens to songs with repetitive phrases and rhythmic patterns
- Explores and experiments with wet and dry media to create artwork
- Creates two- and three-dimensional artwork

Physical Development
- Performs fine-motor tasks that require small-muscle strength and control
- Builds finger dexterity and uses thumb/forefinger in pincer grasp

Unit Components

Story Time Books

Predictable Books

Songs and Poems CD

Picture Cards

Information Book

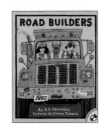

Language and Literacy Assessment Book

Big Book of Poetry

OTHER THEME-RELATED BOOKS

Beil, Karen Magnuson (author) and Paul Meisel (illustrator). *A Cake All for Me!* New York: Holiday House, 1998.
Simple predictable text about a pig who shares his cake with some friends.

Freeman, Don. *Beady Bear.* New York: Puffin Books, 1977.
Moderately difficult text about a boy and his friend, a wind-up bear.

Havill, Juanita (author) and Anne Sibley O'Brien (illustrator). *Jamaica's Find.* Boston: Houghton Mifflin Company, 1993.
Jamaica finds a stuffed dog at a playground. When she returns the toy, she makes a new friend.

Hutchins, Pat. *The Doorbell Rang.* New York: HarperCollins Children's Book Group, 1986.
Simple and predictable text about children who share their cookies with visitors.

Lionni, Leo. *It's Mine!* New York: Knopf Books for Young Readers, 1986.
Moderately difficult text about bickering frogs who at first will not share, but later become friends.

Shelby, Anne (author) and Irene Trivas (illustrator). *Potluck.* New York: Orchard Books, 1991.
Simple text about friends who bring their own unique dishes to a potluck dinner.

UNIT 2 Materials and Resources

To help you plan the unit on friends, here is a list of the basic materials for Center Time and Small Group activities. Many of these materials can be used for other units as well. You often use these materials every day, and they can be recycled for use in the activities. If appropriate, you might want to involve families in helping you gather materials.

Beautiful Junk

Ask parents, friends, or local retail or business office staff to save materials for you.

Cardboard boxes and lids (many sizes)
Empty food containers (soup, cereal, milk, pasta)
Empty toiletry containers (toothpaste, shampoo, lotion)
Paper and plastic grocery bags
Small plastic lids (coffee cans, nut containers)
Paper plates
Aluminum foil
Paper napkins
Paper towels
Empty plastic spice-type bottles with holes in lid for shaking out contents
Grocery store advertisements/flyers
Business advertisement signs (bakery, deli, restaurant)
Trays (polystyrene foam trays with and without divided sections, plastic cafeteria trays)
Small metal cans
Masking tape
Plastic crates

Paper, Tag Board, Stickers

Card weight paper (8 1/2" × 11")
Colored tissue paper (primary colors, secondary colors)
Construction paper (12" × 18" and 9" × 12"; 18" × 24"; 3 packages of each in primary colors, secondary colors, brown, white and black)
Newsprint (for painting activities)
Tag board (manila or white; 9" × 12" and 12" × 18"; 2 packages of each)
Black poster board
Variety of self-adhesive stickers (round and square)
White photocopy paper
White drawing paper (1 ream)
Chart paper
Colored acetate paper

Writing/Drawing/Painting/Collage Materials

Chalk (dust free)
Crayons, markers, pencils, pens
Short dowel rods
Craft sticks
Paint cups (for easel)
Paintbrushes for glue; wooden paintbrushes for easels (various widths)
Plastic paint palettes
Ink stamps (shapes, pictures, letters)
Smocks
Sponges
Easel
Washable tempera paint, primary colors, white and black (4 one-gallon containers of each)
White glue
Glue sticks
Scissors
Clipboards
Shiny materials (sequins, beads)
Ribbons, braided rope, or string
Cotton balls
Buttons

Water/Sand Table Supplies

Liquid dishwashing soap
Pots, pans, dishes
Plastic dishwashing tubs to hold water
Smocks
Sponges
Sand
Variety of molds (gelatin, funnels, measuring cups, melon ball scoops, plastic egg halves, small muffin tins, mini cake tins, mini letter molds)
Spray bottle
Small rocks/gravel (small bag)
Plastic construction vehicles (dump truck, bulldozer, backhoe, roller)
Small shovels or metal spoons
Short dowel rods
Small plastic cars and trucks

Dramatic Play Area

Basic kitchen props
Empty dish detergent bottles
Dish towels
Various pots and pans (cookie sheet, muffin pan, loaf and cake pans)
Paper with "Grocery Store List" printed at the top
Grocery store advertisements
Purses
Wallets
Dress-up clothing (jackets, sweaters)
Play money
Coupons

Writing Center

Ink pads
Upper- and lowercase ink stamps
Stationery
Envelopes
Disposable flash camera
Card-weight paper
Plastic sleeves (photo size)
Audiotape recorder and blank tape
Fancy ink pens
Printed friendship words

Puzzles/Manipulatives Area

Lacing cards
Puzzles: fruits and vegetables, alphabet
Word and picture cards (Unit 2 story words)
Name cards (children's names)
Upper- and lowercase letter tiles
Memory cards (uppercase alphabet, name, Unit 2 storybook pictures)
Large block letters (printed with a computer)
Self-fastening materials
Beads, string, counting objects

Blocks Area

Basic unit blocks
Dollhouse furniture
Small blocks
Small plastic dogs and cats
Construction blocks that snap together
Plastic fruits and vegetables
Cash register
Baskets or play shopping carts (3–4)

Book Area

Information books about music, musical instruments, grocery stores (with photographs), piñatas, Mexican celebrations, road construction and construction vehicles
Children's cookbooks
Simple storybooks, predictable books, alphabet books
Nursery rhymes

Mathematics

Activity Aids 7, 8, 9, 10
Toy cash register
Coins (pennies, nickels, dimes, quarters)
$1 and $5 bills
Stencils for writing numbers
Story mat
Calendar
Screwdriver
Paper towel tubes
Empty tissue boxes

WEEKLY MATERIALS

The following materials are organized by week and are used with specific activities.

Week One

Medium and large bowls (plastic, wooden, metal)

Wooden and metal spoons

Thick plastic bags

Sheets of rubber

Elastic bands

Clear plastic sheeting (designed for table coverings)

Plastic deli containers (quart-size)

Real or toy drum

Various pans (sheet, layer, angel food cake pan, springform; frying pan, bread pan, pizza pan, tart pan, cupcake/muffin)

Printed party invitations (birthday party, wedding)

Pizza dough

White flour

Activity Aids 7, 8

Week Two

Sink mats

Ridged edges of plastic packaging (from colored sticker labels)

Plastic kitchen shelf lining

Fall leaves

Corduroy fabric

Pieces of textured wallpaper

Pennies, nickels, dimes, quarters

$1 and $5 bills

Story mat

Stencils for writing numbers

Week Three

Clay dough (2 batches)

Hot pads

Kitchen timer

Baking items (cookie cutters, rolling pins, pancake turners)

Small shallow dishes

Plastic pizza slicers

Empty shaker-top jars (e.g., grated-cheese containers)

Pennies, nickels, dimes, quarters

$1 and $5 bills

Calendar

Screwdriver

Paper towel tubes

Empty tissue boxes

Printed invitations (birthday party, wedding)

Week Four

Several medium-size plastic bowls

Large mixing bowl

Large plastic pitcher

Lemons (4)

Long handled spoon

Measuring cup (clear, plastic)

Sweetener (honey, maple syrup, sugar)

Plastic juice squeezer (optional)

Store flyers with piñata photos

Piñatas (3 pull string types)

Small treats or toys to stuff piñatas

Activity Aids 9, 10

Plates

Scissors

Bowl

SUGGESTED SUPPLIERS

Lakeshore Learning Materials, 800-778-4456

Discount School Supply, wooden doll families, 800-627-2829

Constructive Playthings, DUPLO™ people, 800-448-4115

Creative Educational Surplus, 800-886-6428

Lauri® Puzzles, 800-451-0520

Kaplaworld.com

Weekly Planner*

	Day 1	Day 2	Day 3
Start-the-Day Centers 30 Minutes **Morning Meeting** 15 Minutes **Center Time** 60 Minutes pp. 12–14	Greet children and open selected Centers. Introduce Center Time activities. **Blocks:** Family Figures, Dollhouse Furniture, Families in a Neighborhood; **Sand and Water:** Washing Dishes; **Dramatic Play:** Washing Dishes and Inviting Friends Over to Play; **Book Area:** Exploring Books; **Art Area/Table:** Making Bowl Drums and Making Stationery; **Art Area/Easel:** Pizza Paintings; **Puzzles and Manipulatives:** Puzzles, Counting Objects, Stringing Beads; **Writing Center:** Writing on Handmade Stationery		
Toileting and Snack 15 Minutes			
Story Time 20 Minutes	**1st Reading** – *The Little Red Hen (Makes a Pizza)* pp. 19–22	**2nd Reading** – *The Little Red Hen (Makes a Pizza)* pp. 26–29	**1st Reading** – *A Letter to Amy* pp. 33–35
Outdoor Play 35 Minutes	**Conversations:** Observe for new friendships; comment to children.	**Conversations:** Note children's motor skills; compliment or support as needed.	**Conversations:** Watch for children helping others. Comment and help each child explain how he or she felt.
Songs, Word Play, Letters 20 Minutes	**Songs:** "If You're Happy"; "Eentsy, Weentsy Spider"; "Five Green and Speckled Frogs"; "Five Little Ducks" **Poems:** "Five Juicy Apples"; "Diddle, Diddle, Dumpling" **Literacy Skills:** If Your Name Starts With [name a letter], Raise Your Hand pp. 23–24	**Songs:** "Down by the Bay"; "If You're Happy"; "Come On and Join In to the Game" **Poems:** "Five Juicy Apples"; "Ten Little Fingers" **Literacy Skills:** Chiming in With Rhyming Words; Those Words Begin With the Same Sound!; Let's Clap Our Names pp. 30–31	**Songs:** "Five Little Ducks"; "Down by the Bay"; "Head and Shoulders, Knees and Toes" **Predictable Book:** *HUSH!* **Literacy Skills:** Chiming in With Rhyming Words; Let's Clap Our Names pp. 36–37
Handwashing/Toileting 10 Minutes			
Lunch/Quiet Time/ Center Time 90 Minutes	**Conversations:** *What makes someone a friend?* Guide discussion; consider if you stay friends if you play with someone else.	**Conversations:** *What kind of food do we have today?* Name foods and their categories. Consider the value of different kinds of food.	**Conversations:** *Little Red Hen wanted help. Have you helped friends do things?* Support recall by noting helpful behaviors you have noted.
Small Groups 25 Minutes pp. 15–17	**Science:** Exploring Pizza Dough **Writing:** Friendship Pictures **Book Browsing:** Exploring Books	**Science:** Exploring Pizza Dough **Writing:** Friendship Pictures **Book Browsing:** Exploring Books	**Science:** Exploring Pizza Dough **Writing:** Friendship Pictures **Book Browsing:** Exploring Books
Let's Find Out About It/Let's Talk About It 20 Minutes	**Social Skills Development: Joining in Play** p. 25	**Making Musical Instruments** p. 32	**Exploring Stationery and Invitations** p. 38
End-the-Day Centers 20 Minutes	Open selected Centers and prepare children to go home.		

*This is a suggested schedule. Adapt to meet the needs of your program.

2nd Reading - *A Letter to Amy* pp. 39–41	**3rd Reading -** *The Little Red Hen (Makes a Pizza)* p. 45 Reread *Peter's Chair* or *Whistle for Willie.*
Conversations: Watch for counting opportunities (hops, times down slide, rungs on the ladder). Count with children.	**Conversations:** Observe for when a child is having a hard time doing something. Help label feelings (*frustrated, annoyed*).
Songs: "Old MacDonald Had a Farm"; "Come On In and Join In to the Game"; "The Wheels on the Bus" **Poems:** "Five Little Owls in an Old Elm Tree"; "Five Juicy Apples" **Literacy Skills:** If Your Name Starts With [name a letter], Raise Your Hand pp. 42–43	**Songs:** "Five Green and Speckled Frogs"; "Come On and Join In to the Game"; "Open, Shut Them" **Predictable Book:** *HUSH!* **Literacy Skills:** Chiming in With Rhyming Words; If Your Name Starts With [first sound in child's name], Raise Your Hand; Guess What Word I'm Saying pp. 46–47
Conversations: *Let's count how many people are at our table.* Encourage counting of varied items on the table.	**Conversations:** *Peter was afraid Amy would not come to his party. Have you been disappointed?* Guide recall; tell a story of your own.
Math: How Many Dinosaurs? **Language & Print Manipulatives:** Simple Puzzles of Fruits and Vegetables, Alphabet Letter Tiles and Storybook Word Cards **Games:** Uppercase Alphabet Memory, Children's Names Memory	**Math:** How Many Dinosaurs? **Language & Print Manipulatives:** Simple Puzzles of Fruits and Vegetables, Alphabet Letter Tiles and Storybook Word Cards **Games:** Uppercase Alphabet Memory, Children's Names Memory
Understanding Feelings: Anticipation of Disappointment p. 44	**Exploring Cooking Pans** p. 48

Half-Day Program Schedule

2 hours 45 minutes

A half-day program includes two literacy circles.

10 min.	**Start-the-Day Centers** Writing Center, Book Area, Puzzles and Manipulatives
10 min.	**Morning Meeting**
60 min.	**Center Time** Include mathematics and science activities from Small Groups. Incorporate Small Groups writing activities at Writing Centers.
20 min.	**Story Time** Use discussion questions from Let's Talk About It to address social-emotional issues and topics from Let's Find Out About It to address concept development.
35 min.	**Outdoor Play**
20 min.	**Songs, Word Play, Letters**
10 min.	**End-the-Day Centers** Writing Center, Book Area, Puzzles and Manipulatives

Connect With Families

- Tell parents that you will be talking about friendship in the classroom. Encourage them to talk with their children about what they played at school, and with whom. Parents might be able to arrange for their child to invite another child in the class to come play.

- If a child has an upcoming play date, suggest that parents talk with the child to plan which toys will be shared and which might need to be put away.

- Give parents a list of empty food cartons that they might contribute to the upcoming grocery store play.

Start-the-Day Centers

- Open two to three Centers (e.g., Puzzles and Manipulatives, Book Area, Writing Center) for children to go to upon their arrival. Spend time with children in the Centers, helping as appropriate and as time allows.

Morning Meeting

- Introduce children to Centers by showing some selected objects from each Center and briefly demonstrating activities to help them make a first choice.

- For example, **Monday:** demonstrate squeezing a wet sponge to make suds at the water table. To show Making Bowl Drums, secure a piece of a plastic bag over the top of a bowl with a rubber band. **Tuesday:** For Pizza Paintings, use red paint on a piece of paper and suggest that it might be tomato sauce and stick some yellow bits of tissue paper onto the red paint, and suggest it might be cheese. **Thursday:** Show examples of paper and cards that children can decorate for stationery in the Art Area. **Friday:** Show examples of decorated stationery that is now in the Writing Center. Explain that they may use the stationery they made, or others made, to write letters and cards. Select other items to show and demonstrate on all mornings.

- Use suggested vocabulary for each Center as you demonstrate activities in a manner that clarifies their meaning for children.

- You might want to modify or substitute an activity to meet your children's needs. For more information on Center Time activities, see the Notes to Teachers on page 49.

▲ Making Stationery

SAND AND WATER

Washing Dishes

Purposes: Observes and explores materials and objects, in the environment. Practices strategies for promoting cleanliness.

Materials: sponges, pots, pans, dishes, liquid dish soap

Suggested Vocabulary: bowl, bubbles, glass, liquid, pan, plate, pot, soap, sponge; clean, pour, rub, wash

- Comment as children play with the materials, that they remind you how the friends in *The Little Red Hen (Makes a Pizza)* washed the dishes.

- Engage children in conversation about their actions. You might say, *Look! When you swish your hand in the water, you get more bubbles.* Or, *Are you washing dishes from breakfast? What kind of food bits are you washing off the dishes?*

- Join play occasionally to model use of materials. For example, *I'm using my sponge to rub the inside of this pot, to make it really clean.*

- Encourage experimentation. You might say, *Oh, a lot of water came out when you squeezed the sponge! What happens when you put it back in the water?*

12

BOOK AREA

Exploring Books

Purposes: Independently chooses to read or to pretend to read books. Understands that pictures, print, and other symbols carry meaning.

Materials: a variety of picture books—storybooks, information books, nursery rhymes

- By now the Book Area will have 25–30 books. Children look at books together, or independently, as they wish.

- Join children for brief periods. Read aloud portions of books if children ask you to. Comment about what they're reading. For example, *Yes, Daniel comes home and says, "Oonga Boonga." What happens then?* Have children continue their retelling.

ART AREA: TABLE

Making Bowl Drums

Purposes: Listens to sounds and sound patterns. Plays simple musical instruments independently and with a group. Follows two-step directions.

Materials: medium and large plastic, metal, and wooden bowls, quart plastic deli containers, strong elastic bands, craft sticks, stickers, markers, pens, short lengths of dowel rods, wooden and metal spoons, thick plastic bags, brown paper shopping bags, sheets of rubber, clear plastic sheeting designed for table coverings

Preparation: Cut panels out of plastic bags and brown shopping bags. Vary sizes to fit over the openings of different-size bowls and plastic containers.

Suggested Vocabulary: drum, musical instrument, rhythm; high, loud, low, quiet, tight; beat, tap

- Remind children about the musical instruments in *The Little Red Hen (Makes a Pizza), Oonga Boonga!,* and *Let's Make Music* as they make their bowl drums.

- Assist those who need it. For example, show a child how to place the plastic bag over the bowl and pull tightly on the edges. Suggest he or she tap the drum and see if making the bag tighter makes the sound deeper. Then see if it makes the same sound as your big drum.

- Encourage children to listen to one anothers' drums.

Making Stationery

Purposes: Uses basic shapes and forms of different sizes to create artwork. Explores and experiments with wet and dry media in a variety of colors. Names letters in their own name.

Materials: 2–3 types of paper (e.g., folded cards, 8 1/2" × 11", smaller sheets), 2 cafeteria trays, 3 small trays for ink stamps (geometric shapes and pictures), 3–6 small polystyrene foam trays, paper towels, markers

Preparation: Put layers of paper toweling on trays to create inking pads. Soak pads with liquid tempera. On some pieces of paper, mark off a 1 1/2" border to indicate where decorations might be placed. Leave others blank. Fold some pieces of heavier paper to make cards. Put paper, shape, and picture stamps on trays within reach of children. Have children wear smocks and put wet paper towels for hand wiping at each place.

Suggested Vocabulary: border, corners, decoration, design, edge, initials, letter, stamp, stationery; bottom, inside, top; print

- Comment that Peter used plain paper to write Amy's invitation in *A Letter to Amy* (if children have heard the story), but sometimes people like to use decorated paper, or stationery.

- Comment about their stationery. You might say, *I see you used the little dog stamps on the corners and markers on the inside of your card.*

- Place finished stationery in Writing Center for later in the week.

ART AREA: EASEL

Pizza Paintings

Purposes: Creates two-dimensional artwork. Explores and experiments with basic shapes and lines in artwork. Builds finger dexterity and uses thumb/forefinger in pincer grasp.

Materials: paint cups, tempera paint (red, green, yellow, black, and blue), 1 large and 4 small easel brushes, large circles of brown construction paper or brown construction paper in its original rectangular shape, bits of yellow and green tissue paper, smocks, easel

Suggested Vocabulary: crust, pan, pizza, pizza pie, sauce, toppings, color names; rectangular, round

- Prompt children to talk about their paintings. You might say, *Tell me about your pizza. It looks delicious.* Or, *That green topping looks yummy. What is it?*

- Encourage children to write their names on paintings. Help with letter formation if they ask. Accept any marks that children create.

Continued on next page

BLOCKS

Family Figures, Dollhouse Furniture, Families in a Neighborhood

SOCIAL STUDIES

Purposes: Engages in socio-dramatic play. Identifies common features in the home. Begins to understand various family structures. Approaches tasks with inventiveness.

Materials: basic unit blocks, dollhouse furniture; small blocks; masking tape; small plastic dogs and cats

Suggested Vocabulary: apartment, bathroom, bedroom, home, house, kitchen, playground, boy, girl, family, aunt, brother, cousin, father, grandfather, grandmother, mother, sister, uncle, friend, neighbor, neighborhood

- Observe children as they explore blocks and use furniture and family figures. You might say, *That's a tall apartment building! Who lives inside?*
- Show children how to make chairs and sofas using masking tape to connect small blocks.
- Comment that it looks like a neighborhood if several children are building separate houses for people.
- Encourage children to share materials fairly, and devise systems that help them (e.g., turns list, equal division of items to start).

PUZZLES AND MANIPULATIVES

Puzzles, Counting Objects, Stringing Beads

Purposes: Observes and explores materials. Performs fine-motor tasks that require small-muscle and control. Makes comparisons among objects.

Materials: Add new puzzles, beads, string, and counting objects to center.

Suggested Vocabulary: beads, necklace, puzzles, string, color names; wooden, pointed, round, straight, same, next to, outside, part of, plastic; count

- Help children who are struggling with puzzles identify where a piece might be placed. As a hint you might ask, *What color piece goes next to this one?* Or, *That piece has a round edge.*
- Encourage children to count (quietly) as they play with materials. For example, *How many buttons do you have in your bowl?* If a child makes errors, scaffold the counting. You might say, *I think there might be more than 5. Let's count together and find out.*
- Ask children to describe their creations. For example, *I see you are using three different beads. I see a yellow sphere first, and then a blue cube,* etc. Scaffold the child's descriptions of the next few beads.

DRAMATIC PLAY

Washing Dishes and Inviting Friends Over to Play

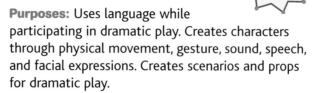
SOCIAL STUDIES

Purposes: Uses language while participating in dramatic play. Creates characters through physical movement, gesture, sound, speech, and facial expressions. Creates scenarios and props for dramatic play.

Materials: basic kitchen props, empty dish detergent bottles, various pots and pans (e.g., cookie sheet, muffin pan, loaf and cake pans), dish towels

Suggested Vocabulary: cake, dish towel, pan, pot, sink, soap, sponge, stove; bake, brush, cook, dry, wash

- Make connections to baking a cake in *A Letter to Amy* or washing dishes in *The Little Red Hen (Makes a Pizza)* as children play freely with the kitchen props.
- Engage children in conversations about their play. You might say, *What are you cooking today? It sure smells delicious!* Or, *You have so many dishes to wash. Did you have a party? Tell me about it.*

WRITING CENTER

Writing on Handmade Stationery

Purposes: Writes for many purposes. Experiments with letter forms by making mock letters and actual letters. Indicates own writing or pretend writing conveys meaning.

Materials: stationery made by children in Art Area, pencils, upper- and lowercase ink stamps, inkpads

Preparation: Place children's stationery from the Art Area in the Writing Area.

Suggested Vocabulary: card, letter, note, initials, pencil, stationery, names; monogrammed

- Ask children about their letters or cards. For example, *Who are you writing this letter to? He/she will be so happy to get it. I see there are lots of blue stars on that card.*
- Accept scribble marks and rudimentary letters, if children are satisfied with them. Help with letter formation if children ask.
- Encourage children to take letters or cards home and deliver them to the intended recipients. Encourage them to deliver others to friends in their class.

Overview of Small Groups

- Each day there are three Small Group activities. The same three activities are made available for three days. Each group of five or six children spends one of the three days in each activity. These work best when children are at tables.

- On Days 1, 2, and 3, children explore the physical properties of pizza dough, draw and discuss pictures of their friends, and spend time browsing books.

- On Days 4 and 5, children count dinosaurs; explore jigsaw puzzles and use letter tiles to build storybook words; and play memory games. These activities will carry over to Day 1 of Week 2.

- Model suggested vocabulary words and phrases in a manner that clarifies their meaning for children.

▲ Exploring Pizza Dough

SCIENCE

Exploring Pizza Dough: Days 1, 2, 3
High support

Purposes: Uses language to describe observations. Describes the physical properties of objects.

Materials: pizza dough, spice bottle (with shaker top), white flour, paper plates, plastic lids (e.g., coffee cans, nut containers) pizza dough ingredients list

Preparation: Make a batch of pizza dough or ask for a donation of a batch from a local pizza parlor. (Recipe: 3 c flour, 2 oz yeast, 1 T milk, 1/4 c olive oil, 1/4 c milk, 1 tsp. salt; Scald the milk, and cool. Dissolve yeast in milk. Add oil to milk, then add dissolved yeast to milk/oil mixture. Mix salt and flour, and then add liquid mixture. Stir to mix thoroughly. Turn out and knead for 20 minutes. Let rise for 3 hours, punch down, and divide into balls.) Divide dough into enough small balls to provide one per child. Keep in a sealed container or bag in the refrigerator until the day of use. Fill a spice bottle with flour. Wash plastic lids thoroughly.

Suggested Vocabulary: crust, dough, flour, shape; sticky; knead, stretch

Procedure

- Show a ball of dough to the children, and tell them that you mixed the ingredients together to make dough, and that they get to explore it today. Demonstrate how dough can be stretched and pulled, before giving it to children. You might say, *I can change the shape of the dough by stretching it out like this.* Show how to make the dough less sticky by working in a small amount of flour.

- Shape the dough over a plastic lid that serves as a model of a pizza pan. You might say, *At pizza parlors, bakers knead the dough until it's flat, then they twirl the dough in the air to stretch it. Spread the dough with your fingers to cover the pan.*

- Have children wash their hands. Then, give each child at the table a plate, a ball of pizza dough, and a plastic lid. Encourage children to explore the properties of the dough. You might ask, *How does the dough feel? Is it warm? Soft? Sticky? What happens when you stretch it too much?*

- Make a connection to how the Little Red Hen rolled, folded, and tossed her dough in *The Little Red Hen (Makes a Pizza)*.

- *EXTRA SUPPORT* Encourage children who are less inclined to explore actively to try new things, such as poking their finger in the dough to make a hole, or patting the dough with their hands.

WRITING

Friendship Pictures: Days 1, 2, 3
Medium support

Purposes: Creates artwork to express thoughts, feelings, and energy. Talks about understandings of relationships among people. Chooses artwork for display in a class book and explains the choices.

Materials: paper, crayons, markers, metal cans

Preparation: Place paper and drawing materials within easy reach of children. Have a notebook ready to record what children say about their pictures.

Suggested Vocabulary: friend; cooperating, drawing, sharing

Continued on next page

15

Procedure

- Join children in a short discussion about school friends. Prompt responses by sharing and asking questions. For example, *When I get together with my friends, I like to go for a walk. What do you like to do with friends?*

- Tell children they are going to draw pictures of things they like to do with their friends. Explain that some pictures are needed to make a class book. Give children the option of including their pictures in the book, or taking them home.

- Children draw freely. Offer encouragement. You might say, *I see you drew yourself and Lee playing jacks.* Record what children say about their pictures as captions. Later, laminate the pictures and assemble a class book. Discuss the pictures with children during informal conversations.

- *SOCIAL-EMOTIONAL SUPPORT* Display the pictures in the classroom with captions. Comment on how they make the classroom bright and colorful. Show drawings to the parents.

BOOK BROWSING

Exploring Books: Days 1, 2, 3
Low support

Purposes: Chooses independently to read or pretend to read books in the book area. Demonstrates self-direction in use of materials.

Materials: Add picture and information books about family, baby care, and musical instruments to the collection.

Suggested Vocabulary: baby, brother, family, father, mother, sister; names of musical instruments, animals, fruits, vegetables, clothing items, vehicles

Procedure

- Have children look at books together or individually. Children can trade books during the period.

- As time allows, observe children as they read and ask questions. For example, *Does anyone you know play music? What's your favorite musical instrument?*

- *ELL* Provide the names or meanings of words or objects in the story as necessary. Have children repeat the words.

- Book Browsing may be paired with other activities so that children remain engaged in small group work. Options are puzzles, writing, computers, or other activities of your choice.

MATHEMATICS

How Many Dinosaurs?: Days 4, 5
High support

Purposes: Uses counting to solve simple addition and subtraction story problems with concrete objects. Listens for numerical information in addition and subtraction story problems and performs the actions described in the story problems.

Materials: Activity Aid 7: dinosaur cut-outs (or plastic dinosaurs), Activity Aid 8: story mat, small bowl

Preparation: Use plastic dinosaurs or photocopy Activity Aid 7 and cut the dinosaur sections along the dotted lines. Prepare one set of the following for each child: Activity Aid 8, story mat, 10 dinosaurs, and a bowl to hold the dinosaurs.

Suggested Vocabulary: count; How many are there altogether?; How many are left?

Procedure

- Give each child a set of materials and explain that they are going to play a dinosaur game. Point to each child's bowl of dinosaurs, forest, and lake (on story mat). You might say, *I am going to tell you stories about dinosaurs that like to eat plants in the forest and drink water in the lake. You can act out the stories with your dinosaurs.*

- Present an addition story problem to children (e.g., 4 dinosaurs + 2 dinosaurs = 6 dinosaurs). Say something like, *Four dinosaurs walk into the forest. Take four dinosaurs out of your bowl and put them into your forest. Now, two more dinosaurs come into the forest to join their friends. Take two more dinosaurs out of your bowl and put them into the forest. How many dinosaurs are in the forest altogether?*

- Present a subtraction story problem similar to the addition problem above (e.g., 5 dinosaurs − 1 dinosaur = 4 dinosaurs).

- *EXTENDING THE ACTIVITY* If time permits, present story problems involving larger sets of 8 to 10 dinosaurs to children who succeed.

Progress Monitoring

Make informal observations and record on copies of pages 158–159 to be used later for a more formal assessment. Note which addition and subtraction problems each child solved correctly. Record the step at which errors were made: (1) constructing the initial set, (2) performing the arithmetic operation, or (3) giving the sum or difference. Record the name of any child who was ready for you to extend the activity upward, and how he or she did on the extension problems.

LANGUAGE AND PRINT MANIPULATIVES

Simple Puzzles of Fruits and Vegetables: Days 4, 5
Low support

Purposes: Uses concrete objects to understand the concepts of part and whole. Tolerates short waiting

periods for turns of teacher attention. Develops independence during activities, routines, and play.

Materials: simple jigsaw puzzles with fruits and vegetables

Procedure

- Some children explore fruit and vegetable jigsaw puzzles as one teacher helps children use the Alphabet Letter Tiles, Storybook Word Cards, and the Memory Game. Another teacher works with children in the Math small group.

Alphabet Letter Tiles and Storybook Word Cards: Days 4, 5

Purposes: Understands the concept of letter and the concept of word. Finds specific letters in words. Recognizes several highly familiar words in books.

Materials: tag board, sets of word cards with words from *The Little Red Hen (Makes a Pizza)* and *A Letter to Amy,* name cards for children in the group, lowercase letter tiles, 4 trays

Preparation: Make word cards selecting from these story words: *cake, candle, cat, dog, envelope, hen, mailbox, pan, parrot, pet, pizza, stamp.* Print words in lowercase letters on tag-board cards with a picture on each. If possible, laminate the cards. Prepare about 6 word cards (3 sets of 2 word cards each). Place word card sets with letter tiles (e.g., plastic or wooden letters, letters printed on tag-board) on a tray.

Suggested Vocabulary: letters, cake, candle, cat, dog, envelope, hen, mailbox, pan, parrot, pet, pizza, stamp; between, first, last, next

Procedure

- Model using letter tiles to create a word by placing a card in front of you on the table. You might say, *I chose the card that says "dog." The first letter is* d. *Let's find* d *on this tray.* Place the letter below the

word card. *The next letter in this word is* o (Point to *o*). *What's the last letter in* dog?

- Give pairs of children a tray with two word cards and the letter tiles needed. Have children work together to create the words on the cards. Encourage them to talk about the letters and words they are using. You might say, *I see you made the word* hen. *What letter is first in that word? In the middle? Last? What letter comes after the* c *in* cake? As children work through the activity, talk about how the words were used in *The Little Red Hen (Makes a Pizza)* and *A Letter to Amy.*

- **ELL** Name alphabet letters as needed and help them identify letters in different ways. For example, *Look, the letter* d *in* dog *has a long line with a closed curve attached at the bottom, and* p *in* pan *has a long line with a closed curve at the top!*

GAMES

Uppercase Alphabet Memory: Days 4, 5
Medium support

Purposes: Associates the name of a letter with its shape. Names many uppercase letters. Participates successfully as a member of a group.

Materials: Uppercase Alphabet Memory Cards

Preparation: Make 3 sets of 8 uppercase Alphabet Memory Cards (each set should contain 4 matches).

Procedure

- Tell children they are going to play a game with letters with a partner. Show children two cards face up and explain that, to play, they turn each one over, face down, on the table. Demonstrate. Explain that for each turn, they will be allowed to turn over two cards. If the cards match, the player can keep the cards face up on the table in front

of them. If they do not match, they should be turned over again, face down.

- Pair children and distribute sets of cards (8 cards with 4 matches). Observe children carefully and coach them to play correctly.

- *EXTRA SUPPORT* Help children who are not sure if the letters match by pointing out what each letter looks like and encouraging them to do the same. You might say, *No, this is* B, *so it doesn't match* P. B *has two round parts on the side* (point to them). P *has only one round part.*

Children's Names Memory: Days 4, 5
Medium support

Purposes: Recognize their own names and the names of others. Names all the letters in their own names and the names of others.

Materials: Name Memory Cards

Preparation: Make 3 sets of 8 Name Memory Cards (each set should contain 4 matches).

Procedure

- Distribute sets of Name Memory Cards to pairs of children. Be sure that the set given to each pair includes both names of the children in the pair and names of two other children in the class. Have children play a memory game as before.

- *EXTRA SUPPORT* Encourage struggling children to compare each letter in one name to each letter in another. For example, *The second letter in* Rob *is* o. *The second letter in* Mike *is* i. *Do they match?*

SUGGESTED RESOURCES

Book

Leuck, Laura. *My Baby Brother Has Ten Tiny Toes.* Minneapolis: Sagebrush Education Resources, 1997.

Developing Children's Language Through Conversation

Often the pictures children draw are about people and things that are interesting and important to them. This week children are drawing pictures of friends. Engage children in conversations about these pictures by saying, *Tell me about your picture.* The response might provide an opening for you to talk with the child about current friends and perhaps about children the child has not yet approached in play settings, but would like to.

Conversations About Friends

This month strive to use informal conversation opportunities to talk with children about their play with others in the classroom. One goal of brief conversations can be to help children become aware of the positive experiences they have had with others during the day. Try to use departure time to help children remember such interactions. If you know that a child played with another child briefly, comment on that and ask the child a question about it to prompt conversation.

Small Groups Time

Use Pictures to Talk About Friends

As children are drawing pictures of friends, move around the table and be alert for opportunities to talk to children about their pictures. Focus on one child at a time. For example: *I'd like to hear about your picture. Can you tell me about it?* You may find other children are listening. Encourage this.

A Model for Conversation

Small Groups: Conversation About Friends

Teacher: *Billy, you have been working a long time on your drawing. Can you tell me about it?*

Billy: Yeah. This is me and Daryl.

Teacher: *Oh, I see. I'm a little curious about this part right here. Can you tell me about it?* (Points to a detail in the picture.)

Billy: That's my dog.

Teacher: *Oh, I didn't know you had a dog. Does your dog have a name?*

Billy: Blacky.

Teacher: *Oh, now I know why you've used your black marker to make him black in your picture. What things do you do with Blacky?*

Billy: We hide his toy and tell him to look for it.

Teacher: (Continues with talk about play with Blacky; also may ask what kind of dog he is; how long they have had him.)

Good Conversations: Mathematics Vocabulary

Talking about shapes is the starting point for learning about geometry. You might begin conversations about shapes during toileting time or other transitions. Look for shapes on the wall, floor, ceiling, the child's clothing, and so on. Name shapes and encourage children to use the words. Provide descriptions of each shape, telling the number of sides and the number of corners.

Social Skills Development: Learning Names

It may take many weeks for some children to learn the names of all the children in the classroom. Children may refer to other children as "he" or "she." Name each child when you take your turn in a conversation.

▶ **Start-the-Day Centers** (see pages 12–14)
Make available two to three Centers as you greet children and their families.

▶ **Morning Meeting** (see page 12)
Gather children and review plans for the day. Orient children to center activities and help them make a first choice. Create a turns list for centers if necessary.

▶ **Center Time** (see pages 12–14)
Children spend time in Centers of their choice.

> **Extending the Book**
> Point to words printed on food containers in pictures to help children who are ready for a challenge to read them with you.

▶ **Story Time: 1st Reading**

The Little Red Hen (Makes a Pizza)

Author: Philemon Sturges
Illustrator: Amy Walrod

Summary: Little Red Hen discovers that she needs a pan and the ingredients to make a pizza, so she asks her friends for help. They are too busy, so Little Red Hen does all the work herself. When the pizza is ready, they gladly accept her invitation to dinner. They also agree to wash dishes.

Theme Link: Friends—Friends often ask one another for help.

Purposes

Listens to stories read aloud. Demonstrates increasing levels of sustained and focused engagement during read-aloud times. Shows a steady increase in the number of words in listening vocabulary. Develops understanding of main events.

Read the Story

As you read, use brief comments to help children notice and track story events and characters' actions. Point to illustrations, use gestures, or briefly explain to help children learn key story words. Quickly define words like *cupboard* whose meanings are not well supported by illustrations.

Suggested Vocabulary

Use these words often in Story Time and throughout the day.

apron something you wear when cooking to keep your clothes clean
cupboard a cabinet where food or dishes are stored
delicatessen a store that sells ready-to-eat foods
delicious tasting very good
dough a soft, thick flour mixture used to make baked goods
fetch to go and get
knead to mix by pushing hard
mozzarella a mild cheese used on pizza
pizza slicer a round knife on a wheel for slicing pizza
rummage search by moving things around
sip to take a very small drink
topping something sprinkled over food

> **English Language Learners**
> Point to some of the food items pictured and say their names slowly and clearly. Invite children to say them with you.

Progress Monitoring

You may photocopy and use pages 158–159 to keep notes on your observations. Note which individual children reveal through facial expressions that they follow and understand story events. Notice whether a child pays attention throughout the story, focuses only after the story is well underway, or loses interest quickly when text reading ends. Note comments, questions, and facial expressions during story reading, to gauge children's understanding of story events. Also monitor understanding by noting responses to follow-up discussion questions. Record your observations.

A MODEL FOR READING: *Use the following model to help you plan your book reading.*

Cover

The title of this book is The Little Red Hen (Makes a Pizza). *(Underline the title.) The author of the story is Philemon Sturges. (Underline name.) The illustrator is Amy Walrod.*

This must be the little red hen. (Point.) It looks like she's mixing something in a bowl. Maybe it's the pizza dough. I wonder who these animals are. (Point to the dog, cat, and duck.) Let's read the book and see.

p. 1 (Read page 1.)

When reading, briefly define *sipped, spied,* and *cupboard.* Use pictures and gestures to support your verbal explanations. Briefly note that tomato sauce made the hen think of pizza because it's always used to make **pizza**.

pp. 2-3 (Read page 2.)

Define *rummaged* in a quick aside. For example: *Little Red Hen* **rummaged** *through her pans–she moved things around as she looked– but she didn't have the right kind. So she yelled out the window to some friends. Let's see who heard her.*

Now read page 3. *That's too bad. None of Hen's friends has a pan for her to borrow. I wonder what she'll do.*

pp. 4-5 (Read page 4.)

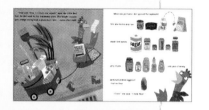

As you read, point to the picture to show a pizza slicer and briefly define *fetch. I see that Hen did* **fetch** *a pizza pan (point to it in the wagon) at the* **hardware store***. She got one and is bringing it home, and I see that she also got a* **pizza slicer** *(point to).*

Now read page 5. *So Little Red Hen has lots of things in her cupboard, but no flour. Flour is a very important ingredient for pizza dough. What do you think she'll do now? (Children respond.) Well, let's see.*

pp. 6-7 (Read page 6.)

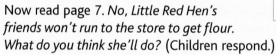
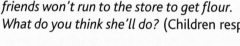

Oh, I see that the duck, the cat, and the dog are still outside. (Point.) Do you think they'll help her this time? (Children respond.)

Now read page 7. *No, Little Red Hen's friends won't run to the store to get flour. What do you think she'll do? (Children respond.)*

pp. 8-9 (Read page 8.)

So Hen went to the store to get the flour— to **fetch** *it herself. Here it is, in this white bag that says* flour *on it. (Point.) And then she sure got a lot of other stuff, didn't she?*

Read page 9. **Mozzarella** *is cheese for the top of the pizza.*

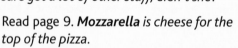

pp. 10-11 (Read page 10.)

*Oh, she's asking her neighborhood friends for help again. She's asking if anyone will go buy the **mozzarella** cheese she needs. Do you think they'll help this time?* (Children respond.)

Read page 11. *Oh, dear. Once again Hen had to go to the store, this time to get some **mozzarella** cheese.*

pp. 12-13 (Read page 12.)

*Hen went to a different store this time, to a **delicatessen**. A **delicatessen** is a store where they sell cheese, meats, and ready-to-eat foods like sandwiches.*

Now read page 13. Define **apron** quickly, as you read, using the picture to support your verbal explanation. *I think the cat, dog, and duck are Hen's friends, but they aren't helpful the way friends should be, are they?*

pp. 14-15 (Read page 14.)

Define **knead** with gestures or words as you read.

*The **dough** is what is used to make the pizza crust, the bottom part of a pizza. You have to make the dough very flat for pizza, so the hen did lots of things to flatten it.*

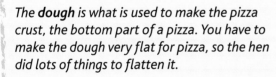

Now read page 15.

pp. 16-17

(Read first sentence on page 16.)

Note that the **topping** is what goes on top of a pizza.

Do you think her friends will offer to help?

Now read page remainder of page 16 and page 17.

pp. 18-19 (Read page 18.)

As you read, use gestures to help children understand action words: grated, sliced, chopped, **sip**.

So the pizza is in the oven baking, and Hen has a few minutes to rest. She has been working hard, so she's a little tired.

Now read page 19. *Mmmm, the pizza smelled really good—**delicious**!*

pp. 20-21 (Read page 21.)

Remember at the beginning of the story, when Little Red Hen said that she would make a lovely little pizza? It ended up as a very big pizza, too big for her to eat by herself.

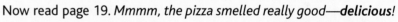

pp. 22–23 **(Read page 22.)**

What do you think Hen is going to do now?
Guide children to guess that she will cut the
pizza using the **pizza slicer** she is holding, as
she asks if anyone wants to eat some pizza.

Next, after you read each animal's name on
page 23, point to the animal and pause to give children time
to answer *yes.*

pp. 24–25 **(Read pages 24 and 25.)**

pp. 26–27 **(Read pages 26 and 27.)**

That's nice. The friends are finally going to
help the little red hen.

page 28 **(Read page 28.)**

Story Discussion

Prompt discussion with questions. For example:

*So that's the story about the hen who made a pizza. Do you think that the duck,
the dog, and the cat acted like good friends of Little Red Hen?* (Children respond.
They may first conclude that the animals were not good friends because they
wouldn't help make the pizza but later decide that they were good friends
because they helped wash the dishes.)

*We need to stop today, but we'll read the story again tomorrow and talk about it
some more.*

▶ Outdoor Play

Invite children to pretend they are the animals at the end of the story
and say "I will" when you call their names today (in threesomes). See
pages 10–11 for suggested conversation topics during this time.

▶ Songs, Word Play, Letters

Today children will be playing word games, singing songs, and reciting poems. Add your favorite game, song, or poem to this collection.

Songs

"If You're Happy"; "Eentsy, Weentsy Spider"; "Five Green and Speckled Frogs"; "Five Little Ducks"

Poems

"Five Juicy Apples"; "Diddle, Diddle, Dumpling"

Literacy Skills

If Your Name Starts With [name a letter], Raise Your Hand

Purposes

Recites songs, rhymes, chants, and poems and engages in language and word play. Communicates using verbal and non-verbal cues. Recognizes own name. Responds to own name and requests for action or information. Identifies the position of steps in a sequence, or objects in a line, pointing to each object and assigning the appropriate ordinal number to it.

Suggested Sequence for Today's Circle

1. "If You're Happy"
2. "Five Juicy Apples"
3. "Eentsy, Weentsy Spider"
4. "Five Green and Speckled Frogs"
5. If Your Name Starts With [name a letter], Raise Your Hand
6. "Diddle, Diddle, Dumpling"
7. "Five Little Ducks"

Materials and Instructional Procedures

IF YOU'RE HAPPY

Materials: CD Track 1, Song Lyrics page 162

Vocabulary: clap, hands, stamp, feet, shout, hurray

Procedure

- Tell children that the first song they are going to sing today is "If You're Happy."

- Sing four verses using clapping hands, stamping feet, tapping toes, and yelling "hurray." Sing slowly enough to give the children a chance to keep up.

FIVE JUICY APPLES

Materials: *Big Book of Poetry*: Poem 5, CD Track 30

Vocabulary: apples, juicy, sitting, store

Procedure

- Review this new poem, and write it on a note card, if you need prompts. Present the poem orally to the children this time, without referring to the printed version. (You will use the *Big Book of Poetry* for this activity tomorrow.)

- Tell children that the second thing we're going to do today is learn a new poem called "Five Juicy Apples." Hold up one hand with splayed fingers and ask children to hold up a hand too.

- Use your own name in the first verse, then a different child's name for the later verses.

- Sing the song one more time, using five different children's names. Tell children, *We'll do that one again tomorrow, and I'll use everyone else's name then.*

EENTSY, WEENTSY SPIDER

Materials: CD Track 5, Song Lyrics page 162

Vocabulary: down, rain, out, sun, up

Procedure

- Tell children that the third thing they are going to do today is sing another song. Place your fingers in the spider position to start the song, and ask, *Do you remember what song we start with our hands together like this?*

- Sing the song, leading the children in the motions.

FIVE GREEN AND SPECKLED FROGS

Materials: CD Track 10, Song Lyrics page 163, flannel board and flannel pieces

Vocabulary: green, speckled, log, delicious, pool, cool

Procedure

- As you place the pieces on the flannel board, ask children if they know what song you are about to sing. After children respond say, *Yes, five green speckled frogs, and I think we have all five here on the log . . . 1, 2, 3, 4, 5* (point and count, as children count). *Yes, all the frogs are here today.*

- Perform the song as usual, using the flannel pieces and pausing to give the children a chance to chime in with the correct number of frogs remaining in the last few verses.

- When removing the frogs, take four off all at once, and say, *Four frogs . . .* and then, as you remove the last frog, say, *. . . and one more makes five frogs.*

IF YOUR NAME STARTS WITH [NAME A LETTER], RAISE YOUR HAND

Materials: uppercase alphabet letter cards (all first letters and first letter combinations such as *Ch, Sh,* and *Th* found in children's names), children's name cards (written conventionally, with only first letter capitalized)

Vocabulary: name, letter, begins, touch, ear

Procedure

- Tell children, *Next, we're going to play the name game. You probably remember that I hold up a letter* (pick a letter). *If your name begins with the letter I usually say, "raise your hand." But today, you can touch your ear instead of raise your hand. This is a new way to do this game.*

- Play one round of the game. For children who don't respond when the first letter of their name is called, hold up their name card and point to the letter at the beginning. Say, *Nancy, your name* (point to *N*) *begins with* N, *so touch your ear.*

DIDDLE, DIDDLE, DUMPLING

Materials: *Big Book of Poetry*: Poem 2, CD Track 27, flannel board and flannel pieces

Vocabulary: bed, off, on, son, stockings

Procedure

- Recite the poem once. Point to the appropriate parts of the flannel board scene as you proceed.

- Pause before saying the words *on* and *off* to give the children a chance to chime in.

- Show the *Big Book of Poetry* illustration to the children, and point to the socks and shoes. The poem from the book will be used in a later activity.

FIVE LITTLE DUCKS

Materials: CD Track 11, Song Lyrics page 163

Vocabulary: out, over, far away, back

Procedure

- Say, *I'm going to give you a hint about the last song we are going to sing today. It has a hand motion like this* (four fingers together, up and down to touch your thumb), *and we say "quack, quack, quack" while we do that. Who remembers?*

- Sing the song as usual.

▶ **Lunch and Quiet Time**

This time is set aside for lunch, quiet time, and center activities. See pages 10–11 for suggested conversation topics during this time.

▶ Small Groups

For information on small groups, refer to pages 15–17.

▶ Let's Talk About It

Social Skills Development: Joining in Play

Purposes

Interacts appropriately with other children. Tells a personal narrative.

Procedure

- Remind children that in the book *The Little Red Hen (Makes a Pizza)*, the little red hen asked the animals to help her do lots of things, and most of the time they did not help her. Of course, she was not hurt or scared, she just wanted others to help her cook pizza—to do what she wanted to do.

- Encourage children to discuss helping and joining play. For example: *Can you remember a time today, or another day, when you wanted somebody to help you do something that you wanted to do—maybe build something with blocks or play family in the house—but no one would join you to help you do that? What did you do?*

- Help children who wish to respond to express themselves by asking clarifying questions. Also repeat their comments in a clear, well-formulated manner if necessary. Focus on positive efforts or guide toward effective steps that might have been taken. Be careful not to allow this to become a case of children assigning blame or reliving a conflict.

- Suggest ways children can join others in play. Here's an example: *What if children are playing family in the house, and you want to play, too? If you say, "I want to be the mother," and somebody else is already playing that part, that child might say, "No, you can't be the mother. I am!" If there isn't a baby, you might say, "Okay, then I'll be the baby." Then you should do what the mother tells you. That's what babies do, and a play mother won't want you to be her baby if you don't really act like one.*

- For more information on Let's Talk About It, see page 49.

Connect With Families

Send a note home asking parents to save food cartons for the children's upcoming grocery store play. Suggest such things as pasta, rice, and cereal boxes; pudding or gelatin boxes; boxes from frozen foods; and yogurt and cottage cheese containers.

▶ End-the-Day Centers

Children choose one of the open Centers (writing, books, puzzles/manipulatives). As children leave for home, tell them that tomorrow you will read the book about the little red hen and her pizza again.

▶ **Start-the-Day Centers** (see pages 12–14)
Open selected Centers as you greet children.

▶ **Morning Meeting** (see page 12)
Review plans for the day. Orient children to center activities.

▶ **Center Time** (see pages 12–14)
Children spend time in Centers of their choice.

▶ **Story Time: 2nd Reading**

The Little Red Hen (Makes a Pizza)

Author: Philemon Sturges
Illustrator: Amy Walrod

Purposes

Recalls some main events when asked, "What is happening in this story?" Links characters' basic emotions to their actions. Uses own experiences to understand characters' feelings and motivations. Expresses the main idea of a story or other text in a way that shows increasing understanding.

Read the Story Again

This time reconstruct the story with children. Prompt children's recall of events and the main character's actions by asking, *What is happening here? What did Little Red Hen do next?* Follow up on children's answers by rereading the text or discussing story events, using the most appropriate strategy to help children understand the story sequence on each page.

Suggested Vocabulary

Use these words often in Story Time and throughout the day.

apron something you wear when cooking to keep your clothes clean

cupboard a cabinet where food or dishes are stored

delicatessen a store that sells ready-to-eat foods

delicious tasting very good

dough a soft, thick flour mixture used to make baked goods

fetch to go and get

knead to mix by pushing hard

mozzarella a mild cheese used on pizza

pizza slicer a round knife on a wheel for slicing pizza

rummage search by moving things around

sip to take a very small drink of something

topping something sprinkled over food

Extending the Book

For children who are ready for a challenge, write Hen's favorite expression, *Cluck,* on a card, and hold it up for them to read every time you come to this word in the book.

English Language Learners

After you finish the story, go back and point to some pictures showing what the little red hen's friends are doing when they refuse to help her. Help children name the activities, such as jumping rope, reading, running, splashing, playing.

Progress Monitoring

Be aware of cues to individual children's understanding. Notice which children respond to the story events with smiles, frowns, giggles, and shaking heads. Notice any quizzical looks as well. To help you gauge understanding, note which children answer questions posed during this reading. Record your observations on copies of pages 158–159.

A MODEL FOR READING: *Read all the text on each page. When you read it will vary, depending on the flow of conversations with children.*

Cover

*We read this book the other day, so you know that the **title** of the book is . . . (pause) The Little Red Hen (Makes a Pizza). (Underline the title with your finger as you read it.) Today we're going to read and talk about the story again.*

p. 1

*You might remember that Hen was hungry, and when she began looking through her **cupboard** for something to eat, she **spied** something that made her think of pizza. Do you remember what it was? (Point to the can of tomato sauce to help prompt response.) Yes, she **spied** a can of tomato sauce. We use it when we make pizza.*

Read page 1.

But it wasn't all that easy for Little Red Hen to make pizza, was it? What problem did she keep having? Guide children to recall that she didn't have many of the things she needed to make pizza.

pp. 2–3

*What was the first thing Little Red Hen realized she needed but didn't have? (Point to the pans.) Right, she found that she needed a pizza pan after **rummaging** through her pan drawer.*

Read page 2. *Did any of her friends have a pizza pan? (no) No, they didn't.*

Read page 3.

pp. 4–5

*So what did the little red hen decide to do? (Children respond.) That's right. She decided to **fetch** one—go get one herself.*

Read page 4. *What kind of store did she visit? (a hardware store) That's right, a **hardware store**. Hen put all of the things she bought there in her wagon. Point to **pizza slicer**, nails, hammer, broom, and plant food as you name them. In Peter's Chair we also talked about how Peter's father probably got pink paint at a **hardware store**. A **hardware store** sells a lot of different things.*

*Okay, so then, Hen looked in her **cupboard** to see if she had the ingredients she needed to make pizza. Read page 5.*

So what was her first idea about how to get flour? (Children respond.) Let's see if you are right.

pp. 6–7

Read page 6. *Yes, you were right. She asked her friends to go to the store for her.*

Read page 7. *So what did she say that she would do?* Turn page.

pp. 8–9

That's right. Read first line on page 8. *And she had to go to a different store this time, not a hardware store, but a store that we sometimes call a grocery store. What kind of store is it? (a supermarket)*

Read the rest of page 8.

Read page 9. Slow down to let children fill in the word ***mozzarella***. *Remember? **Mozzarella** is a kind of cheese you sprinkle on top of pizza.*

pp. 10-11

What's happening now? Support children's recall of the hen's request for help and her friends' lack of response.

Read page 10 and all but the last line on page 11. *So what did Little Red Hen decide to do?* (to get it herself) *That's right. She decided to* **fetch** *the* **mozzarella** *herself. She's going to a lot of trouble to make this pizza, isn't she?*

pp. 12-13

Read page 12 and define **delicatessen.**

She certainly bought a lot of things!

Now that Hen finally has everything she needs, she's ready to make her pizza. What will she make first? Prompt **dough** by providing clues, such as, *it's the part we make with flour and then roll out and toss in the air.* If children say "crust," explain that, when baked, the **dough** becomes the crust.

Now read page 13.

pp. 14-15

Read page 14. *So she mixed flour and other stuff to make the* **dough,** *and then it rose, which means that the* **dough** *got bigger.*

Read page 15. *Maybe you've seen people spin pizza* **dough** *around in the air. They throw it up and spin it and then catch it to make the* **dough** *get round and flat.*

pp. 16-17

What was the next part of the pizza that Hen prepared? (Lead children to recall **toppings** were next, the things that go on top of the crust.)

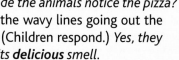

Read pages 16 and 17.

pp. 18-19

As you read page 18, help clarify the meanings of *chopped, grated, sliced,* with gestures.

What made the animals notice the pizza? Point to the wavy lines going out the window. (Children respond.) *Yes, they smelled its* **delicious** *smell.*

Read page 19.

Then comment that finally, Hen got to rest for a while.

pp. 20-21

Read page 21.

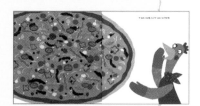

Wow! It's huge, isn't it? What do you think is going through Hen's mind right now? Look at her face. Guide answers toward Hen's realization that she couldn't eat it all, and her idea to invite her friends to dinner.

pp. 22–23

Read pages 22 and 23.

And what did they all say? (Yes.) They all said yes.

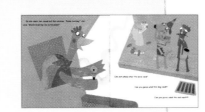

pp. 24–25

Read pages 24 and 25.

Did the animal friends help? (Children respond.)

pp. 26–27

Read pages 26 and 27, pointing to the pictures.

p. 28

Read page 28.

Story Discussion

Prompt discussion with questions like these.

Were you surprised that Little Red Hen offered some pizza to the other animals, given that they had not helped her make it? Would you have given them any? Why? Note that Hen must have known her friends were playing and she liked making pizza herself anyway. Friends keep asking friends to do things with them.

We'll talk more about the surprise ending on another day.

▶ Outdoor Play

Dismiss children by the initial sounds of their names: *If your name starts with /f/ like* fetch . . . *If your name starts with /m/ like* mozzarella . . . and so on. See pages 10–11 for suggested conversation topics during this time.

▶ Songs, Word Play, Letters

Today children will be playing word games, singing songs, and reciting poems. Add your favorite game, song, or poem to this collection.

Songs

"Down by the Bay"; "If You're Happy"; "Come On and Join In to the Game"

Poems

"Ten Little Fingers"; "Five Juicy Apples"

Literacy Skills

Chiming in With Rhyming Words; Those Words Begin With the Same Sound; Let's Clap Our Names

Purposes

Recites songs, rhymes, chants, and poems, and engages in language and word play. Says the words that complete rhymes, in a group. Uses new words in meaningful ways. Separates words into syllables. Responds to own name and requests for action or information. Follows two-step directions.

Suggested Sequence for Today's Circle

1. "Down by the Bay"
2. "Come On and Join In to the Game"
3. "Ten Little Fingers"
4. "Five Juicy Apples" (and Chiming in With Rhyming Words)
5. "If You're Happy" (and Those Words Begin With the Same Sound!)
6. Let's Clap Our Names

Materials and Instructional Procedures

DOWN BY THE BAY

Materials: CD Track 3, Song Lyrics page 162, flannel board and flannel pieces

Vocabulary: bay, watermelons, snake, cake, frog, dog, mouse, house

Procedure

- Sing the song with "dog kissing the frog," the "snake eating a cake," and "a bear combing his hair," placing the appropriate flannel pieces on the board for each verse. Remove the pieces for each verse before putting on the new ones.

- Sing a new verse, using body gestures to portray new words (e.g., "fly" and "tie" or "cow" and "bow").

COME ON AND JOIN IN TO THE GAME

Materials: CD Track 20, Song Lyrics page 163

Vocabulary: clap, come, join, game, sneeze, blink

Procedure

- Tell children that the next song is a new one. Sing the song for the first time and model the motions. Sing only three verses ("clapping," "blinking," "sneezing"). Go slowly enough so that children can keep up.

- Tell children that they will sing that song again another day, and that the next thing they are going to do is recite a poem that they already know.

TEN LITTLE FINGERS

Materials: *Big Book of Poetry*: Poem 1, CD Track 26

Vocabulary: fingers, fold, high, low, open, shut, tight, together, wide

Procedure

- Wiggle the fingers of both of your raised hands, and ask children if they can guess what the poem is. Wait a moment for a response; if no one answers or someone gives an incorrect guess, continue, "*Ten . . . Little Fingers.*"

- Present the poem, leading the children in the finger movements.

- Show children the *Big Book of Poetry* illustration for this poem, and talk about it.

FIVE JUICY APPLES (AND CHIMING IN WITH RHYMING WORDS)

Materials: *Big Book of Poetry*: Poem 5, CD Track 30

Vocabulary: apples, juicy, pair, grocer, store

Procedure

- Display the *Big Book of Poetry*. Say, *Remember the poem we learned yesterday, called "Five Juicy Apples"? We're going to do that poem again today.*

- Hold up one hand with splayed fingers to count down from five to zero, to prompt children to hold up a hand in the same way. Proceed as usual, using a different child's name each time. Be sure you use names of children you didn't use on Monday.

- After reciting the poem once, say, *Let's do that again,* and, this time, use any names that haven't yet been used today, and weren't used on Monday, so that everyone will have had a turn when you finish today.

- As you recite the poem again, linger on the first sound of the second word in rhyming pairs (e.g., *store/four; be/three; through/two; pair/there*) so that children can chime in.

IF YOU'RE HAPPY (AND THOSE WORDS BEGIN WITH THE SAME SOUND!)

Materials: CD Track 1, Song Lyrics page 162

Vocabulary: clap, hands, tap, toes, smack, lips

Procedure

- Lead children in singing two verses of the song as usual, using "clap hands" and "tap toes" as the motions.

- After singing two verses, stop and say, *I noticed that some of the words in that song begin with the same sounds.* Happy *and* hands *have the same sound at the beginning:* /h/ happy *and* /h/ hand. Tap *and* toes *also have the same sound at the beginning:* /t/ tap *and* /t/ toes. *That's interesting, isn't it? Some words start with the same sound.*

- Sing one more verse using "smack your lips" as the verse and motion, and comment that these words do not start with the same sound.

LET'S CLAP OUR NAMES

Vocabulary: clap, game, names

Procedure

- Tell children that next, they're going to play a clapping game. *First you say a name, and then you clap the parts you hear in the name. This is how you do it.*

- Model the game first, using names that are not any of the children's (e.g., Priscilla, Anthony, Thomas). First say the name slowly, emphasizing the syllables. Then, say the name again, this time clapping with each syllable.

- Go around the circle, saying each child's name slowly, breaking it into syllables, then saying the name again, clapping once for each syllable. All children should join in clapping each child's name.

- If a child has trouble clapping names, keep going. Children get practice with the group and should not be singled out. Try to do everyone's name in one session so no one feels left out.

Progress Monitoring

Make informal observations to be used later for a more formal assessment. Note which children are clapping the syllables of names without any difficulty, and which ones are struggling. Note whether a child focuses on an activity quickly, participates in the singing, and attempts hand/finger/body motions. Is anyone attentive, but not actively participating? Is anyone unfocused or withdrawn? Note which children chime in to recite the poetry and which indicate with facial expressions, nods, or words that they recognize the similar beginning sounds you point out in "If You're Happy."

▶ Lunch/Quiet Time/Centers

This time is set aside for lunch, quiet time, and center activities. See pages 10–11 for suggested conversation topics during this time.

▶ Small Groups

For information on small groups, refer to pages 15–17.

▶ Let's Find Out About It

Making Musical Instruments

Purposes

Listens to explanation of multi-step directions. Listens to sounds, sound patterns, or songs. Understands comparisons made among objects.

Materials

books: *The Little Red Hen (Makes a Pizza), Oonga Boonga, Let's Make Music;* books with pictures of drums; real or toy drum

Suggested Vocabulary

Use these words in the discussion: beat, musical instrument, percussion, rhythm; high, hollow, loud, quiet; close, seal

Procedure

- Displays illustrations of the saxophone in *The Little Red Hen (Makes a Pizza)* and Grandpa's harmonica in *Oonga Boonga*

- Point out that one musical instrument they have not seen in any of the stories they've read so far is the drum. Use resource books to show pictures of drums. Point out a drum's main characteristics (hollow inside, tops or sides covered with a strong material to pound or tap on).

- If you have a real drum, show it to the children. Allow children a chance to thump on it one at a time.

- Show children the directions in *Let's Make Music* for making a drum bowl. Review the directions and demonstrate the three simple steps. Tell children that soon they will be able to make bowl drums in Centers, if they would like to do that.

> **English Language Learners**
>
> Use a real drum or a bowl drum to demonstrate words like *beat, loud,* and *quiet.* Help children say the words.

Outdoor Play

Take drums outside for a drumming parade.

> **Extending the Activity**
>
> Beat on appropriate objects in the classroom with hands or drumsticks. Invite children who are ready for a challenge to describe the different sounds.

SUGGESTED RESOURCES

Books

Cox, Judy (author) and Elbrite Brown (illustrator). *My Family Plays Music.* New York: Holiday House, 2003.

Hayes, Ann (author) and Karmen Thompson (illustrator). *Meet the Orchestra.* New York: Voyager Books, 1991.

▶ End-the-Day Centers

Children spend time in open Centers. As children leave for home, say something that will help each child look forward to the next day. For example, tell children that tomorrow they will read a new book, *A Letter to Amy,* about a boy who invites a special friend to his birthday party.

▶ **Start-the-Day Centers** (see pages 12–14)
Direct children to two to three open Centers.

▶ **Morning Meeting** (see page 12)
Gather children and review plans for the day.

▶ **Center Time** (see pages 12–14)
Children spend time in Centers of their choice.

▶ **Story Time: 1st Reading**

A Letter to Amy

Author: Ezra Jack Keats

Summary: Peter writes his friend Amy a special invitation to his birthday party. On his way to the mailbox, the letter blows out of his hand and he knocks Amy down trying to get it back. Peter worries that Amy won't come to his party but she does, which makes Peter very happy.

Theme Link: *Friends*—People can have a variety of friends, both boys and girls. Sometimes, we are not sure whether someone will be our friend or do things with us.

Purposes

Listens to stories read aloud. Demonstrates increasing levels of sustained and focused engagement during read alouds. Shows increase in words in listening vocabulary. Develops comprehension of the story's main events.

Read the Story

Read with expression to show Peter's range of emotions in this story. For example, your voice can convey Peter's desperation as he tries to retrieve the invitation, as well as his worry and indecision about the right moment to bring out the cake. To help children learn new story words, use gestures and pantomime, point to illustrations, and give short explanations. Repeat key words as you sum up story events.

Suggested Vocabulary

Use these words often in Story Time and throughout the day.

candles solid pieces of wax with wicks, burned to give light
hopscotch a game played by hopping on numbered squares on the ground
invite to ask someone to come to a place or an event
parrot a tropical bird with bright feathers
reflection an image thrown back by something shiny, such as a mirror or water
seal to close tightly
spoiled ruined; no good
stamp a small piece of paper stuck to an envelope that shows you have paid to have the letter delivered
stare to look with a long, steady gaze
wish to have a strong desire or hope for something

Extending the Book

Children who are ready for a challenge can help you read the book's title. Underline the words with your finger as you read them slowly with children.

English Language Learners

Hold up a stamp and an envelope for children to see and pronounce the words slowly and clearly.

Progress Monitoring

Watch for cues to children's understanding. Do children come to this new story with enthusiasm? Do individual children attend throughout the reading? Notice which children nod or call out answers to participate in discussions. You may want to record your observations on pages 158–159.

A MODEL FOR READING: *Use the following model to help you plan your book reading. You might want to write reminders to yourself on sticky notes.*

Cover

*The **title** of this book is* A Letter to Amy. *The person who wrote this story is Ezra Jack Keats. He also made the pictures for the story.*

We know the main character in this story— the boy right here. (Point.) *We've read other stories about him. Do you remember him?* (Children respond.) *Yes, it's Peter. We read the story* Whistle for Willie, *when Peter was a little boy, and then we read* Peter's Chair, *when Peter was a little older and had a baby sister. In this story, Peter has learned to write, so he's older than you, maybe in first or second grade.*

Now let's read the book to find out what happens to Peter in this story.

pp. 2–3 (Read page 3.)

*After you read the word **stared**, say that it means Peter just looked at the paper for a while.*

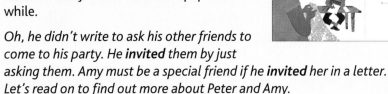

*Oh, he didn't write to ask his other friends to come to his party. He **invited** them by just asking them. Amy must be a special friend if he **invited** her in a letter. Let's read on to find out more about Peter and Amy.*

pp. 4–5 (Read page 4.)

*We always need a postage **stamp** (point to it in the picture) on things we mail. That's how we pay for mailing a letter.*

pp. 6–7 (Read page 7.)

Point and comment, I think Amy must have lived pretty close to Peter. He walked past her window on his way to the mailbox.

I see that Willie went with Peter, after all. Point to the dog Willie.

pp. 8–9 (Read page 9.)

Oh, the book tells us that Peter was kind of worried about something. He was worried the boys might say something about inviting Amy, a girl.

pp. 10–11 (Read pages 10 and 11.)

Point to letter, floating in the wind, as you read.

pp. 12–13 (Read pages 12 and 13.)

Point to hopscotch game as you read the words. Complete page and comment, Maybe something has blown out of your hand on a windy day. Sometimes it's hard to get it back again. Let's see if Peter can catch it in his hand (point to Peter's hand).

pp. 14–15 (Read pages 14 and 15.)

pp. 16–17 (Read page 16.)

That was lucky! Amy didn't see the name and address on the letter. She didn't find out that it was for her.

pp. 18–19 (Read page 18.)

Point to the mailbox as you say the word. *Oh, look at Amy. She's holding her back with her hand. Why do you think she's doing that?* (Children may suggest that she hurt herself when she fell down.)

pp. 20–21 (Read page 20.)

This is Peter's reflection right here. (point)— *the picture of him in the puddle. The puddle is sort of like a mirror, but the reflection is pretty blurry.* Ask, *How do you think Peter was feeling right then?* Help children realize the possible range of Peter's emotions—sadness, disappointment, worry, and regret for bumping into Amy.

pp. 22–23 (Read page 22.)

He sounds pretty sad and worried, doesn't he?

pp. 24–25 (Read pages 24 and 25.)

I think he was still hoping that Amy would come to the party. But then, after the other children shouted to bring the cake out now, he changed his mind and said, "All right, bring it out now." I guess he stopped hoping that Amy would come.

pp. 26–27 (Read pages 26 and 27.)

Well, Amy did come, and she brought her pet, too. Point at Peter's expression and comment, *I think Peter is feeling pretty happy now.* Quickly turn the page and continue the story.

pp. 28–29 (Read pages 28 and 29.)

As you read the word **candles**, point to the picture of them on page 29.

The birthday child gets to make a wish before blowing out the candles. A wish is something you really want.

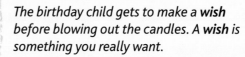

Story Discussion

Prompt discussion with questions. For example:

Peter bumped into Amy and knocked her down, but he didn't do it on purpose, did he? It was an accident. Do you think Amy understood that? Guide a short discussion about accidental versus intentional actions.

We need to stop for today. We'll read this story again another day.

▶ Outdoor Play

Use clothes colors to dismiss a few children at a time to cubbies to put on outdoor clothing: *If you are wearing anything that is brown, you may get up and go put your jacket or sweater on.* See pages 10–11 for suggested conversation topics during this time.

▶ Songs, Word Play, Letters

Today children will be playing word games, singing songs, and reciting poems. Add your favorite game, song, or poem to this collection.

Songs

"Five Little Ducks"; "Down by the Bay"; "Head and Shoulders, Knees and Toes"

Predictable Book

HUSH!

Literacy Skills

Chiming in With Rhyming Words; Let's Clap Our Names

Purposes

Says words that complete rhymes, in a group. Recites songs, rhymes, chants, and poems, and engages in language and word play. Listens to a variety of genres read aloud: predictable texts books and poems. Identifies the position of objects in a line, assigning the appropriate ordinal number to it. Responds to own name and requests for action or information. Separates words into syllables.

Suggested Sequence for Today's Circle

1. "Five Little Ducks" (and Chiming in With Rhyming Words)
2. HUSH!
3. "Down by the Bay" (and Chiming in With Rhyming Words)
4. "Head and Shoulders, Knees and Toes"
5. "Let's Clap Our Names"

Materials and Instructional Procedures

FIVE LITTLE DUCKS (AND CHIMING IN WITH RHYMING WORDS)

Materials: CD Track 11, Song Lyrics page 163

Vocabulary: out, over, far away, back

Procedure

- Tell children that the first song they are going to sing today, is "Five Little . . ." (pause to let children chime in, and make quacking sounds to give them a hint) . . . Ducks!

- Sing the song as usual, using hand motions to show the hills and the quacking. Sing the song again, but this time, linger briefly on the first sound of the second word of a rhyming pair (e.g., day/away; quack/back) so that children can chime in on these words.

HUSH!

Materials: book: HUSH!

Vocabulary: weeping, wind, mosquito, sleeping, lizard, creeping

Procedure

- Show children the cover of HUSH! and read the title. Ask, What does the word hush mean? That's right, it means to be quiet.

- Read the book once, keeping the natural rhythm of the verse. Point to pictures to identify objects named. Comment occasionally about what the baby is doing.

- After reading, ask children if they thought that was a funny book, and ask why. Tell children they'll read it again on another day.

DOWN BY THE BAY (AND CHIMING IN WITH RHYMING WORDS)

Materials: CD Track 3, Song Lyrics page 162, flannel board and flannel pieces

Vocabulary: grow, go, snake, cake, frog, dog, mouse, house

Procedure

- Say something like, *Let's sing that song about the silly animals down by the bay.*

- Sing the song, as before.

- Linger briefly as you say the first sound in the second word of rhyming pairs (e.g., *grow/go; snake/cake*) so that children can chime in.

HEAD AND SHOULDERS, KNEES AND TOES

Materials: CD Track 4, Song Lyrics page 162

Vocabulary: head, shoulders, knees, toes, eyes, ears, chin, nose

Procedure

- Sing the song as usual, touching the different parts of your body as you sing about them except for substituting *chin* for *mouth*. Jut out your own chin when you name it.

LET'S CLAP OUR NAMES

Procedure

- Tell children that next they are going to play the same clapping game they played yesterday. *First I say a name, then you clap the parts you hear in the name.*

- Go around the circle, saying each child's name slowly, breaking it into syllables, then saying the name again, clapping once for each syllable. All children may join in clapping each child's name.

- If children start to clap as you say a name the first time, remind them to listen first before clapping.

▶ Lunch and Quiet Time

This time is set aside for lunch, quiet time, and center activities. See pages 10–11 for suggested conversation topics during this time.

▶ **Small Groups**

For information on small groups, refer to pages 15–17.

▶ **Let's Find Out About It**

Exploring Stationery and Invitations

Purposes

Understands that print carries meaning. Understands that we write for many purposes.

Materials

book: *A Letter to Amy;* variety of printed party invitations, stationery, letter stamps for monogram, stamps to decorate stationery, a letter written on stationery, clipboard, paper, marker

Suggested Vocabulary

Use these words throughout the discussion: address, decoration, envelope, initials, invitation, message, monogram, stationery

Procedure

● Show children a variety of printed invitations. Explain that an invitation is a special kind of card or letter used to let people know you are having a party or other special event that you would like them to attend.

● Explain that in *A Letter to Amy,* Peter didn't use a printed invitation to invite Amy to his party. Instead, he wrote on plain paper and used a plain envelope. Show the picture in the story where Peter is writing the letter, and the envelope when it is blown out of his hand.

● Tell children that we can use a letter to invite someone to something; we don't need to buy printed invitations.

● Show some examples of stationery. Explain that, sometimes, when we write a letter, we use a special kind of paper called stationery. Stationery often is decorated.

English Language Learners

As you show sample invitations to children, say words such as *invitation, stationery,* and *monogram* several times. Invite children to say the words with you.

● Say that stationery can be used to write an invitation, a thank-you note, or just a nice letter to someone. If appropriate, share a letter that a parent wrote to you (a thank-you note, for example), or some other letter you received on stationery.

● Explain that people sometimes use monogrammed stationery. Write a few children's names on paper mounted on a clipboard. Write the first letters of the first, middle, and last names. Then, write the letters as a group. Ask the child to name the letters, as you point. Help, if needed, and explain that this group of letters is a person's monogram.

● Use letter stamps to put your initials on paper to show how to make monogrammed stationery. Use a picture stamp to decorate the border of the stationery. Tell children they will make their own stationery later.

Extending the Activity

Ask children who are ready for a challenge what information they would need to include on a birthday party invitation.

Center Time Connections

Children can make stationery in an art table activity.

Progress Monitoring

Notice which individual children lose interest and which ones listen attentively throughout. Who uses new words in spoken vocabulary, and who seems eager to make a monogram? Note who asks questions or offers personal experience with stationery and writing for a purpose.

▶ **End-the-Day Centers**

Children choose among open Centers. As children leave for home, say something that will help each one look forward to the next day. For example, tell children who are on the turns list for the art table tomorrow that they will make stationery and write on it.

▶ **Start-the-Day Centers** (see pages 12–14)
Direct children as they arrive to two to three open Centers.

▶ **Morning Meeting** (see page 12)
Orient children to center activities, consulting the turns list if necessary.

▶ **Center Time** (see pages 12–14)
Children spend time in Centers of their choice.

▶ **Story Time: 2nd Reading**

A Letter to Amy
Author: Ezra Jack Keats

Purposes
Recalls some main events when asked, "What is happening in this story?" Links characters' basic emotions to their actions. Uses own experiences to understand characters' feelings and motivations. Shows increasing understanding of story events.

Read the Story Again
This time reconstruct the story with children. Prompt children's recall of events by asking, *What is happening here?* or *What did Peter do next?* Help children understand Peter's reasons for his actions, such as why he wanted to wait to bring out the cake during his party.

Suggested Vocabulary

Use these words often in Story Time and throughout the day.

candles solid pieces of wax with wicks, burned to give light

hopscotch a game played by hopping on numbered squares on the ground

invite to ask someone to come to a place or an event

parrot a tropical bird with bright feathers

reflection an image thrown back by something shiny, such as a mirror or water

seal to close tightly

spoiled ruined; no good

stamp a small piece of paper stuck to an envelope that shows that you have paid to have the letter delivered

stare to look with a long, steady gaze

wish to have a strong desire or hope for something

Extending the Book

For children who are ready for a challenge, point to the word *We-e-el-l* on page 3 and read it in a drawn-out way. Have children imitate you. Tell them that it is a different way of saying *well* and that it means that Peter is thinking hard about what he is about to say.

English Language Learners

Point out the raincoat on the page where Peter's mother tells him to wear it. Repeat the word, and have children say it with you.

Progress Monitoring

Notice which children react positively, with recognition and delight, indifferently, or negatively to the story ("Not that one again!"). Notice individual answers to questions. Record your observations on copies of pages 158–159.

A MODEL FOR READING: *Use the following model to help you reconstruct the story with children. Read the text on each page. When you read it will depend on the flow of conversation with children.*

Cover

We read this book the other day, so you know that the title of the book is . . . (Pause.) *Right? A Letter to Amy. Today we're going to read the story again.*

pp. 2-3

Ask, *What's happening here, at the beginning of the story?* (Point to Peter writing.) *Yes, Peter's writing a letter to his friend Amy, and he's telling his mother.* Ask, *Why is he writing to Amy?* (Children respond.) *Yes, he's writing to **invite** her, to ask her to come to his birthday party.*

Read page 3.

*Did Peter write a letter to anyone else to **invite** them to his party?* (No.) *Why did Peter decide to write to Amy instead of just asking her, the way he had **invited** other children?* (Children respond.) *Yes, to make it more special. He wanted Amy to know he really wanted her to come.*

pp. 4-5

Read first sentence on page 4. Comment that **sealed** means Peter licked the flap and stuck it down tightly.

Read until "He did, and started to leave." Ask, *What two things did Peter's mother remind him to do?* Help children understand that invitations need to say when the party is and that letters need stamps. Point to the stamp and comment, *We need a **stamp** to pay for mailing letters. The mail carrier won't deliver a letter without a postage **stamp** on it.*

Read the rest of the page.

pp. 6-7

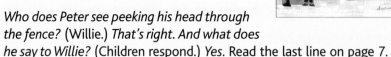

Read first two lines on page 6. Then, ask, *Where is Peter now?* (Children respond.) *Yes, he's on the way to the mailbox.*

Who does Peter see peeking his head through the fence? (Willie.) *That's right. And what does he say to Willie?* (Children respond.) *Yes.* Read the last line on page 7.

pp. 8-9

Read page 9.
The wind caught Peter's letter. Does Peter try to get it back? (Point to Peter and the letter as children respond.) *Yes.*

pp. 10-11

Read pages 10 and 11.

pp. 12-13

Read pages 12 and 13.

*A **hopscotch** game* (point) *is a kind of sidewalk game. It looked like Peter was going to be able to grab the letter, but then what happened?* (Point to the picture on page 13 as children respond.) *Yes, it flew away again, and Peter ran after it again.*

And whom does Peter see, as he runs after his letter? (Children respond.) *Yes, Amy.*

pp. 14-15

Read pages 14 and 15; then define **spoiled**.

pp. 16–17

Amy didn't see the letter, because Peter caught it just in time, but then what happened? (Point to page 17 as children respond.) *Yes, Amy fell down. And what made her fall? That's right. Peter bumped into her by accident, which means he didn't mean to.*

Read page 16.

"In his great hurry," means that Peter was trying to get his letter before Amy could see that it was for her. Then he bumped into her.

Look at Amy's face. (Point.) *How do you think she's feeling right now?* (Children respond.) *Yes, she looks like she's a bit angry and upset, or maybe really surprised that Peter bumped into her.*

pp. 18–19

What's happening here? (Children respond.) *Yes, Peter is putting his letter in the mailbox, and Amy is running away. Read text.*

pp. 20–21

Read page 20.

Now Peter is worried that Amy won't come to his party. He thinks she might think that he ran into her on purpose.

pp. 22–23

Read page 22.

Why did Peter sound sad when he answered his mother's question? (Children respond.)

pp. 24–25

What is happening here? Why do Peter and the boys have hats on? (Children respond.) *Yes, it's the day of the party, and the boys Peter **invited** are there. Who isn't there yet?* (Children respond.) *Right, Amy.*

Read pages 24 and 25.

At this point Peter doesn't know that Amy is on her way. Look at Peter's face. How is he feeling? (Children respond.)

pp. 26–27

Read pages 26 and 27.

pp. 28–29

Read pages 28 and 29.

Story Discussion

Prompt discussion with questions. For example:

Usually, when we accidentally bump into someone, we say, "Oh, I'm sorry. Excuse me!" But Peter didn't say that to Amy. Why not? (Children respond.) Guide toward understanding that he was preoccupied with mailing the letter.

Okay, we need to stop for today, but we'll read this story again another day.

▶ Outdoor Play

To dismiss children a few at a time, hold up and name uppercase letters that are at the beginning of children's names. Say, *If your name starts with ____, you may go put your jacket on now.* See pages 10–11 for suggested conversation topics during this time.

▶ Songs, Word Play, Letters

Today children will be playing word games, singing songs, and reciting poems. Add your favorite game, song, or poem to this collection.

Songs

"The Wheels on the Bus"; "Come On and Join In to the Game"; "Old MacDonald Had a Farm"

Poems

"Five Little Owls in an Old Elm Tree"; "Five Juicy Apples"

Literacy Skills

If Your Name Starts With [name a letter], Raise Your Hand

Purposes

Recites songs, rhymes, chants, and poems, and engages in language and word play. Identifies the position of items in a series and objects, assigning the appropriate ordinal number to it. Listens with increasing attention. Responds to own name and requests for action or information. Shows a steady increase in the number of words in his or her listening vocabulary. Communicates using verbal and non-verbal cues.

Suggested Sequence for Today's Circle

1. "The Wheels on the Bus"
2. "Five Little Owls in an Old Elm Tree"
3. "Come On and Join In to the Game"
4. If Your Name Starts With [name a letter], Raise Your Hand
5. "Five Juicy Apples"
6. "Old MacDonald Had a Farm"

Materials and Instructional Procedures

THE WHEELS ON THE BUS

Materials: CD Track 7, Song Lyrics page 163

Vocabulary: wheels, bus, round, town, up, down, horn, box, wiper, glass, driver, back

Procedure

- First, sing verses that children already know, leading them in the appropriate motion for each verse.

- Introduce additional verses by singing and modeling the motion. Sing slowly enough for them to keep up.

FIVE LITTLE OWLS IN AN OLD ELM TREE

Materials: *Big Book of Poetry*: Poem 7, CD Track 32

Vocabulary: big, elm, owls, round, tree

Procedure

- Review the poem and write it on a small note card if you need prompts.

- Present the poem orally to children once. Then, show children the *Big Book of Poetry* illustration, and say, *Here are the little owls. Let's count them.* Point as children help recite number words.

- Say the poem again, this time pointing to the appropriate pictures in the illustration (e.g., as you say "blinking" and "winking"). Look at the illustration again, and ask children how many owls are not winking or blinking. Point them out to confirm: "1, 2, 3."

COME ON AND JOIN IN TO THE GAME

Materials: CD Track 20, Song Lyrics page 163

Vocabulary: clap, hands, come, join, game, sneeze, jump, high, yawn, stretch

Procedure

- Tell children that the third thing they are going to do is sing "Come On and Join In to the Game," which they sang once last week. Sing the first two verses ("clapping," "sneezing") slowly and model the motions.

- Then, ask children to stand up, telling them that they are going to sing another verse and do a jumping action. Sing the jumping verse of the song ("jump high with me"), and then ask children to sit down again.

- Say something like, *That jumping made me a little tired so now you can yawn and stretch with me in the last verse.*

IF YOUR NAME STARTS WITH [NAME A LETTER], RAISE YOUR HAND

Materials: alphabet cards and children's name cards

Vocabulary: ear, hand, letter, name, raise, touch

Procedure

- Tell children that the next thing they are going to do is play the name game again. You might say, *Remember that I hold up a letter, and usually you raise your hand. Today, though, I want you to blink your eyes like the little owl in our poem.* Pick a letter. Proceed as usual, except say, *blink your eyes.*

- Play one round of the game. For children who don't respond when the first letter of their name is called, hold up their name card and point to the first letter. For example, say, *Nancy, your name* (point to *N*) *begins with* N, *so you can blink your eyes, too.*

- Do the letter for everyone's name so no one feels left out.

FIVE JUICY APPLES

Materials: *Big Book of Poetry*: Poem 5, CD Track 30

Vocabulary: apples, juicy, sitting, store

Procedure

- Say, *Let's do the "Five Juicy Apples" chant next.* Proceed as usual, using a different child's name each time. Hold up one hand with splayed fingers to count down from five to zero.

- Linger on the first sound of the second word in rhyming pairs (e.g., *store/four; be/three; through/two; pair/there*) so children can chime in.

- Repeat the chant two times today, and tell children who did not get turns today that they will do the poem again next week, so they will get turns then.

OLD MACDONALD HAD A FARM

Materials: CD Track 6, Song Lyrics page 162, flannel board and pieces for the song

Vocabulary: farm, chick, duck, cow, horse, goat, pig, sheep

Procedure

- Say something like, *It's been a long time since we sang "Old MacDonald Had a Farm." I'm going to put the animals up that are on the farm today, and you can name them as I do that.* Place the animals one at a time, and name any that children cannot name.

- Tell children that they will sing about the animals in the order they are up on the flannel board. Point to each one as you say, *The cow first, the duck second, the horse third, and the goat fourth* (or whatever animals are up). Be sure to use the ordinal number terms (e.g., first, second) to help children learn them.

- Remove animals from the board one at a time. Ask children to name the animals again as you remove them.

▶ Lunch/Quiet Time/Centers

This time is set aside for lunch, quiet time, and center activities. See pages 10–11 for suggested conversation topics during this time.

▶ Let's Talk About It

Understanding Feelings: Anticipation of Disappointment

Purposes

Interacts appropriately with other children. Communicates using verbal and non-verbal cues.

Procedure

- Remind children that in the book *A Letter to Amy,* Peter was not sure on the day of the party that Amy would actually come. You might say, *It's hard sometimes to invite someone to a party or to play with you. Sometimes you're not sure whether the person will be able to come, and you know you will be disappointed if that happens.*

- Ask about children's experiences with invitations. For example, *Have you ever been a little unsure about inviting someone to do something with you, because you wondered whether they would want to, and you knew you'd be a little disappointed if they said no?*

- Engage a few children in a discussion. If no one has ideas or if you worry this topic might not work, ask if they have ever been disappointed when they did not get to do something with a friend or family member.

- Support children who want to tell about a time when this happened to them. For example:

  Jamil: Well, one time I invited Adam over, but he couldn't come. His mommy said, "no." I cried.

  Teacher: *Yes, it is disappointing when someone can't play. I hope you were able to invite Adam to play another day.*

- Sum up the discussion. For example, you might say, *Feeling disappointed is hard, isn't it? Usually our friends want to play with us. But sometimes it doesn't work out for that day and we have to try again on another day.*

▶ End-the-Day Centers

Children spend time in open Centers of their choice. As children leave for home, say something that will help each child look forward to the next day. For example, tell children who like singing, *Tomorrow we'll have fun singing "Five Green and Speckled Frogs."*

▶ **Start-the-Day Centers** (see pages 12–14)
Children to spend time in selected Centers.

▶ **Morning Meeting** (see page 12)
Review plans for the day with children and consult the turns list.

▶ **Center Time** (see pages 12–14)
Children spend time in Centers of their choice.

▶ **Story Time: 3rd Reading**

The Little Red Hen (Makes a Pizza)
Author: Philemon Sturges

Read the Story Again

In this reading, invite children to chime in with short parts of the story. This gives children the opportunity to practice saying many of the new words. Prompt recall by lingering over the first sound of a word or first word or two in a phrase. Also cue children by pantomiming words like *stirred, kneaded,* and *pounded.* Children may also wish to chime in on repeated words and phrases like *cluck* and *"Not I," said the (duck, dog, cat).*

If there is time to read a second book, children might enjoy revisiting *Peter's Chair* or *Whistle for Willie* from Unit 1.

Story Discussion

Prompt discussion with questions. For example: *After everyone had finished eating the delicious pizza, Hen asked,* "Who will help me do the dishes?" (Show page.) *But then we see on the next page that the cat, dog, and duck are doing the dishes. Do you think Hen told the other animals to do dishes? Or is it more likely that the* animals offered? (There's no one right answer, because we don't really know.)

Words and Phrases for Chiming In
(Vocabulary words appear in **dark** type.)

cupboard, **tomato sauce** – p. 1
pizza – pp. 1, 2, 13, 14, 15, 18, 19, 22, 24
rummaged – p. 2
"Not I," said the [dog] – pp. 3, 7, 11, 13, 16
. . . then, I'll **fetch** one myself – pp. 4, 8, 11
hardware store – p. 4
pickled eggplant – pp. 5, 12, 18
flour – pp. 5, 6, 8
. . . stuck her head out the window – pp. 6, 10, 13, 16, 22
Hello – p. 6
supermarket – p. 8
mozzarella – pp. 9, 10, 12, 18
delicatessen – p. 12
apron – p. 13
dough – pp. 14, 15, 18
sip – p. 1
delicious – p. 19
YES! – p. 24
I will. – pp. 26, 27
they did – p. 28

Extending the Book

Print "Not I," on a card, and ask children who are ready for a challenge to say the phrase *"Not I," said the dog* (cat, duck) when you hold up the card.

English Language Learners

Repeat the phrases *good morning, hello, good afternoon,* and *good evening* when they appear in the story and encourage children to chime in on them.

▶ **Outdoor Play**

Use sounds from story words to dismiss children. For example: *If your name starts with /d/ like* dog *and* duck. . . *If your name starts with /h/ like* hen . . . and so on. See pages 10–11 for suggested conversation topics during this time.

▶ Songs, Word Play, Letters

Today children will be playing word games, singing songs, and reciting poems. Add your favorite game, song, or poem to this collection.

Songs

"Five Green and Speckled Frogs"; "Come On and Join In to the Game"; "Open, Shut Them"

Predictable Book

HUSH!

Literacy Skills

Chiming in With Rhyming Words; If Your Name Starts With [first sound in child's name], Raise Your Hand; Guess What Word I'm Saying

Purposes

Recites songs, rhymes, chants, and poems, and engages in language and word play. Listens with increasing attention. Listens to a variety of genres read aloud: predictable textbooks and poems. Communicates using verbal and non-verbal cues. Segments first sounds in words.

Suggested Sequence for Today's Circle

1. "Five Green and Speckled Frogs"

2. "Come On and Join In to the Game"

3. HUSH! (and Chiming in With Rhyming Words)

4. If Your Name Starts With [first sound in child's name], Raise Your Hand

5. "Open, Shut Them"

6. Guess What Word I'm Saying [and Little Red Hen (Makes a Pizza)]

Materials and Instructional Procedures

FIVE GREEN AND SPECKLED FROGS

Materials: CD Track 10, Song Lyrics page 163, flannel board and flannel pieces

Vocabulary: green, speckled, log, delicious, pool, cool

Procedure

- As you place the pieces on the flannel board, ask children if they know what song you are about to sing.

- Tell children that, yes that is the name of the song, but, unfortunately, one frog is sick today, so can't play on the log and in the pool. Ask children what they think the song should be called today.

- Perform the song, using only four flannel pieces and, sing, *Four green and speckled frogs . . .* in the first verse, instead of five.

COME ON AND JOIN IN TO THE GAME

Materials: CD Track 20, Song Lyrics page 163

Vocabulary: clap, come, join, game, sneeze, jump, bow, low

Procedure

- Tell children that, next, they are going to sing "Come On and Join In to the Game" again. Sing the first two verses ("clapping," "sneezing") slowly, and model the motions.

- Stand up and ask the children to stand up too. Sing a third verse ("jump high with me"), and then a fourth ("bow low like me"). Model the motions as you sing. Go slowly enough so children can keep up.

- Ask children to sit down, and tell them that next you are going to read the book HUSH!

HUSH! (AND CHIMING IN WITH RHYMING WORDS)

Vocabulary: weeping, wind, mosquito, sleeping, nearby, lizard, creeping

Materials: book: HUSH!

Procedure

- Read the book aloud, keeping the natural rhythm of the verse. Point to pictures to identify objects named.

- As you read, linger on the first sound in the second of a pair of rhyming words to signal children to chime in with you (e.g., *peep-ing/sleeping, cry/nearby, squeaking/sleeping, beeping/sleeping*).

IF YOUR NAME STARTS WITH [FIRST SOUND IN A CHILD'S NAME], RAISE YOUR HAND

Vocabulary: hand, name, raise

Procedure:

- Tell children that the next thing they are going to do is play a game with their names. Tell them that, this time, instead of holding up letters, you are going to say sounds.

- Model game for children, by using a first sound not used in the children's names. You might say *I'm going to say a sound, such as /t/, /t/. Let's pretend that someone named Tanika is in our class. If I said /t/ and then said "If your name starts with /t/, raise your hand," then Tanika would raise her hand. I'm going to say some sounds that I know are at the beginning of your names. When I say a sound, think about your own name. If it begins with the sound I say, then raise your hand. I'll help you, if you need help. I will say enough sounds so everyone will have a turn today to raise a hand.*

- Proceed with the game, using first sounds found in names of children in the group. Hang on to the sound long enough to give children time to compare it to the beginning sound in their name.

- If a child does not respond, say something like, *Misty, your name starts with /m/. Misty, /m/* (draw out the /m/ sound in the letter and in her name to provide very explicit help), *so you can raise your hand.*

- Be sure to say the target sound (/m/, /m/) and not the letter name (*m*).

OPEN, SHUT THEM

Materials: CD Track 9, Song Lyrics page 163

Vocabulary: open, shut, clap, in, lap, creep, chin

Procedure

- Sing the song with the children as before, modeling the hand motions.

- An alternative song with a lot of body movement is "Shake Your Sillies Out." A source for this song is provided at the right.

GUESS WHAT WORD I'M SAYING [AND *THE LITTLE RED HEN (MAKES A PIZZA)*]

Vocabulary: hen, pizza, pans, duck, bowl, jars, jam, dough

Materials: book: *The Little Red Hen (Makes a Pizza)*

Procedure

- Say something like, *You know this book. It's The Little Red Hen (Makes Pizza). I'm going to say some words that are in this book in a funny way, a way that is not quite right. I want you to say the words the right way. For example, If I say "lit-"* (pause) *"-tle," you say "little."*

- Repeat with *tasty: ta-* (pause) *-sty, lovely: love-* (pause) *-ly, morning: morn-* (pause) *-ing, window: win-* (pause) *-dow,* and *olives: ol-* (pause) *-ives,* or other two-syllable words from the book you think children would like.

- Wait for children to raise their hand to guess the word, or go child by child around the circle. Do just a few words unless children show great interest.

SUGGESTED RESOURCES

Book

Raffi. "Shake My Sillies Out." In *The Raffi Singable Songbook,* (New York: Crown Publishers Inc., 1980).

CD

Raffi. "Shake My Sillies Out." *More Singable Songs.* Raffi. Rounder Records compact sound disc. 1996.

▶ Lunch and Quiet Time

This time is set aside for lunch, quiet time, and center activities. See pages 10–11 for suggested conversation topics during this time.

▶ Small Groups

For information on small groups, refer to pages 15–17.

▶ Let's Find Out About It

Exploring Cooking Pans

Purposes

Listens with increasing attention. Understands the proper use of tools and equipment. Begins to understand the properties associated with objects. Develops understanding of different kinds of texts.

Materials

books: *The Little Red Hen (Makes a Pizza)*, *A Letter to Amy*, children's cookbook; muffin or cupcake, a variety of pans (muffin, loaf, pizza, cookie sheet), loaf of bread, grocery store ads

Suggested Vocabulary

Convey word meanings by using them appropriately in today's discussion.

cake pan, directions, frying pan, loaf pan, mold, muffin pan, pizza pan, recipe

Procedure

- Bring in a variety of pans to show children. Show a few distinctive pans (muffin, bread, cake), and ask children if they know what kind of food is cooked in them. Explain that each pan has a specific use.

- Show a muffin and a loaf of bread, and then show the pans in which they were baked. Point out how the baked items take the shape of the pans in which they are cooked.

- Look through a children's cookbook and point out pictures showing prepared foods in baking or cooking pans. Read brief directions in different recipes that specify the types of pans needed.

> **English Language Learners**
>
> As you discuss different types of pans, say the name of each pan slowly. Invite children to say the names with you a second time.

- Go to page 2 in *The Little Red Hen (Makes a Pizza)*. Point out a few pans and ask, *What kind of pan is this one?* Provide the name if no one knows.

- Explain that sometimes a recipe calls for a specific kind of pan. A person needs to shop for it if they don't have it. Point out that in *The Little Red Hen (Makes a Pizza)*, the little red hen had to buy a pizza pan before she could make her pizza. Sometimes people can use something they already have, for example a cookie sheet instead of a pizza pan.

Small Groups Connections

Place pans in the dramatic play area and at the art table for play with sculpting dough.

> **Extending the Activity**
>
> For children who are ready for a challenge, show some unusual kinds of pans, such as Angel Food, bundt, or shortbread cookie pan molds.

Connect With Families

In a note to families, explain that this week, children read a story called *The Little Red Hen (Makes a Pizza)* and talked about helping. Give parents ideas for ways that children can help with meals at home. For example, children might help set the table or tear lettuce for a salad. Provide parents with some of the new words children are learning and ask them to listen to see if they are used at home.

SUGGESTED RESOURCES

Books

Watt, Fiona (author) and Stephen Cartwright and Molly Sage (illustrators). *Farmyard Tales Children's Cookbook*. London: Usborne, 2002.

Wilkes, Angela. *First Cookbook*. London: Usborne, 2001.

▶ End-the-Day Centers

Children can choose among open Centers. As children leave for home, say something that will help each child look forward to next week. For example, tell children that next week they can play with pans and cooking tools at the sand table.

Notes to Teachers

Here are some tips and suggestions that might be helpful.

Center Time

Dramatic Play

- Encourage children who are playing parents in the house area to have their doll babies play together. Provide baby toys (e.g., rattles, cloth books) to support such play. Coach children in how to have their babies "talk" to one another. As appropriate, also encourage children who are playing parents to do as friends do, by going together to take their "children" to visit the library, or for a walk "around the block."

Let's Talk About It

- Specific ideas for Let's Talk About It topics are provided in the Weekly Planner. Remember that the schedule suggests topics after a Story Time book has been read at least twice.

- Many of the ideas provided are based on topics that come up in storybooks. Others address social-emotional situations that arise frequently in preschool classrooms.

- The schedule provided should be used as a guide and should not be adhered to rigidly, given that it makes more sense to discuss a topic as it relates to the actual life of the classroom.

Looking Ahead

Looking Ahead to Unit 3, Wind and Water

- In the Unit 3 storybook *Gilberto and the Wind,* a story character sweeps leaves that have fallen to the ground. Gather some fall leaves with children, if you can, and save these (in between sheets of waxed paper) for showing later when you read the book.

Looking Ahead to Unit 6, Things That Grow

- Collect pine cones in the fall, if you can, and store in plastic bags. If you make a jack-o-lantern with children, be sure to save pumpkin seeds.

- If children are served fresh fruit for snacks or lunch, have them start saving seeds from apples.

- Gather small twigs and sticks, and harvest some grass and dry it. These supplies will come in handy for a nest-making activity.

- Be on the lookout in the fall for abandoned birds' nests in shrubs and trees. It's great to be able to show children the real thing when you discuss nests.

Weekly Planner

	Day 1	Day 2	Day 3
Start-the-Day Centers 30 Minutes **Morning Meeting** 15 Minutes **Center Time** 60 Minutes pp. 52–54	Greet children and open selected Centers. Introduce Center Time activities. **Blocks:** Materials for Making a Playground; **Sand and Water:** Making Sand Molds; **Dramatic Play:** Grocery Shopping Props; **Book Area:** Exploring Books; **Art Area/Table:** Making Stationery, Making Crayon Rubbings; **Art Area/Easel:** Drawing with Chalk; **Puzzles and Manipulatives:** Letter Tiles and Word Cards, Alphabet and Name Memory Games; **Writing Center:** Writing on Handmade Stationery, Writing Captions for Class Photo Album		
Toileting and Snack 15 Minutes			
Story Time 20 Minutes	**4th Reading** – *The Little Red Hen (Makes a Pizza)* Read another book of your choice. p. 60	**1st Reading** – *Matthew and Tilly* pp. 64–67	**2nd Reading** – *Matthew and Tilly* pp. 71–73
Outdoor Play 35 Minutes	**Conversations:** Observe children who struggle with following rules. Praise their successes.	**Conversations:** Use varied verbs to describe actions: *jump, leap, climb, balance, skip.*	**Conversations:** If there is a conflict, support discussion of what occurred. Do not force an apology, but do get children to recognize each other's hurt feelings.
Songs, Word Play, Letters 20 Minutes	**Songs:** "Down by the Bay"; "Come On and Join In to the Game"; "The More We Get Together" **Predictable Book:** *Golden Bear* **Literacy Skills:** Those Words Rhyme!; Interesting-Sounding Words pp. 61–62	**Songs:** "Five Green and Speckled Frogs"; "Head and Shoulders, Knees and Toes" **Poems:** "Three Little Monkeys"; "Ten Little Fingers" **Literacy Skills:** Guess What Word I'm Saying; Interesting-Sounding Words pp. 68–69	**Songs:** "Old MacDonald Had a Farm"; "Bingo"; "The More We Get Together" **Predictable Book:** *Golden Bear* **Poems:** "Mix a Pancake" **Literacy Skills:** Those Words Rhyme!; If Your Name Starts With [name a letter], Clap Just Once pp. 74–75
Handwashing/Toileting 10 Minutes			
Lunch/Quiet Time/ Center Time 90 Minutes	**Conversations:** *What are some things you like to do with your friends at home?* Ensure different children get turns to talk.	**Conversations:** *What are some words that name actions we do at mealtime?* (Verbs you may use: *eat, chew, cut, slice, chop, hold, open.*)	**Conversations:** *Have you had a fight like Matthew and Tilly and then gotten back together?* Guide recall; avoid reviving bad feelings.
Small Groups 25 Minutes pp. 55–58	**Mathematics:** How Many Dinosaurs? **Science:** Sorting Items for Grocery Store Play **Language and Print Manipulatives:** Simple Puzzles of Fruits and Vegetables, Alphabet Letter Tiles and Storybook Word Cards **Games:** Uppercase Alphabet Memory, Children's Names Memory	**Science:** Sorting Items for Grocery Store Play **Language and Print Manipulatives:** Uppercase and Lowercase Matching, Lauri® Lacing Cards, Match Pictures and Words from *Matthew and Tilly* **Book Browsing:** Exploring Books	**Science:** Sorting Items for Grocery Store Play **Language and Print Manipulatives:** Uppercase and Lowercase Matching, Lauri® Lacing Cards, Match Pictures and Words from *Matthew and Tilly* **Book Browsing:** Exploring Books
Let's Find Out About It/ Let's Talk About It 20 Minutes	Grocery Stores and Grocery Lists p. 63	Finding Things in a Grocery Store p. 70	Grocery Store Jobs p. 76
End-the-Day Centers 20 Minutes	Open selected Centers and prepare children to go home.		

Day 4	Day 5
3rd Reading – *A Letter to Amy* p. 77 Read another book of your choice.	**4th Reading** – *A Letter to Amy* p. 81 *Read A Cake All for Me!, The Doorbell Rang, Jamaica's Find*, or another book of your choice.
Conversations: Gently enter and extend, modeling possible roles and dialogue.	**Conversations:** Talk with children about their weekend plans. Be sensitive to privacy issues.
Songs: "Five Little Ducks"; "Story-Character Bingo"; "Five Green and Speckled Frogs" **Predictable Book:** *HUSH!* **Literacy Skills:** I'm Thinking of __ Clue Game pp. 78–79	**Songs:** "Down by the Bay"; "What Are You Wearing?"; "Head and Shoulders, Knees and Toes" **Poems:** "Mix a Pancake"; "Five Juicy Apples"; "Three Little Monkeys" **Literacy Skills:** Those Words Begin With the Same Sound!; Alphabet Memory Pocket Chart Game pp. 82–83
Conversations: *Do you go to the store with someone from your family?* Discuss doing errands with family members.	**Conversations:** *What did you do in Center Time this week?*
Language and Print Manipulatives: Uppercase and Lowercase Matching, Lauri® Lacing Cards, Match Pictures and Words from *Matthew and Tilly* **Book Browsing:** Exploring Books	**Mathematics:** Matching, Identifying, and Counting Coins/Making Play Money Bills **Language & Print Manipulatives:** Making Store Signs **Book Browsing:** Exploring Books
Building Friendships: Talking About Play Interests p. 80	**Work Friends** p. 84

Half-Day Program Schedule

2 hours 45 minutes
A half-day program includes two literacy circles.

10 min.	**Start-the-Day Centers** Writing Center, Book Area, Puzzles and Manipulatives
10 min.	**Morning Meeting**
60 min.	**Center Time** Include mathematics and science activities from Small Groups. Incorporate Small Groups writing activities at Writing Centers.
20 min.	**Story Time** Use discussion questions from Let's Talk About It to address social-emotional issues and topics from Let's Find Out About It to address concept development.
35 min.	**Outdoor Play**
20 min.	**Songs, Word Play, Letters**
10 min.	**End-the-Day Centers** Writing Center, Book Area, Puzzles and Manipulatives

Connect With Families

- Remind parents that children are welcome to use the classroom lending library. Tell parents to ask their children about how this works, and to tell their children that they would be very happy to read a book that the child brings home.

- Send home the words to the poems "Five Juicy Apples" and "Three Little Monkeys" (*Big Book of Poetry*, Poems 5 and 6) so that parents can learn the words. Suggest that parents ask their children to teach them the motions that go along with these poems.

Start-the-Day Centers

- Open two to three Centers (e.g. Puzzles and Manipulatives, Writing Center, Book Area) for children to go to upon their arrival. Spend time with children in the Centers, helping as appropriate and as time allows.

Morning Meeting

- Introduce children to Centers by showing some selected objects from each Center and briefly demonstrating activities to help them make a first choice.

- For example, **Monday:** You might want to show the alphabet letter stamps that have been added to the Art Table and model use of the shopping list materials from Dramatic Play. **Tuesday:** Show children illustrations from *Golden Bear,* and then suggest they draw with chalk like the illustrator did on the new paper at the easel. **Wednesday:** Show the new molds that have been added to the sand table. **Thursday:** Show some photos for the class photo album in the Writing Center. Tell children to look for themselves in the photos and to think of captions that describe them. **Friday:** Show some samples of the easel pictures made with chalk. Be sure to show a variety (e.g., those that resemble the *Golden Bear* illustrations and others that have original themes).

- Use the suggested vocabulary for each Center as you demonstrate activities.

- You might want to modify or substitute an activity to meet your children's needs. For more information on organizing and adapting Center Time activities to your classroom, see Notes to Teachers on page 85.

▲ Making Sand Molds

SAND AND WATER

Making Sand Molds

SCIENCE

Purposes: Observes and explores materials and objects in the environment. Uses a variety of tools and materials to strengthen hand grasp, flexibility, and coordination. Describes physical properties of materials.

Materials: sand, spray bottle with warm water, variety of molds (e.g., gelatin molds, funnels, measuring cups, melon ball scoops, plastic egg halves, small muffin tins, mini cake tins, mini letter molds, pieces of cardboard larger than the molds

Preparation: Spread sand into bottom of water table and moisten it with warm water. Place a few sand molds, spoons, and scoops at each place. Add new molds and remove old ones as the week progresses. Spray sand periodically as children play, to keep it damp enough to form good molds.

Suggested Vocabulary: mold, shape; dry, moist, packed; crumble, dump, fill, jiggle, overturn, tap

- Observe and comment about children's molds. For example, *You're working very hard filling up that mold. What kind of shape are you making?*

- Provide assistance as needed. You might say, *Can I help you tap the mold and overturn it to see the shape you made? Sometimes the sand crumbles a bit so we need to add a little warm water to make it work again.*

BOOK AREA

Exploring Books

Purposes: Independently chooses to read or pretends to read books. Understands that pictures, print, and other symbols carry meaning. Recalls some main events when retelling stories, using pictures as prompts.

Materials: Add *The Little Red Hen (Makes a Pizza)* and *A Letter to Amy* to the collection.

- Encourage children to explore books together or independently.

- Listen and comment as children retell stories. You might say, *Those animals never want to help, do they?* Talk with children after they have finished retelling a story. You might say, *If you had been Little Red Hen, would you have invited the animals to come have pizza?*

ART AREA: TABLE

Making Stationery

- Continue activity from Week 1 (page 13). Add alphabet stamps, list of children's names with first initials in boldface, initials alone (optional). Encourage children to make monogrammed stationery if they like.

Making Crayon Rubbings

Purposes: Explores and experiments with dry media to create artwork. Observes and explores materials, objects, in the environment.

Materials: ridged edges of plastic packaging from colored sticker labels, sink mats, pieces of plastic kitchen shelf lining, fall leaves, pieces of corduroy

fabric, pieces of textured wallpaper, clipboards (for securing both the backing board and the piece of paper for the rubbing), trays or dishes for crayon pieces, pieces of cardboard, poster board, glue, white photocopy paper, markers

Preparation: Glue objects, such as leaves and pieces of fabric, shelf lining material, and bath mats, on cardboard or poster board backing. Remove paper wrappers from crayons and arrange a collection of colors in small dishes or trays.

Suggested Vocabulary: clipboard, design, pattern, rubbings, texture, wrappings; bumpy, over, under; insert, removed

- Assist children who need help. Show how to secure items on a clipboard, and how to hold the crayon and rub it sideways to produce a rubbing.

- Observe and engage children in conversations about their crayon rubbings. You might say, *I can tell that's a rubbing of a leaf by its shape.* Or, *That's a bumpy one isn't it? That picture is so interesting. Can you tell me how you made it?*

- Ask children to write their names on their pictures. Provide help if children ask for it.

- Display drawings on a bulletin board in the center.

ART AREA: EASEL

Drawing With Chalk

Purposes: Creates two-dimensional artwork. Explores and experiments with dry media to create artwork. Explores and experiments with basic shapes and lines in artwork.

Materials: colored chalk, brightly colored construction paper (18" × 24"), smocks, easel

Suggested Vocabulary: chalk; blurred, dark, hard, light, sharp, soft, thin, wider; blend

- Talk with children about their drawings. You might say, *I see you've used many different colors in your drawing. Oh, something interesting happened here, when you blended two colors.* Or, *I notice you are drawing with the chalk on its side. It makes wider lines that way, doesn't it?*

- Ask children to sign his or her painting with markers or chalk. Provide help if needed.

- Send the drawings home with children at the end of the day.

BLOCKS

Materials for Making a Playground

Purposes: Performs fine-motor tasks that require small-muscle strength and control. Creates simple representations of home, school, or community. Uses words and seeks adult help in conflict resolution.

Materials: Add to existing materials: construction blocks that snap together, blue construction paper, and other items that you think might add to the play

Suggested Vocabulary: Add these words to those introduced in Week 1 (page 13): ladder, playhouse, pool, slide, swing, toys; climb, jump.

- Suggest to children, if it seems appropriate, that they create a community pool and climbing structures for the playground with paper and construction blocks.

Continued on next page

- Observe children and talk with them about their buildings. You might say, *Tell me about what you have built here. It looks very interesting.* Or, *That pool looks like fun. I'd like to jump in! Can grownups swim there or just kids?*

- Help children resolve conflicts and negotiate differences. For example, you might say, *I think that was an accident. Lisa didn't mean to step on and tear your pool. Here, let's get some tape to fix it. Maybe Lisa would like to help us.*

PUZZLES AND MANIPULATIVES

Letter Tiles and Word Cards; Alphabet and Name Memory Games

Purposes: Names many uppercase letters. Builds finger dexterity and uses thumb/forefinger pincer grasp.

Materials: Add to materials from Week 1 (page 14): alphabet letter tiles, storybook word cards (with a picture as clue), uppercase alphabet memory game cards, children's names memory cards

Vocabulary: Add these words to those introduced in Week 1 (page 14): alphabet, game, letter, name, picture, story, tile, word; uppercase, round, straight

- Ask children to name letters and describe their features if time permits. You might say, *This letter has all straight lines. What letter is it?*

- Help children identify storybook words on cards. For example, *What is this picture? Its name starts with /k/. It is something we eat at a birthday party.* (cake) *What letter do we use to write /k/? Right,* K. *Do you see that letter here?*

- Ask questions as children play the Name Memory game. For example, *Oh, whose name is that?* Or, *Oh, that's Mandy's name, with* M *at the beginning. I wonder where the match is?*

DRAMATIC PLAY

Grocery Shopping Props

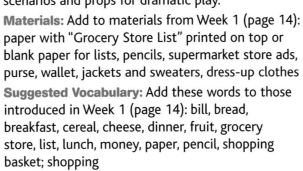

Purposes: Creates characters through physical movement, gesture, sound, speech, and facial expressions. Creates scenarios and props for dramatic play.

Materials: Add to materials from Week 1 (page 14): paper with "Grocery Store List" printed on top or blank paper for lists, pencils, supermarket store ads, purse, wallet, jackets and sweaters, dress-up clothes

Suggested Vocabulary: Add these words to those introduced in Week 1 (page 14): bill, bread, breakfast, cereal, cheese, dinner, fruit, grocery store, list, lunch, money, paper, pencil, shopping basket; shopping

- Encourage children to make a list of items they need from the store, then pretend to go shopping to try to find all the items.

- Make connections to shopping scenes in *The Little Red Hen (Makes a Pizza)* as they play freely with grocery store props.

- Observe and engage children in conversation. You might say, *I think I'll go with you to the grocery store, if you don't mind. I need to jot down a few things on a list first. Can you wait just a minute?*

WRITING CENTER

Writing on Handmade Stationery

Continue activity from Week 1 (page 14).

Writing Captions for Class Photo Album

Purposes: Composes and dictates or writes messages. Interacts appropriately with other children by cooperating, helping, sharing, and expressing interest. Asks and answers questions.

Materials: disposable flash camera, or photos taken in classroom settings, card-weight paper for mounting photos, plastic sleeves to enclose photos, machine to laminate finished photo album pages, markers, paper

Preparation: Take photos of children engaged in activities and interacting with friends in a variety of settings. Mount two photos with small bits of masking tape to a card-weight backing, and slip them into a plastic sheet protector. The photos will be used to make three class photo albums in Small Groups.

Suggested Vocabulary: album, author, camera, caption, cooperation, film, flash, friendship, photograph; develop, help, make up, share

- Invite children to find themselves and their friends in the photos, and think about what they would like to say about them. You might say, *Who were you playing with at the water table?* Or, *This is a picture of you and Samantha pretending to buy groceries.* Or, *Who is in this photo?* Or, *What was happening here?*

- Write the captions children dictate, as time permits.

Unit 2 • Week 2
Small Groups

Small Groups Overview

- Each day there are three different Small Group activities. The same three activities are made available for three days, and each group of five or six children spends one of the three days in each activity. Small groups work best when children are at tables.

- On Day 1, complete the rotation of children through the three groups from Days 4 and 5 of Week 1.

- On Days 2, 3, and 4, children sort food containers, match letters, words and pictures, play with lacing cards; and spend time browsing fiction and information books in the book area.

- On Day 5, children learn to identify, match, and count money; create grocery store signs; and browse two new predictable books that have been added to the collection.

- Use suggested vocabulary words and phrases in a manner that clarifies their meaning for children.

▲ Grocery Store Play

MATHEMATICS

How Many Dinosaurs?: Day 1 `High support`

- Proceed with activity from Days 4 and 5 of Week 1 (page 17). You might say, *Last week you might have noticed some children playing a game with dinosaurs. Now it's your turn.*

LANGUAGE AND PRINT MANIPULATIVES

Simple Puzzles of Fruits and Vegetables: Day 1 `Low support`

- Proceed with activity from Week 1, Days 4 and 5 (page 17). Tell children it is their turn today to play with the puzzles of fruits and vegetables.

Alphabet Letter Tiles and Storybook Word Cards: Day 1 `Medium support`

- Proceed with activity from Week 1 (page 17). Tell children it is their turn today to play with letters to make storybook words.

GAMES

Uppercase Alphabet Memory: Day 1 `Medium support`

- Proceed with activity from Week 1, Days 4 and 5 (page 17). Tell children that today it is their turn to play the Alphabet Memory Game.

Children's Names Memory: Day 1

- Proceed with activity from Week 1, Days 4 and 5 (page 17). Tell children that today it is their turn to play the Name Memory Game.

SCIENCE

Sorting Items for Grocery Store Play: Days 2, 3, 4 `Medium support`

Purposes: Locates objects in a familiar environment. Makes comparisons among objects and sort things into categories. Participates successfully as a member of a group. Recognizes several highly familiar words in the environment.

Continued on next page

Materials: food, toiletry, and household item containers collected from home, plastic fruits and vegetables, boxes or box lids (long and wide, but not very tall), plastic grocery bags, supermarket advertising flyers, poster or tag board, glue

Preparation: Assemble materials you've collected. Use large boxes or box lids to hold the groups of like items after children have sorted them. Make large signs for the following categories: Dairy Products, Personal Care Items, Canned Fruits and Vegetables, Baking Items and Mixes, Pasta and Dried Grains, Cereals, Crackers, and Cookies, Frozen Foods. Decorate these signs with colored pictures from supermarket ads.

Suggested Vocabulary: box, dairy, fruits, grains, grocery store, jar, label, mix, pasta, personal care products, produce, vegetables, directions, frozen; belongs with, inside

Procedure

- Tell children they will organize items for a play grocery store. Remind them they discussed how items are organized in a grocery store in Let's Find Out About It (page 63).

- Decide on 3 to 4 signs for each day's small group, and place one sign in a box lid or box. Give pairs of children cartons of items from these categories and have them sort them into piles.

- Read and explain the meaning of the signs with children. You might say, *The word* produce *means fruits and vegetables. That's why there are pictures of apples and broccoli on this sign. What other foods would go in this box? That's right, carrots and apples would. How about cookies? Cookies aren't a fruit or vegetable, right? Which box would cookies go in?* Help children find the sign that says *Cereal, Cookies, Crackers,* and has pictures of

these items on it. As you discuss individual items, model placing them in the appropriate boxes.

- *Extra Support* Point out clues to help children identify items and decide which box they belong in. Explain that they can use a process of elimination to decide where to put each item. For example, you might say, *Tell me about the picture on the front of that box. That's right, it's a picture of a muffin. Now let's look at each sign to see where it belongs.* Or, *Is it a fruit or vegetable? No? Well, is it a frozen or canned food? No? Well, do you think it is a baking item or mix? That's right! This is a mix you can use to bake muffins, so it belongs in this box.*

- *ELL* Discuss with children some of the foods they eat at home. You might ask, *Do you eat this cereal at home? No? What kind do you eat?* Or, *Do you like corn? What other vegetables do you like?*

- If time permits after items have been sorted, review the contents of each box. You might say, *Let's see what things we'll be able to sell in our grocery store. Let's start with dairy products.* Have children identify each item in the box. Help, as needed, to move things along.

LANGUAGE AND PRINT MANIPULATIVES

Uppercase and Lowercase Matching: Days 2, 3, 4

Medium support

Purposes: Associates the name of a letter with its shape. Recognizes uppercase and lowercase letter pairs.

Materials: tag board, marker, double-sided tape (or similar), laminating machine (optional)

Preparation: Make multiple copies of upper- and lowercase letter tiles from tag board. Mount 6

uppercase tiles on the left-hand column of two pieces of tag board. These are the background boards. Laminate background boards and letter tiles, if possible. Use self-fastening material on the background board and the backs of tiles, so that lowercase tiles can be stuck next to their uppercase match.

Suggested Vocabulary: letter, letter names; lowercase, uppercase; match

Procedure

- Tell children they are going to play a matching game with letters. Explain that letters can be written two ways: uppercase and lowercase. Show a letter tile of an uppercase and lowercase *g* to provide an example. You might ask, *Does anyone know what letters these are? That's right, they are both g's. This g is bigger than the other g. It's called uppercase G. The smaller g is called lowercase g.*

- Give two pairs of children a background board and point to the uppercase letters in the left column.

- *Extra Support* As you work with children, say the letter names and have children repeat them with you several times.

- *Extra Support* If children are having difficulty matching letters, point out a critical feature of the letter and trace the letter shape with your finger as you describe it. For example, *This is an uppercase N. It has three straight lines* (point to lines) *1, 2, 3. A lowercase n doesn't look like the uppercase N. The lowercase n has one straight line, and one curved line.*

Lauri® Lacing Cards: Days 2, 3, 4
Medium support

Purposes: Builds finger dexterity and uses thumb/forefinger pincer grasp.

Materials: Lauri® or other similar grasp lacing cards

Preparation: Place 3–4 lacing cards and laces on a tray. One pair of children can share these materials at a time.

Suggested Vocabulary: hole, lace, loops, shoelace; through; weave

Procedure

- Describe materials. For example, *This is called a lace. It's like the shoelaces you use to tie your shoes. Does anyone have shoes with laces on them?* Show a lacing card. You might say, *This is called a lacing card because you can weave a lace through the holes in it the same way you weave your shoelaces through the holes in your shoes.*

- Thread the lace through a few holes and describe your actions: *First I take the tip of the lace and push it through the hole. Then I pull it out through the next hole, like this, then in again through another hole. When I'm finished lacing, I'll have a special design.* Give the tray of lacing cards to the pair of children who will start with it.

- *SOCIAL-EMOTIONAL SUPPORT* Children may find different ways to weave laces through the cards. Accept each child's style. There's no one right way.

- *EXTRA SUPPORT* If children have difficulty holding the cards and lacing at the same time, suggest that they take turns with their partner.

Match Pictures and Words From Matthew and Tilly: Days 2, 3, 4

Purposes: Recognizes familiar words in books. Uses pictures to understand a book. Says new words and dialogue from stories. Understands that pictures, print, and other symbols carry meaning.

Materials: book: *Matthew and Tilly,* tag board, crayons or markers, laminating machine (optional),

Picture Cards: bike, cash register, crayon, ice-cream cone, lemon

Preparation: Make 2 sets (2–3 matches each) of word cards from tag board. Laminate the word cards, if possible. Use the following words from *Matthew and Tilly*: *bike, cash register, crayon, ice-cream cone, lemon.* Use the corresponding Picture Card to match each word.

Suggested Vocabulary: bike, cash register, crayon, ice-cream cone, lemon, lemonade; sell

Procedure

- Show picture and word matching materials to children. Identify a picture first, say its name, isolate the first sound in its name, and name the letter the word starts with. Then, find that word from among the word cards. Provide a copy of the book *Matthew and Tilly.* Have children look at the Picture Cards, talk about them, and find the place in the story where they appear. They can also look at the word cards that go with the pictures.

- *ELL* Remove the word cards, and have children focus only on the Picture Cards. Help children identify the pictures. Encourage them to name the pictures and talk about the item as it appeared in the story.

BOOK BROWSING

Exploring Books: Days 2, 3, 4

Purposes: Children hold a book upright and turn its pages from front to back while reading or pretending to read. Chooses independently to read or pretend to read books in the book area.

Materials: Add *The Little Red Hen (Makes a Pizza), A Letter to Amy,* and *Feast for 10* to the collection from Week 1.

Procedure

- Pair children to look at books together, or let children look at books individually. Have enough books to meet the interests of children.

- Encourage children to talk with one another about what they are reading.

- *EXTRA SUPPORT* Read portions of a book to children, or ask them about the illustrations.

- Book Browsing may be paired with other activities so that children remain engaged in small group work. Options are puzzles, writing, computers, or other activities of your choice.

MATHEMATICS

High support

Matching, Identifying, and Counting Coins/Making Play Money Bills: Day 5

Purposes: Knows that letters are different from numbers. Counts objects in a set. Writes for different purposes.

Materials: toy cash register, pennies, nickels, dimes, and quarters, $1 and $5 bills, play money coins, green construction paper, markers, guides for writing numbers 1 or 5, small dishes

Preparation: Cut green construction paper into rectangular pieces that resemble dollar bills. Draw an oval in 4 corners of one side of each piece, large enough for children to write *1* or *5* inside it. Prepare for each child 6–8 coins in a small dish. Include at least one coin of each kind in each dish.

Suggested Vocabulary: bills, cash register, coins, compartments, dime, nickel, penny, quarter

Procedure

- Tell children that before they can play store like Matthew in *Matthew and Tilly,* they need to learn about using a cash register. Point to the picture of the cash register in the book.

- Put the toy cash register on the table, open it, and point out the compartments for holding different kinds of money. Show children some of the play coins and bills and explain that when they play store they use pretend money, like this because real money could get lost.

- Show examples of real coins (quarter, dime, nickel, and penny) and name them. Give each child a small dish with 6–8 coins. You might say, *Inside your dish are some coins. We're going to find out what kinds of coins you have and how many you have.* Tell children to put together coins that are the same on the table. Go around the table and ask each child how many quarters, nickels, dimes, and pennies each has. Help children recall the names of each coin.

- Collect coins and show children an example of a $1 and $5 bill, pointing out the numbers on each one. You might say, *Is this a one- or five-dollar bill? How can you tell?* Hand out the green pieces of paper and explain that you need their help to turn them into pretend bills for their store. Point out the ovals on the paper and explain that they will write a *1* or *5* in each of them. Accept numbers even if they are rudimentary marks.

- *EXTRA SUPPORT* For children struggling with forming the number 5, demonstrate on a separate piece of paper as they watch. Have them attempt it one step at a time.

Progress Monitoring

Make copies of pages 158–159 to use as you record children's progress. Note which children know what the number *5* looks like, and the orientation they use to write it. Note which children enjoy and can use the picture and word matching cards successfully.

LANGUAGE AND PRINT MANIPULATIVES

Making Store Signs: Day 5

Medium support

Purposes: Children read environmental print, and identify letters. Writes for a specific purpose. Interacts appropriately with other children by cooperating, helping, sharing, and expressing interest.

Materials: 3 sheets of card-weight paper, glue sticks, large block letters (printed with computer), 7–8 large sheets of tag or poster board, scissors, 8–10 poly-styrene foam trays, supermarket advertisements

Preparation: Print out these words using block letters in a large font: *GROCERY STORE OPENING SOON, OPEN, CLOSED.* Make several copies of the letters, cut them out in blocks (rather than around the edges of letters), and arrange them in piles by letter. Trace light pencil lines on the poster board to show where the letters should be placed. The *OPEN* and *CLOSED* signs should be a quarter of a sheet of poster board with one word on each side. Make simple models of each sign on the card-weight paper on the computer. Cut out supermarket ads, sort by types of food, and place in trays.

Suggested Vocabulary: advertisements, business hours, display, notices, sale, sequence, signs; arrange, decorate

---

Procedure

- Tell children they are going to make signs for the grocery store.

- Have each pair of children create one sign. Provide the pairs with materials to make their sign and give them a model to follow. Read the models aloud. Show the pencil guidelines and instruct children to paste the letters that match the model onto the poster board. The children who make the *OPEN* and *CLOSED* sign can also help cut out food pictures to decorate the other signs.

- Observe and comment about children's work and encourage conversation. For example, *I see you found three letters for your sign already: G, R, and O. Tim, look at the model. Which letter comes next?*

- *ELL* Talk with children about the pictures they find. Repeat English words several times.

- *SOCIAL-EMOTIONAL SUPPORT* Encourage efforts as children work. Help as needed. When signs are finished, hang them up and praise children's work.

- Book Browsing may be paired with other activities so that children remain engaged in small group work. Options are puzzles, writing, computers, or other activities of your choice.

SUGGESTED RESOURCES

Books

De Bourgoing, Pascale and Gallimard Jeunesse (authors) and P. M. Valet (illustrator). *Fruit.* New York: Scholastic, 1991.

Ehlert, Lois. *Eating the Alphabet: Fruits and Vegetables from A to Z.* San Diego: Harcourt Children's Books, 1989.

Falwell, Cathryn. *Feast for 10.* Boston: Houghton Mifflin Company, 1993.

Developing Children's Language Through Conversation

One way that children gain the ability to control their own behavior is by learning to recognize and name different feelings. Recognizing and naming the emotions of characters in books is one way to help build children's vocabulary for talking about feelings. You can also help children identify and name their own emotions. Brief interactions that occur as children arrive and leave provide an opportunity to help children describe how they are feeling.

Mathematical Knowledge

There are many opportunities to help children learn concepts of number. For example: (1) encourage children to count actions, such as jumping; (2) after counting with children, reiterate "how many" were just counted. (*One-two-three-four. You did four jumps*); use ordinal numbers to describe steps in a sequence: First *we will line up*, Second *we will get quiet, and* third *we will go outdoors.*

Arrival and Departure

Use Vocabulary to Talk About Emotions

When children arrive, they bring with them a broad range of emotional states. As you greet a child, you are likely to note if a child is in good spirits or seems to be unhappy or tired. Welcome the child and honestly ask how he or she is feeling. Follow up your question by noting your guess about those feelings, commenting on cues you saw in the child's face or body that suggested those feelings. Help children use precise and varied words to describe feelings (pleased, expectant, excited, tired, angry, sad, shy) by using these words as you talk with them.

A Model for Conversation

Arrival and Departure: Naming Emotions

Teacher: *Good morning, Rosa. It's nice to see you today.*

Rosa: Hi. (in a quiet, sad voice)

Teacher: *How are you today?*

Rosa: Bad.

Teacher: *Oh, I'm sorry to hear that. I thought your face looked sad, or maybe mad. What's the matter?*

Rosa: My sister hit me.

Teacher: *Oh my, does it hurt?*

Rosa: Not now.

Teacher: *Oh, good. Do you want to talk more about it, or would you like to look at books or work on a puzzle?*

Rosa: Yeah. She wanted the chair, and I was there first.

Teacher: *Oh, I see. When was this, at breakfast?*

Rosa: Yes, and my mom said, "No! Don't hit her. You can sit over here."

Teacher: *Oh, I see. Sounds like your mommy helped you.*

Rosa: Yes. (goes off to the Puzzles and Manipulatives Center)

Good Conversations: Building a Science Vocabulary

Careful observation and precise description of objects and events is the starting point for science. To help children attend to different properties of objects (size, color, texture), model use of precise words to describe these properties.

Self-Regulation: Using the Turns List

If a child is having trouble waiting for a turn in a center, help him or her understand how the turns list works. Be sure that child's name is on the list, then help the child count how many children are listed ahead of her or him. Assure a turn tomorrow if a child does not get one today.

▶ **Start-the-Day Centers** (see pages 52–54)

Make two to three Centers available as you greet children and their families.

▶ **Morning Meeting** (see page 52)

Review plans for the day with children and orient them to center activities. Create a turns list for Centers if necessary.

▶ **Center Time** (see pages 52–54)

Children spend time in Centers of their choice.

▶ **Story Time: 4th Reading**

The Little Red Hen (Makes a Pizza)

Author: Philemon Sturges

Read *The Little Red Hen (Makes a Pizza)* Again

Ask all children to say the words that the animal friends speak. You take the role of Little Red Hen. Encourage children to say "Yes," enthusiastically when they respond to the offer of pizza, and to say "I will" affirmatively when they answer about helping with the dishes. When speaking Little Red Hen's part, be sure to raise your voice a bit, as if calling to the animals from your window.

Taking On the Roles of Story Characters

Duck, Cat, Dog:

Not I. — pp. 3, 7, 11, 13, 16

Yes! – p. 25

I will. – p. 27

Story Discussion

Prompt discussion with questions like these:

Let's suppose that, the next day, the dog decided to make a pizza because he had enjoyed the pizza so much at Hen's house. He asked Hen what he needed to make pizza, and if she would lend him some of her cooking things. Do you think she would help the dog? If yes, what might she put in her red wagon for him to borrow? Children might mention pizza pan, bowl, and pizza slicer. Use pictures to prompt naming of other items: wooden spoon, measuring spoons and cups, rolling pin, apron.

Other Book Suggestions

If you think a fourth reading of *The Little Red Hen (Makes a Pizza)* will not hold children's interest, substitute *Potluck* (see page 7) or another theme-related book. *Potluck* is about two children who invite all of their friends to their house for a potluck dinner.

Making Connections: Suggest that it might have been easier for Hen to organize a potluck than to cook pizza by herself. Ask, *What if Hen had invited Duck, Cat, and Dog to a potluck dinner and each one brought a dish that begins with the same letter as his or her name? What might each of them have brought for the meal?*

▶ **Outdoor Play**

Use color matches to dismiss children. For example, *If you are wearing something yellow like Duck's yellow feathers . . . If you are wearing something blue like Cat's fur . . .* and so on. For more information on Outdoor Play, see the Notes to Teachers on page 85. Also, see pages 50–51 for suggested conversation topics during Outdoor Play.

▶ Songs, Word Play, Letters

Today children will be playing word games, singing songs, and reciting poems. Add your favorite game, song, or poem to this collection.

Songs

"Down by the Bay"; "Come On and Join In to the Game"; "The More We Get Together"

Predictable Book

Golden Bear

Literacy Skills

Those Words Rhyme!; Interesting-Sounding Words

Purposes

Recites songs, rhymes, chants, and poems and engages in language and word play. Listens with increasing attention. Listens to a variety of genres read aloud: stories, songs, rhymes, poems. Speaks clearly so that their words can be understood by peers and adults.

Suggested Sequence for Today's Circle

1. "Down by the Bay"

2. *Golden Bear* (and Those Words Rhyme!)

3. "Come On and Join In to the Game"

4. Interesting-Sounding Words [and *The Little Red Hen (Makes a Pizza)*]

5. "The More We Get Together"

Materials and Instructional Procedures

Down by the Bay

Materials: CD Track 3, Song Lyrics p. 162, flannel board and flannel pieces

Vocabulary: grow, go, snake, cake, frog, dog, mouse, house

Procedure

- Tell children that the first song they're going to sing today is that song about those silly animals down by the bay.

- Make up some new verses, such as "goat driving a boat" or "fish making a wish." Suggest the name of the animal and see if children can come up with an action that rhymes. Have some in mind as it can be hard for children to think of them.

- As you sing, linger on the first sound of the second word of a rhyming word pair (e.g., *grow/go; snake/cake*) so that children can chime in on these words.

Golden Bear (and Those Words Rhyme!)

Materials: book: *Golden Bear*

Vocabulary: golden, bear, everywhere, dancing, stair, rocking

Procedure

- Show children the cover of *Golden Bear,* point to and read the title, and then read the book, keeping the natural rhythm of the verse. Point to pictures to identify objects named.

- When you finish reading, go back to some of the pages and read them again. After reading each one say something like, *I noticed two words that have the same sound at the end— words that rhyme:* stair and chair.

- Read a couple more pages with rhyming word pairs (e.g., *rug/bug*; *seeds/weeds*) and invite children to tell you which words rhyme. You might need to identify them, and then ask children to repeat them. Tell children that you will do more rhyming words on another day.

COME ON AND JOIN IN TO THE GAME

Materials: CD Track 20, Song Lyrics page 163

Vocabulary: clap, come, join, game, sneeze, yawn, jump, snap, fingers

Procedure

- Tell children that they are going to sing "Come On and Join In to the Game" next. Sing four or five verses ("clap," "sneeze," "yawn," "jump," and "snap fingers") and model the motions. Children should follow your lead with words and motions.

INTERESTING-SOUNDING WORDS [AND THE LITTLE RED HEN (MAKES A PIZZA)]

Materials: *The Little Red Hen (Makes a Pizza)*, clipboard and paper

Vocabulary: mozzarella, delicatessen, pepperoni

Procedure

- Tell children that next they're going to talk about some interesting-sounding words in the book *The Little Red Hen (Makes a Pizza)*.

- You might say, Mozzarella *is an interesting-sounding word. Let's say it. Mozz-a-rell-a.* Mozzarella *is a long word, isn't it?* Mozzarella *is a kind of cheese you put on pizza.* Mozzarella *starts with* /m/ *and we write it with the letter* M. *Write an* m *so children can see it.*

- You might say, *Another interesting word is* pepperoni. *Let's say it together. Pepp-er-o-ni.* Pepperoni *starts with* /p/, *and we write that sound with the letter* P. *Write* p *so children can see it.*

- You might say, *A third word that I think sounds interesting is* delicatessen. *Let's say that one together too: Del-i-ca-tess-en. The Little Red Hen bought her mozzarella cheese and her pepperoni at a delicatessen, which is a kind of store.* Delicatessen *starts with* /d/, *and we use the letter* D *to write that sound. Write* d *so children can see it.*

- Tell children that some words are really fun to say, and they'll talk about some more interesting-sounding words on another day.

THE MORE WE GET TOGETHER

Materials: CD Track 13, Song Lyrics page 163

Vocabulary: together, happier, friends

Procedure

- Tell children that the next song is about having friends and making new friends. Tell children that a friend is someone you like and want to spend time with.

- Sing the song as usual.

▶ Lunch/Quiet Time/Centers

This time is set aside for lunch, quiet time, and center activities. See pages 50–51 for suggested conversation topics during this time.

▶ Small Groups

For more information on Small Groups, see pages 55–58.

▶ Let's Find Out About It

Grocery Stores and Grocery Lists

Purposes

Listens with increasing attention. Understands that print carries meaning. Develops understanding of different kinds of texts. Shows interest and curiosity in learning new concepts.

Materials

book: *The Little Red Hen (Makes a Pizza)*; sample grocery list, supermarket ads

Preparation

Prepare a sample grocery list with large printing that includes milk or eggs, canned corn, peaches, and macaroni noodles.

Suggested Vocabulary

Use these words in sentences to make their meanings clear: ads, aisle, cashier, groceries, ingredients, list, supermarket

Procedure

- Explain that most people buy their food at a grocery store or supermarket. Turn to the page in *The Little Red Hen (Makes a Pizza)* where the hen goes to the supermarket to buy flour for her pizza dough. Point out some of the other items in her shopping cart (maple syrup, olive oil, bagels, peaches).

- Tell children that different kinds of food items are found in different parts of a supermarket, so that people will know where to find each kind of food. Briefly ask children, *What other things are found near corn flakes? Milk? Broccoli?*

> **English Language Learners**
>
> Point to and read each item on the grocery list. Then say each item's name a second time and invite children to say the words with you. For a few items, also say the name in the child's first language.

- Show children the shopping list you have prepared. Make a large version so they can see it easily, and hold it up. Read it and briefly mention that you will need to visit the dairy aisle where milk and eggs are kept cold. Point out you will also have to visit the canned goods aisle and the aisle that has pasta and dried noodles.

- Show children supermarket ads (from newspapers) that will also be placed in the Dramatic Play area. Read about some of the specials and show children where you are getting the information that you read to them.

- If you have time, explain that a lot of people keep track of things they need at the supermarket by keeping a list. Then, when people want to cook something special, such as a pizza or a birthday cake, they check to see if they have all the ingredients they need. If they don't, they add the items they need to the list and bring it to the supermarket. Once they find an item at the store, they cross it off the list. Point out that if the Little Red Hen had made a list, she probably wouldn't have had to go back to the store so many times.

- Tell children that they can make a list and pretend to go to a grocery store to shop during Center Time this week.

> **Extending the Activity**
>
> For children who are ready for a challenge, look through *The Little Red Hen (Makes a Pizza)* and use the illustrations to help them read the names of some food items with you.

Center Time Connections

Place grocery list paper and supermarket ads in the Dramatic Play area.

▶ End-the-Day Centers

Put the shopping list you used in Let's Find Out About It in the Writing Center for children to look at and read, if they wish. As children leave for home, say something that will help each child look forward to the next day. For example, tell children they will be reading a new book tomorrow about two good friends who don't always want to play together.

▶ **Start-the-Day Centers** (see pages 52–54)
Children may visit open Centers as you greet other arrivals.

▶ **Morning Meeting** (see page 52)
Review plans for the day with children and orient them to center activities.

▶ **Center Time** (see pages 52–54)
Children spend time in Centers of their choice.

▶ **Story Time: 1st Reading**

Matthew and Tilly

Author: Rebecca C. Jones
Illustrator: Beth Peck

Summary: Matthew and Tilly are friends. They do many things together. One day Matthew accidentally breaks one of Tilly's crayons. Tilly gets angry and they have an argument. The children stay angry for a while, but they soon realize that playing alone is not much fun. Finally, they both say they're sorry and begin playing together again.

Theme Link: Friends—Friends sometimes get angry with each other, but good friends make up.

Purposes

Listens to stories read aloud. Demonstrates increasing levels of sustained and focused engagement during read aloud times. Shows a steady increase in the number of word in listening vocabulary. Comprehends story's main events.

Read the Story

Read with feeling to show characters' excitement or boredom with events, and also to show Matthew's and Tilly's anger after the crayon breaks. Point out the city setting, with its stores, apartment buildings, and sidewalks. To help children learn new vocabulary words, provide brief explanations and use the words again as you discuss story events.

Suggested Vocabulary

Use these words often in Story Time and throughout the day.

brave showing courage
cash register a box that rings up sales and holds money in stores
chew to move your jaws up and down on food or gum
customer a person who buys something
hide-and-seek a game where children hide and one child tries to find them
rescue to save from danger or harm
stomped hit feet down hard while walking
together with someone else

Extending the Book

For children who are ready for a challenge, underline the word *together* with your finger each time you read it and encourage children to read it with you.

English Language Learners

As you read, point to story words shown in the illustrations, such as *bikes, lemonade, ice-cream cones, lady, kitten, tree,* and *crayon.* Repeat longer words and have children say them, too.

Progress Monitoring

Do children come to this new story with curiosity and enthusiasm? (*Hey! A new book! What's it called?*) Note which individual children attend throughout the reading and whose attention wavers. Note which children nod or offer comments that show they understand events in the story. Record your observations on copies of pages 158–159.

A MODEL FOR READING: *Use the following model to help you plan your book reading.*

Cover

*The **title** of this book is Matthew and Tilly. The person who wrote the story—the **author**—is Rebecca Jones, and the person who drew the pictures—the **illustrator**—is Beth Peck.*

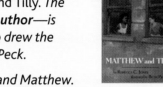

I think these children must be Tilly and Matthew. This boy must be Matthew, because Matthew is a boy's name. And this girl must be Tilly.

Maybe they live next door to each other in an apartment building. Looks like they are talking to one another. Maybe they are planning some things to do together. Let's read the story to find out what happens with Matthew and Tilly.

p. 1 (Read page 1.)

*Oh, Matthew and Tilly are friends. We see them sharing an umbrella here, as they walk down the street **together**. They probably do a lot of things **together** if they are friends. Let's see.*

pp. 2-3 (Read pages 2 and 3.)

*Do you know the game of **hide-and-seek**? It looks like Tilly is hiding back here, where Matthew can't see her. (Point.) Matthew must go find her—must **seek** her. That's why the game is called **hide-and-seek**. Tilly is hiding just around the corner. He'll probably find her soon.*

pp. 4-5 (Read pages 4 and 5.)

When someone says, "when business is slow," they mean when someone is trying to sell something and no one wants to buy it. What did Matthew and Tilly sometimes sell? (lemonade) Yes, and sometimes no one wanted to buy it, so they played games on the sidewalk. (Point.)

It looks like Tilly is playing a game like one we saw in the story A Letter to Amy. Do you see the squares here, drawn in chalk? (Point.) The game is called hopscotch. To play, you hop from square to square.

pp. 6-7 (Read page 6.)

Here are Matthew and Tilly inside a store that sells ice cream. It looks like they both are eating ice-cream cones. (Point.) Mmmm. Matthew and Tilly do a lot of fun things together, don't they? They seem to be good friends.

pp. 8-9 (Read page 8.)

*Oh, sometimes kittens climb up trees (point to the kitten on page 9), but then they don't know how to get down. They get stuck up there, and they might fall. It's kind of dangerous for them. So Matthew and Tilly used a stepladder (point) to get the kitten—they **rescued** it for a lady. That was very helpful.*

pp. 10-11 (Read page 10.)

Here's the bubble gum machine. (Point.) *You put money in and the gum comes out.*

Why did the lady give Matthew and Tilly some money? Guide children to understand that people sometimes pay children who help them out. The children would help anyway, but it's nice when the adult gives them some money for a treat.

Read page 11. When you come to **chew** demonstrate by moving your jaws.

Sounds like Matthew and Tilly might have been a little scared at first to go up into the tree to **rescue** *the kitten. But they did it anyway. They were* **brave**.

pp. 12-13 (Read page 12.)

Uh-oh. Maybe this is one of those times when Matthew and Tilly got tired of each other and didn't want to be **together** *for a while, even though Matthew broke the crayon by accident. He didn't mean to.*

pp. 14-15 (Read page 15.)

They are having an argument. They are calling each other names, aren't they? Do you remember another story we read a few weeks ago, when one child called another child a name? (Children respond.) *Yes, Kate called Noisy Nora a name.*

pp. 16-17 (Read page 16.)

Matthew banged his feet as he stepped on each step: **stomp, stomp***. He doesn't look very happy, does he?*

pp. 18-19 (Read page 19.)

pp. 20-21 (Read first paragraph.)

Point to the **cash register**. Briefly define **customer** as you read. Then read the rest of the page.

He didn't have anyone to buy something in his play store; he had no **customers***. It's not much fun to have a store without* **customers**.

pp. 22-23 (Read pages 22 and 23.)

It sounds like Tilly is still angry with Matthew. She's still calling him bad names in her thoughts. But she's not having much fun alone either, is she? She looks kind of bored and sad to me.

pp. 24–25 **(Read pages 24 and 25.)**

Oh, so they both said they were sorry. I wonder what will happen next.

pp. 26–27 **(Read pages 26 and 27.)**

Oh, good!

p. 28 **(Read page 28.)**

So that's the story about two good friends who had an argument once, and stayed mad for a while, but then they got over being mad, and played together again.

Story Discussion

Prompt discussion with questions. For example:

Do you think that Tilly really thought Matthew had broken her crayon on purpose, or was she just so upset that she said he had? Guide children toward understanding that sometimes we know something is an accident, but we think someone should have been more careful. Or sometimes we are so upset we want to blame someone.

We will read this story another day, but Story Time is over for today.

▶ **Outdoor Play**

Hold up crayons one at time and say, *If you are wearing [color], you may go get your jacket or sweater.* See pages 50–51 for suggested conversation topics during this time.

▶ Songs, Word Play, Letters

Today children will be playing word games, singing songs, and reciting poems. Add your favorite game, song, or poem to this collection.

Songs

"Five Green and Speckled Frogs"; "Head and Shoulders, Knees and Toes"

Poems

"Three Little Monkeys"; "Ten Little Fingers"

Literacy Skills

Guess What Word I'm Saying; Interesting-Sounding Words

Purposes

Recites songs, rhymes, chants, and poems and engages in language and word play. Listens with increasing attention. Speaks clearly so that their words can be understood by peers and adults. Begins subtracting to solve story problems using concrete objects. Counts up to ten objects in a set.

Suggested Sequence for Today's Circle

1. "Five Green and Speckled Frogs"
2. "Three Little Monkeys"
3. "Ten Little Fingers"
4. Guess What Word I'm Saying (and *A Letter to Amy*)
5. "Head and Shoulders, Knees and Toes"
6. Interesting-Sounding Words (and *A Letter to Amy*)

Materials and Instructional Procedures

FIVE GREEN AND SPECKLED FROGS

Materials: CD Track 10, Song Lyrics page 163, flannel board and flannel pieces

Vocabulary: green, speckled, log, delicious, pool, cool

Procedure

- Set up and perform the song as usual, using the flannel pieces to show the motions in the song, and pausing to give the children a chance to chime in with the correct number of frogs remaining.

- Now that children are quite familiar with this song, they will probably sing most of the words in all verses.

THREE LITTLE MONKEYS

Materials: *Big Book of Poetry*: Poem 6, CD Track 31

Vocabulary: catch, crocodile, monkeys, swinging, tree

Procedure

- Review the poem and write it on a small note card, if you need prompts.

- Tell children that you are going to teach them a new poem today called "Three Little Monkeys."

- Hold up one hand with three fingers extended, with thumb and little finger clasped over one another, beneath them.

- Show children how to move their hand back and forth.

- Chant the poem, and, as you chant, fold back one of the three fingers with each verse. Go slowly so that children can do the poem and motions with you.

- Show children the *Big Book of Poetry* illustration and point out the three little monkeys swinging on the tree branches and the crocodile beneath them in the water. Suggest that maybe the monkeys should find someplace else to play!

TEN LITTLE FINGERS

Materials: *Big Book of Poetry*: Poem 1, CD Track 26

Vocabulary: fingers, little, shut, tight, wide

Procedure

- Wiggle your fingers, as you have done before, to signal children that "Ten Little Fingers" is what they will do next.

- After the children finish the poem, ask them to hold one hand up, and use the index finger of the other hand to count the five fingers on it. Do it with children to model. Then, switch hands, and count fingers of the second hand, continuing with "6, 7, 8, 9, 10." Go slowly enough so that children can keep up with you.

- Feel free to add or substitute other counting chants or poems. Try to adapt suggested instructional strategies.

GUESS WHAT WORD I'M SAYING (AND *A LETTER TO AMY*)

Materials: book: *A Letter to Amy*

Vocabulary: writing, letter, envelope, mail

Procedure

- Hold up book and say something like, A Letter to Amy *is a book we've been reading, and I'm going to say some words from it in a funny way, a way that is not quite right. I want you to say the words the right way.* For example, *If I said* p- (pause) -arty, *you would say* party.

- Say some words in the "funny way" and wait for children to say the word in the usual way. You might want to say, *m* (pause) *-ail*, *r-* (pause) *-ain*, *w-* (pause) *-illie*; and *w-* (pause) *-ind*. Repeat each word before children guess.

- Go child by child around the circle, to give turns, or just allow children to call out together, if they think they know the word. Do not pressure a child to respond. Provide added support to those children you expect will need it. For example, give hints about possible words.

- After children guess a word, use the word in a sentence to convey its meaning. For example, *Yes,* rain *was the word I was saying. It started to rain when Peter went to mail his letter to Amy, didn't it?*

- Use more words, if children like this game, and want to play longer.

HEAD AND SHOULDERS, KNEES AND TOES

Materials: CD Track 4, Song Lyrics page 162

Vocabulary: head, shoulders, knees, toes, eyes, ears, mouth, nose

Procedure

- Sing the song and do the motions as usual. Do the song a second time, humming the tune and touching the body parts, without saying the words.

- Substitute another movement song if you wish.

INTERESTING-SOUNDING WORDS (AND *A LETTER TO AMY*)

Materials: book: *A Letter to Amy,* clipboard, paper, and marker

Vocabulary: envelope, hopscotch

Procedure

- Tell children that some words are interesting to hear and to say. Tell children that you think *envelope* is an interesting word to say because it has three different parts. You might say, *Let's say it together, en-ve-lope.*

- You might say, Hopscotch *is another interesting word to say. How many parts does it have? Let's say it, and clap it. Right, two parts:* hop-scotch.

- *What about the word* Saturday? *Let's say and clap it too:* Sat-ur-day. It has three parts. Saturday *starts with /s/ and we use* s *to write* /s/. *The letter S looks like this*. Write s, so children can see it.

- Invite children to say other long words and divide them. If a child provides a short word, compare it with a long word already discussed. For example, Tiger *is not as long a word as* crocodile, *but it's still interesting to say.*

Progress Monitoring

Make informal observations to be used later for a more formal assessment. You may wish to use copies of pages 158–159. Note whether individual children clapped the syllables with you, or said the syllables clearly. Which children remained engaged during the word guessing game? Which children guessed the words quickly? Which children did not guess any words at all? Which children followed along easily with the finger counting game? Did anyone get lost? Is anyone having trouble keeping up with you on "Head and Shoulders, Knees and Toes"?

▶ Lunch/Quiet Time/Centers

This time is set aside for lunch, quiet time, and center activities. See pages 50–51 for suggested conversation topics during this time.

▶ **Small Groups**

For information on Small Groups, see pages 55–58.

▶ **Let's Find Out About It**

Finding Things in a Grocery Store

Purposes

Understands that print carries meaning. Develops understanding of different kinds of texts. Develops understanding of how objects are sorted. Develops understanding of relationship to buying and selling.

Materials

book: *The Little Red Hen (Makes a Pizza)*; a book with photographs of a grocery store interior

Suggested Vocabulary

Use these words in the discussion in ways that make their meanings clear: *aisle, grocery, label, shelves, supermarket; organized; buy, trade*

Procedure

- Remind children that in *The Little Red Hen (Makes a Pizza)*, the hen shopped at a supermarket. Point out that she had to find the ingredients for her pizza dough on the supermarket shelves.

- Explain that supermarkets are organized with similar kinds of foods placed together on shelves. Different kinds of soups are stacked together. Different kinds of bread are stacked together, and so on. This helps people find the things they need.

- Look through a book with photos of a supermarket such as *A Busy Day at Mr. Kang's Grocery Store*. Point out the signs, the aisles, and the organization of items in the store. Read a few signs and explain that the words on them help people find things. Also point out the labels on cans and other items.

> **English Language Learners**
>
> When you use key vocabulary, such as *supermarket, grocery store*, or *aisle*, say the words slowly and repeat them so that children can say them with you.

Small Groups Connections

Children will make money, sort food containers, and make signs in activities scheduled for Small Groups.

Center Time Connections

Provide grocery list paper and supermarket ads in the Dramatic Play area.

Story Time Connections

You may want to read *A Busy Day at Mr. Kang's Grocery Store* (see below) after the third reading of *Matthew and Tilly* on Week 3, Day 5.

SUGGESTED RESOURCES

Books

Flanagan, Alice K. (author) and Christine Osinski (illustrator). *A Busy Day at Mr. Kang's Grocery Store.* New York: Scholastic, 1996.

Hoena, B. A. *A Visit to the Supermarket.* Mankato, MN: Capstone Press, 2004.

Johnston, Marianne. *Let's Visit the Supermarket.* New York: The Rosen Publishing Group, Inc., 2003.

> **Extending the Activity**
>
> For children who are ready for a challenge, help them read labels on the food boxes you've placed in the Puzzles and Manipulatives Center.

▶ **End-the-Day Centers**

Children spend time in open Centers. As children leave for home, say something that will help each child look forward to the next day. For example, tell children who enjoy singing that tomorrow they will sing "Down by the Bay" again.

▶ **Start-the-Day Centers** (see pages 52–54)
Open two to three Centers for children.

▶ **Morning Meeting** (see page 52)
Orient children to center activities and check the turns list.

▶ **Center Time** (see pages 52–54)
Children spend time in Centers of their choice.

▶ **Story Time: 2nd Reading**

Matthew and Tilly

Author: Rebecca C. Jones
Illustrator: Beth Peck

Purposes

Recalls some main events when asked, "What is happening in this story?" Links characters' basic emotions to their actions. Uses own experiences to understand characters' feelings and motivations. Expresses the main idea of a story or other text in a way that shows increasing understanding. Expands expressive vocabulary.

Read the Story Again

This time reconstruct the story with children. Prompt children's recall of events and characters' actions by asking, *What is happening on this page? What did Matthew and Tilly do next?* Help children connect events and Matthew's and Tilly's feelings.

Suggested Vocabulary

Use these words often in Story Time and throughout the day.

brave showing courage
cash register a box that rings up sales and holds money in stores
chew to move your jaws up and down on food or gum
customer a person who buys something
hide-and-seek a game where children hide and one child tries to find them
rescue to save from danger or harm
stomped hit feet down hard while walking
together with someone else

> **Extending the Book**
>
> Ask children if they can remember another story in which there was name-calling. Ask if Nora "got even" with Kate, the way Matthew "got even" with Tilly.

> **English Language Learners**
>
> Invite children to repeat the words *stomped* and *rescued* with you.

Progress Monitoring

Check children's understanding. Who calls out answers to questions? Who predicts what will happen next? Who infers Tilly's and Matthew's feelings? Does anyone misunderstand links between actions and feelings (For example, "Matthew doesn't like girls, so he's not going to play with Tilly.")? Record your observations using copies of pages 158–159.

A MODEL FOR READING: *Read all the text on each page. When you read it will vary, depending on the flow of your conversations with children.*

Cover

We read this story once before, so you know that the title of the book is . . . (Underline the title with your finger and wait for children to read it.) *Yes,* Matthew and Tilly. *Today we're going to read the story again and talk more about what happens.*

p. 1

Read page 1.

pp. 2-3

What are they doing here? (Point to Matthew on a bicycle.) *Yes, they are riding their bikes.* Read page 2.

Point to Tilly on page 3. *What were they playing here, when Tilly went back here to hide?* (Children respond.) *Yes, a game of* **hide-and-seek***. Tilly hid, and Matthew looked for her.* Now read page 3.

pp. 4-5

Over here, (point to lemonade stand) *there's a pitcher and some glasses on a little box, and there's a sign in back of it.* (Point to the sign.) *What did they sell sometimes?* (Children respond.) *Yes, lemonade.*

Read pages 4 and 5.

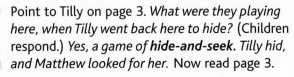

pp. 6-7

What are they doing here? (They're eating ice cream.) *Yes, they're eating ice-cream cones.*

Read page 6.

pp. 8-9

Point to the ladder on page 9. *And what are they doing with the stepladder?* (Children respond.) *Yes, they're* **rescuing** *a kitten—getting a kitten out of danger.*

Read page 8.

pp. 10-11

And what are they doing here? (Children respond.) *Yes, they're riding a horse by the gum machine. The lady gave them some money for* **rescuing** *the kitten, and they bought some bubble gum. Now they're riding on a play horse.*

Read pages 10 and 11. Stress the word *chewed* as you read and ask children to make chewing motions with you.

pp. 12-13

Point to the picture on page 13. *What's happening here?* (Children respond.) *Yes, Matthew and Tilly are playing with Tilly's crayons—they're drawing.*

Read page 12. *And then what happened?* (Children respond.) *Yes, Matthew broke a crayon, and Tilly got mad. The children quarrelled.*

pp. 14–15

Read page 15. *Oh, dear. They really are mad at each other, aren't they? How do we know they are really, really mad?* (Lead them to comment on the children's angry faces and postures, as well as on their words.)

pp. 16–17

What's happening here? (Matthew is sitting on the stairs.) *Yes, he got angry and ran up the stairs, and now he's sitting there.*

Read page 16.

pp. 18–19

Read page 19.

Now Tilly's playing alone.

pp. 20–21

What's Matthew doing here? (Children respond.) *Yes, he's playing store. There's his **cash register**. Is he having fun?* (Children respond.) *Do you think he's missing his friend Tilly by now?*

pp. 22–23

Point to Tilly on page 22. *What's happening here?* (Children respond.) *Yes, Tilly is sitting by herself. Do you think she's missing her friend Matthew by now?*

Read page 23. *They miss each other, don't they?*

pp. 24–25

Now what's happening? (Children respond.) *Yes, Matthew is looking out his window and thinking about Tilly, and Tilly is looking up at Matthew.*

Read page 25.

pp. 26–27

Read page 26.

p. 28

Read page 28.

Story Discussion

Prompt discussion with questions. For example:

Sometimes children don't have someone to play with when they are not at school, and they are kind of lonely, like Matthew and Tilly were when they were mad and playing alone. Sometimes children pretend they are playing with someone, or they use a stuffed animal or doll in their play. Have you ever done that?

▶ Outdoor Play

Use the first sounds in Matthew's and Tilly's names, to dismiss children. If no one's name starts with these sounds, comment on that. Then use first sounds in key story words—*kitten, chew, rescue*—as appropriate, to dismiss other children. See pages 50–51 for conversation topics.

▶ Songs, Word Play, Letters

Today children will be playing word games, singing songs, and reciting poems. Add your favorite game, song, or poem to this collection.

Songs

"Old MacDonald Had a Farm"; "Bingo"; "The More We Get Together"

Predictable Book

Golden Bear

Poem

"Mix a Pancake"

Literacy Skills

If Your Name Starts With [name a letter], Clap Just Once; Those Words Rhyme!

Purposes

Recites songs, rhymes, chants, and poems, and engages in language and word play. Responds to own name and requests for action or information. Communicates using verbal and non-verbal cues. Names some uppercase letters.

Suggested Sequence for Today's Circle

1. "Old MacDonald Had a Farm"
2. "Bingo"
3. "Mix a Pancake"
4. "The More We Get Together"
5. *Golden Bear* (and Those Words Rhyme!)
6. If Your Name Starts With [name a letter], Clap Just Once

Materials and Instructional Procedures

OLD MACDONALD HAD A FARM

Materials: CD Track 6, Song Lyrics page 162, flannel board and pieces for the song

Vocabulary: farm, chick, duck, cow, turkey, goat, horse, pig, sheep

Procedure

- Sing as usual, adding a couple of new animals this time, if you can.

BINGO

Materials: CD Track 2, Song Lyrics page 162, flannel board and felt letters

Vocabulary: farmer, dog, clap, letter, name, replace

Procedure

- As you place the letters *B, I, N, G, O* on the board, have children join you in naming them.

- Sing the song as usual, removing one letter for each verse and replacing each letter with a clap.

MIX A PANCAKE

Materials: *Big Book of Poetry*: Poem 8, CD Track 33

Vocabulary: mix, pancake, fry, pan, stir, toss

Procedure

- Review the poem and write it on a small note card, if you need prompts.

- Tell children they're going to learn a new poem today called "Mix a Pancake."

- Present the poem orally to children, and perform appropriate motions.

- Show children the *Big Book of Poetry* illustration and point to aspects of the illustration that match the words in the verses. For example, *Here's the bowl of pancake batter right here, with the spoon for mixing. And here's the skillet that the cook fried the pancakes in, right here. Wow, this is a giant pancake up here that the cook has just flipped. I hope he can catch that one.*

THE MORE WE GET TOGETHER

Materials: CD Track 13, Song Lyrics page 163

Vocabulary: together, happier, friends

Procedure

- Tell children that next they are going to sing the song about friends, "The More We Get Together."

- Sing both verses of the song with children.

GOLDEN BEAR (AND THOSE WORDS RHYME!)

Materials: book: *Golden Bear*

Vocabulary: golden, bear, everywhere, dancing, stair, rocking

Procedure

- Show children the cover of *Golden Bear,* and ask them if they remember the name of this book. Point to *G* in *Golden* and sound it out as a clue. Do the same for *B* in *Bear*.

- Read the book, keeping the natural rhythm of the verse. Point to pictures again, to help children link names to objects depicted. Go back to a few pages and reread those verses. Comment on the rhyming words.

- Say something like, *The words* rug *and* bug *have the same sound at the end. They rhyme. Some words do not have the same sound at the end, like* bear *and* rocking. *They don't rhyme. But* rug *and* bug *rhyme, and so do* bear *and* chair. *It's fun to find words that rhyme, isn't it?*

- Go to a few other pages with a rhyming pair and read them. This time, ask children if they think any words you have just read rhyme—have the same sound at the end. If children do not respond quickly, read the verse again, lingering a bit on the rhyming words, to emphasize them. If children still do not respond, say the words one after the other. For example, Ice *and* twice *sound the same at the end. They rhyme.*

- Stop while children are still enjoying the game, and tell them you'll do more rhymes on another day.

IF YOUR NAME STARTS WITH [NAME A LETTER], CLAP JUST ONCE

Materials: alphabet cards, children's name cards

Vocabulary: letter, name, raise

Procedure

- Tell children that you are going to play the name game with letters again. This time, though, tell children to clap just once instead of touching their ear or raising their hand. Also say that you might say to clap more than once, so they need to listen.

- Play one round of the game. Sometimes, instead of saying *Clap just once,* say, *Clap two times* or *Clap three times.* Most children will probably know the first letter in their own names by now, but keep the name cards handy, just in case.

▶ Lunch/Quiet Time/Centers

This time is set aside for lunch, quiet time, and center activities. See pages 50–51 for suggested conversation topics during this time.

▶ **Small Groups**

Refer to pages 55–58 for information about Small Groups.

▶ **Let's Find Out About It**

Grocery Store Jobs

Purposes

Listens with increasing attention. Begins to understand the various kinds of work people do outside their homes.

Materials

book: *Matthew and Tilly;* cardboard box filled with one type of food item, paper and plastic grocery bags

Suggested Vocabulary

Use words in context to make their meanings clear: bagger, cashier, cash register, customer, delivery, scanner, stocker

Procedure

- Remind children that in *The Little Red Hen (Makes a Pizza),* the hen had to find things on the supermarket shelves before she could buy them. Explain that putting the items on the shelves is the job of some people who work in the supermarket. These people are called *stockers.*

- Bring in a box filled with one type of food item, such as soup or pudding. Explain that a delivery person brings the food to the stores in boxes. A stocker unpacks the items and places them on the shelves.

- Tell children that shoppers need to pay for the items they buy. A cashier passes the items over a scanner or rings them into a cash register. The shoppers give the cashier money, and the cashier puts it into the cash register. Point out the cash register in Matthew's play store in *Matthew and Tilly.*

> **English Language Learners**
>
> Repeat the names of supermarket jobs as you discuss them, and help children say the names.

- Ask, *What do we put groceries in so we can carry them home?* Confirm that food items are put into bags. Show children brown paper bags and plastic bags from local grocery stores.

- Ask children if they ever noticed a person putting food into bags for shoppers after the cashier rings in the items. Explain that this person is called a *bagger,* and this is another important job at the supermarket.

- Tell children that in the play store they will set up in their classroom, they will need people for all these important jobs. Remind children that Matthew in *Matthew and Tilly* tried to play store, but he couldn't really play by himself. He needed someone to shop in his play store—to be a customer—while he played cashier.

- Explain that to set up a play store, teachers and children must gather food containers and organize them, just like in a real supermarket. Tell children that this is why they are sorting food cartons in a Small Groups activity.

> **Extending the Activity**
>
> For children who are ready for a challenge, write *bagger, stocker,* and *cashier* on a piece of paper. Provide tag board pieces for children to make nametags with these words.

Progress Monitoring

Which children remain focused and engaged while hearing about the various supermarket jobs? Which children nod or speak up to show an understanding of what each worker does? Record your observations on copies of pages 158–159.

▶ **End-the-Day Centers**

Children spend time in open Centers. As children leave for home, tell them that they will learn new verses to the "Bingo" song tomorrow, using some words from the book *A Letter to Amy.*

▶ **Start-the-Day Centers** (see pages 52–54)
Children spend time in two to three open Centers as they arrive.

▶ **Morning Meeting** (see page 52)
Orient children to center activities and help them make first choices.

▶ **Center Time** (see pages 52–54)
Children spend time in Centers of their choice.

▶ **Story Time 3rd Reading**

A Letter to Amy
Author: Ezra Jack Keats

Read the Story Again

In the third reading of *A Letter to Amy*, linger over beginning sounds as you read to invite children to chime in. This gives children the opportunity to practice saying many of the new words. If some children want to chime in on other words or phrases besides those suggested here, that's fine. After reading, thank children for helping to read the story and tell them they did a wonderful job.

Story Discussion

Prompt discussion with questions. For example:

I'm really glad, and I bet you are too, that Amy did come to Peter's birthday party. I was thinking, though, about Peter's feelings, had Amy decided not to come. Do you think Peter would have gotten over being a little sad, and that he would have had a happy time at his party? If the children do not say it, suggest

that, sometimes, even though we have felt really disappointed about something for a little while, we are able to have a good time.

Words and Phrases for Chiming In

(Vocabulary words appear in **dark** type.)

inviting, stared – p. 3
special – p. 3
envelope – p. 4
sealed it – p. 4
WILL YOU PLEASE COME TO MY BIRTHDAY PARTY. PETER. – p. 4
stamp – p. 4
parrot – pp. 7, 27
hopscotch game – p. 12
Amy – p. 14
spoiled – p. 15
mailbox – p. 18
reflection, all mixed up – p. 20
cake – p. 25
HAAPPY BIRRRTHDAY, PEEETERRR! – p. 27
candles – pp. 28, 29
wish – p. 28

> **Extending the Book**
>
> For children who are ready for a challenge, point to the words in the illustration of the mailbox on page 18. Invite children to read the words on the box as you underline them with your finger, and help sound out the letters.

> **English Language Learners**
>
> After children have chimed in, add comments that repeat the key words, such as *Yes, Peter's mother lit the* **candles**. *The* **candles** *are here on the cake.*

▶ **Outdoor Play**

Write *Peter* and *Amy* on cards. Point to letters one by one. Children whose names begin with those letters leave for play first. Hold up letters from your own set to dismiss remaining children. See pages 50–51 for suggested conversation topics during this time.

▶ Songs, Word Play, Letters

Today children will be playing word games, singing songs, and reciting poems. Add your favorite game, song, or poem to this collection.

Songs

"Five Little Ducks"; "Bingo"; "Five Green and Speckled Frogs"

Predictable Book

HUSH!

Literacy Skills

I'm Thinking of _____ Clue Game

Purposes

Recites songs, rhymes, chants, and poems, and engages in language and word play. Uses new words in meaningful ways. Listens with increasing attention. Uses ordinal numbers to indicate position of items.

Suggested Sequence for Today's Circle

1. "Five Little Ducks"
2. "Story-Character Bingo" (and *A Letter to Amy*)
3. *HUSH!*
4. "Five Green and Speckled Frogs"
5. I'm Thinking of ___ Clue Game [and *The Little Red Hen (Makes a Pizza)*]

Materials and Instructional Procedures

FIVE LITTLE DUCKS

Materials: CD Track 11, Song Lyrics page 163

Vocabulary: out, over, far away, back

Procedure

- Sing the song as usual.

- Feel free to sing a favorite song of your own instead of this one.

STORY-CHARACTER BINGO (AND *A LETTER TO AMY*)

Materials: book: *A Letter to Amy*, name cards, flannel board and flannel letters

Preparation: Make a card with *Peter* printed on it, in all uppercase letters. Make a set of flannel letters for *Peter* and mount them on a square of felt.

Vocabulary: letter, boy, first, second, third, fourth, fifth

Procedure

- Tell children that you are going to sing "Bingo," but instead of singing about the farmer's dog, you are going to sing about the boy who is the main character in a story book. Show the cover of *A Letter to Amy*, point to the picture of Peter, and ask if they can guess who they are going to sing about.

- Show children the card with *Peter* on it, and tell them that it says, *Peter*. Using the card as a guide, ask children to help you select the flannel letters to spell *Peter*. Point to the P in *Peter* and say something like, Peter *begins with* P, *so the first letter we need on our flannel board is* P. *Here it is*. Then, point to the second letter in *Peter* and ask, *What is the second letter in Peter?* Put the E up next. Continue with T, E, and R. As you point to the specific letter, ask something like, *What is the third letter we need? The fourth? The fifth?*

- Tell children that the song has the same tune as "Bingo," but different words. It goes like this: *There was a boy who mailed a note (letter) and* Peter *was his name-o.* P-E-T-E-R (three times), *and* Peter *was his name-o.*

- Then, sing the song with the children, substituting a clap for missing letter just as they do with "Bingo."

HUSH!

Materials: book: *HUSH!*

Vocabulary: whispering, leaping, sweeping, buffalo, lean, skinny

Procedure

- Show children the cover of *HUSH!* and ask if they remember its title. Children will probably say the word in a voice louder than a whisper. Follow with, *Yes, HUSH!* said in a whisper, as you put your index finger to your own mouth. Point out the mother doing the same on the book cover.

- Ask children why the mother is whispering the word. Children may remember that there's a baby in the book who is supposed to be sleeping.

- You might ask children about the meaning of *hush* which is used in another story they have heard many times called *Noisy Nora*.

- Read *HUSH!* as you did the last time. Linger on the first sound of *sleeping* every time it comes up, so that children can join you on this word. Do the same with *nearby*.

- Comment as you read about the where-abouts and actions of the baby in the story.

- When finished reading the book, go back through it and comment about some of the words. As you explain a word's meaning, point to the appropriate picture. For "a lean black cat," you might say, *Lean means the cat is skinny, not fat.* For "don't come leaping," you might say, *This means stop making those big jumps, little frog.* For "don't come sweeping," you might say, *This means, Mr. Buffalo, stop swishing your tail like that. It's noisy and it's making the straw fly all over the place.*

FIVE GREEN AND SPECKLED FROGS

Materials: CD Track 10, Song Lyrics page 163, flannel board and flannel pieces

Vocabulary: green, speckled, log, delicious, pool, cool

Procedure

- Put three frogs up, and tell the children that the other frogs (don't say how many) are a little bit late getting to the pond this morning. Ask children how many frogs are late. After children guess, put the two frogs up on the log, say *two*, and then point to the original three, as you say *three* (very brief pause). Then quickly add, *four, five*, as you count on to include the two tardy frogs.

- Perform the song as usual. Substitute other counting songs of your own, and apply some variations to enhance children's understanding of number relationships.

I'M THINKING OF __ CLUE GAME [AND *THE LITTLE RED HEN (MAKES A PIZZA)*]

Materials: *The Little Red Hen (Makes a Pizza)*, Picture Cards: pizza, bowl, saxophone, money

Vocabulary: pizza, bowl, toppings, crust

Procedure

- Show children the book cover, and tell them they are going to play a clue game with words from the story. Remind them to listen to all the clues, and to think for a little bit before raising their hands when they have an idea. Tell them that other children might still be thinking so it's important to just raise their hand and not shout out ideas.

- For *pizza*, use these clues: *This word is the name of a kind of food that Little Red Hen was making. This food has a crust and toppings. When we say this word, we hear two parts*

(clap two times). If children need another clue, say, *This word begins with /p/.*

- For *bowl*, use these clues: *Little Red Hen mixed her dough ingredients in one of these. These are round.* If children need another clue, say, *The word I'm thinking of begins with /b/.*

- Do another word or two from the book, (e.g., *cheese, saxophone, money*) if children are interested.

- After they figure out each word, show the picture card if there is one, to reinforce the meaning of the word.

Progress Monitoring

Make informal observations to be used later for a more formal assessment. You may wish to use copies of pages 158–159. Note which children remained engaged during the clue word game, and which children figured out the words. Note which children stayed engaged when you explained some words from *HUSH!* Note which letters various children identified in *Peter*, in the variation on "Bingo." Did anyone know right away that it was two frogs that were late for the log? Did anyone use their own fingers to keep track of the items as they counted up before you put the two late frogs on the board?

▶ Lunch/Quiet Time/Centers

This time is set aside for lunch, quiet time, and center activities. See pages 50–51 for suggested conversation topics during this time.

▶ **Small Groups**

For information on Small Groups, refer to pages 55–58.

▶ **Let's Talk About It**

Building Friendships: Talking About Play Interests

Purposes

Interacts appropriately with other children. Listens with increasing attention.

Preparation

Take six or seven photos of different situations where children are playing together.

Procedure

- Show children the photos you have taken of them playing together. Then let the children tell what they were playing or doing in the photos. Be sure to include as many children as possible in the photos you choose.

- Use the photos to help children learn about each other's play interests. Point out similarities in interests when photos allow. For example:

   Oh, Keisha, I see that you and Sarah were playing in the blocks together. I know that many of you like to play blocks, and it's nice that you have so many friends to play that with.

   Jack, you painted a picture of the little red hen's pizza, and so did Tiffany. Sometimes it's fun to paint pictures at the easels with a friend.

▲ Photos of class activities can help children recognize similar play interests.

▶ **End-the-Day Centers**

Some children can go to the Writing Center to look at more photos and to think of captions for them. Say something that will help each child look forward to the next day. For example, tell children that you will be choosing a book to read tomorrow and it will be a surprise.

▶ **Start-the-Day Centers** (see pages 52–54)
Open two to three Centers for morning play.

▶ **Morning Meeting** (see page 52)
Orient children to center activities.

▶ **Center Time** (see pages 52–54)
Children spend time in Centers of their choice.

▶ **Story Time: 4th Reading**

A Letter to Amy
Author: Ezra Jack Keats

Read *A Letter to Amy* Again
Ask all children to say the words that Peter speaks as you read the story again. You take the role of Peter's mother and the other story characters. Encourage children to speak Peter's lines with the appropriate emotions.

Story Discussion
Prompt discussion with questions. For example: *You might remember that Eddie said, "A girl—ugh!" when Amy arrived. Which one of the boys shown on the page with Peter* (hold up page) *do you think is Eddie? Why?* Guide children toward understanding that his expression shows his feelings. *Do you think all the other boys agreed with Eddie's reaction to Amy? Why or why not?* Help children to base their answers on characters' expressions.

Taking On the Roles of Story Characters
Peter: I'm writing a letter to Amy. I'm **inviting** her to my party. – p. 3

We-e-el-l, this way it's sort of **special.** – p. 3
WILL YOU PLEASE COME TO MY BIRTHDAY PARTY. PETER. – p. 4
Now I'll mail it. – p. 4
It looks like rain. You'd better stay in, Willie. – p. 4
Willie! Didn't I tell you to stay home? – p. 7
Now she'll never come to my party. – p. 20
Yes. – p. 22
All right, . . . bring it out now. – p. 25

Other Book Suggestions
If you think a fourth reading of *A Letter to Amy* will not hold children's interest, read another theme-related book, such as *A Cake All for Me!* (see page 7). This story is about a pig who makes a cake, thinking at first that he'll eat it all by himself. When three friends show up, he shares it with them.

Making Connections: Ask children if they think the pig was making a cake for his birthday. Hint at absence of candles as a clue. Comment that people often eat cake, even when it isn't someone's birthday. Ask children if they think the pig should offer his friends a second piece of cake or eat the rest himself.

▶ **Outdoor Play**
Name items of clothing to dismiss children to go to cubbies to get on their jackets or sweaters. For example, *If you are wearing a long-sleeved shirt today . . . If you are wearing white socks today . . .* and so on. See pages 50–51 for suggested conversation topics during this time.

▶ Songs, Word Play, Letters

Today children will be playing word games, singing songs, and reciting poems. Add your favorite game, song, or poem to this colllection.

Songs

"Down by the Bay"; "What Are You Wearing?"; "Head and Shoulders, Knees and Toes"

Poems

"Mix a Pancake"; "Five Juicy Apples"; "Three Little Monkeys"

Literacy Skills

Those Words Begin With the Same Sound!; Alphabet Memory Pocket Chart Game

Purposes

Recites songs, rhymes, chants, and poems, and engages in language and word play. Names many uppercase letters. Segments the beginning sounds in words.

Suggested Sequence for Today's Circle

1. "Down by the Bay"
2. "What Are You Wearing?"
3. "Mix a Pancake"
4. "Head and Shoulders, Knees and Toes"
5. "Five Juicy Apples"
6. "Three Little Monkeys" (and Those Words Begin With the Same Sound!)
7. Alphabet Memory Pocket Chart Game

Materials and Instructional Procedures

DOWN BY THE BAY

Materials: CD Track 3, Song Lyrics page 163, flannel board and flannel pieces

Vocabulary: grow, go, snake, cake, frog, dog, mouse, house

Procedure

- Sing the song as usual.

- Think of some new verses (e.g., "sheep riding in a jeep" or "pig dancing a jig"). For flannel pieces, use those from "Old MacDonald" and just move them appropriately or do hand motions to portray the actions (e.g., holding a steering wheel for sheep verse; moving pig in jig fashion).

- Substitute another rhyming song if you prefer.

WHAT ARE YOU WEARING?

Materials: CD Track 14, Song Lyrics page 163

Vocabulary: wearing, day, long, shirt, pants

Procedure

- Tell children that you are going to teach them a new song today, called "What Are You Wearing?"

- Sing a verse, using the name of a child in the circle. *[Child's name] is wearing a [color] shirt, a [color] shirt, a [color] shirt. [Child's name] is wearing a [color] shirt all day long.*

- Tell children that you are going to go around the circle and sing to each child.

- When you're finished, you might sing "Willoughby, Wallaby, Woo," which also uses children's names in a funny way. A source for this song is listed on page 83.

MIX A PANCAKE

Materials: *Big Book of Poetry*: Poem 8, CD Track 33

Vocabulary: fry, mix, pan, pancake, stir, toss

Procedure

- Show children the *Big Book of Poetry* illustration and ask them if they remember the name of this poem. If they are unable, read the title. Point to *M* when you read *Mix*, and sound it out; do the same with *P* in *Pancake*.

- Present the poem orally, as before, going slowly enough for children to say *pancake* with you each time it comes up.

HEAD AND SHOULDERS, KNEES AND TOES

Materials: CD Track 4, Song Lyrics page 162

Vocabulary: head, shoulders, knees, toes, eyes, ears, mouth, nose

Procedure

- Sing the song as usual, and model the motions.

FIVE JUICY APPLES

Materials: *Big Book of Poetry*: Poem 5, CD Track 30

Vocabulary: apples, juicy, sitting, store

Procedure

- Show children the poem in the *Big Book of Poetry*. Point out the five juicy apples in the illustration.

- Linger on the first sound of the second word in a rhyming pair (e.g., *store/four, be/three, through/two, pair/there*) so that children can chime in.

- Repeat three times to use every child's name. Or, tell children you'll do the poem again the next day, to give the rest of the children a turn so they don't feel left out.

THREE LITTLE MONKEYS (AND THOSE WORDS BEGIN WITH THE SAME SOUND!)

Materials: *Big Book of Poetry*: Poem 6, CD Track 31

Vocabulary: monkeys, catch, crocodile, swinging, tree

Procedure

- Show children the *Big Book of Poetry* illustration for the poem, and ask or tell the name of this poem.

- Present the poem orally, as before, using hand and fingers to represent the monkeys.

- When you finish, you might say, *Some words in this poem start with the same sound.* Crocodile *and* catch *start with the same sound, don't they? They both start with /k/. They have the same sound at the beginning.* Me *and* monkey *also start with the same sound . . . /m/, me; and /m/, monkey.*

- You might also say, *Some words in the poem do not start with the same sound.* Monkey *and* crocodile *don't start with the same sound, do they? But* crocodile *and* catch *have the same sound at the beginning.*

- Summarize by saying something like, *Some words start with the same sound, and some words don't. Words are interesting in that way.*

ALPHABET MEMORY POCKET CHART GAME

Materials: two sets of uppercase alphabet letter cards and a poster board chart with one pocket for each child in the class (from Unit 1)

Vocabulary: pocket, chart

Procedure

- Use the pocket chart as before in Unit 1. Select as many letters as there are children in your class. Place letters from one set in the pockets on the chart, hiding the letter, when you prepare materials for the day.

- Tell children that they are going to play the alphabet memory game they played a few weeks ago. Hand out letters that match letters you've put in the pocket chart, one per child. Remind children that the pockets have matches for letters they are holding.

- Read the numbers on the pockets, *one, two, three,* and so on, as you point to each one, to review numeral recognition. There should still be a small picture sticker on each pocket too, for children who want to name it when they select a pocket. If necessary review the names of the objects pictured, but encourage use of numerals.

- Go around the circle, giving each child a turn to choose a pocket. If there is a match, give the matching card to the child. Say, *Yes, this is the other* B *that matches your* B. If there is not a match, put it back in the pocket and say, *I'll bet someone else is watching.* Continue until all children have found their match.

SUGGESTED RESOURCES

Book

Raffi. "Willoughby, Wallaby, Woo." In *Raffi's Singable Songbook.* New York: Crown Publishers Inc., 1980.

CD

Raffi. "Willoughby, Wallaby, Woo." *Singable Songs for the Very Young.* Raffi. Rounder Records sound compact disc. 1996.

▶ **Lunch/Quiet Time/Centers**

This time is set aside for lunch, quiet time, and center activities. See pages 50–51 for suggested conversation topics during this time.

▶ Small Groups

For information on Small Groups, refer to pages 55–58.

▶ Let's Find Out About It

Work Friends

Purposes

Develops understanding of relationships among people. Demonstrates increasing levels of sustained and focused engagement during read–aloud times. Begins to understand the various kinds of work people do outside their homes.

Materials

book: *Road Builders*

Suggested Vocabulary

Define these words as you read so their meanings are clear: backhoe, bulldozer, cement mixer, cherry-picker trucks, chute, grader, gutters, pickup truck, power shovel; dumps, packs, pours

Procedure

- Mention that children often make friends at school or in their neighborhood. Explain that grown-ups make friends, too, sometimes at school if they still go to school, sometimes in the neighborhood, and often at work. Invite children's observations.

- Tell children you are going to read a book to them called *Road Builders*. Explain that road builders are the grown-ups who operate the heavy equipment needed to build the roads we drive on. Point out that the road builders must work well together to get the work done. They get to know one another as they work, and often they become friends.

> **English Language Learners**
>
> Repeat the names of the road building equipment as you point them out in the book *Road Builders*. Help children say the names with you.

- Read *Road Builders*. As you read, point out the equipment as it is named in the book, and mention how the road builders work together.

- On the last page, where it shows the road builders riding together in a truck, mention that it looks as if they are friends. Discuss why they look like they might be friends.

Center Time Connections

Children can play with road-building vehicles in the sand table and can pretend that they are road builders, working together with their friends.

> **Extending the Activity**
>
> Point out the plan the road worker holds up in *Road Builders*, and provide simple plans on big pieces of paper for use in the sand table play.

Connect With Families

In a note home, tell families that children have been sorting food containers and making signs for a play grocery store they will set up the following week. Suggest that they bring their child along to help pick out produce at the grocery store. They can also show their child how to use the store's scale to weigh the fruits and vegetables.

▶ End-the-Day Centers

Provide pieces of white card-weight paper cut into the shape that is suitable for rolling to make cones. Any child who is interested can color these orange with a marker or crayon at the Writing Center.

As children leave for home, tell them that on Monday, you'll be reading a story about a funny lion named Dandelion who gets all dressed up to go to a party.

Notes to Teachers

Here are some tips and suggestions that might be helpful.

Center Time

Sand and Water Table—Success in Making Sand Molds

- Children can become frustrated if their sand molds fall apart or aren't formed well. Be sure to keep sand at an appropriate dampness for making molds. If it becomes too dry, the molded form falls apart as soon as it is dumped out. If the sand is too wet, it often sticks to the mold and is hard to dump out.

- Coach children in turning a mold over quickly, and tapping it sharply on the receiving surface.

Dramatic Play—Modeling Print Props

- Join Dramatic Play, as appropriate, and model looking through the supermarket food ads, and using grocery-list-making materials. When these items are first added to the house play area, the grocery store will not yet be available in the Blocks area.

- Tell children they can go anywhere in the classroom on a "just pretend" shopping trip.

Writing Center—Modeling Use of Stationery Supplies

- Use classroom stationery to write a letter to each child in the class. You will need to write most of these when children are resting, or before or after the school day.

- Show a sealed envelope with a child's name on it at Morning Meeting, when you introduce the activity. Tell children you are writing letters to everyone, and will leave them in their cubbies or take-home boxes.

Outdoor Play

Encouraging Gross Motor Play

- Some children shy away from climbing, riding wheel toys, swings, and other activities that require use of gross motor skills. Be observant for such children, and encourage them to spend at least some of their outdoor play time in some gross motor activity.

- Accompany him or her to the climber and offer to stand nearby while the child climbs. Invite the child to use a tricycle, and offer to push a bit from behind. Offer to push the child on the swing, and then coach him or her in learning how to pump.

- If an inactive child appears to be tired, or without normal energy, talk to the parent about your observations.

Weekly Planner

	Day 1	Day 2	Day 3
Start-the-Day Centers 30 Minutes **Morning Meeting** 15 Minutes **Center Time** 60 Minutes pp. 88–90	Greet children and open selected Centers. **Blocks:** Materials for Making a Playground, Setting Up and Shopping at the Grocery Store; **Sand and Water:** Road Construction Vehicles; **Dramatic Play:** Grocery Store Play; **Book Area:** Exploring Books; **Art Area/Table:** Making Clay Dough Cookies, Making Clay Dough Pizza; **Art Area/Easel:** Easel Painting with a Basic Set of Colors; **Puzzles and Manipulatives:** Beginning Sound Pictures, and Letter Font Matching; **Writing Center:** Recording Captions for Class Photo Album		
Toileting and Snack 15 Minutes			
Story Time 20 Minutes	1st Reading – *Dandelion* pp. 95–99	2nd Reading – *Dandelion* pp. 103–107	1st Reading – *Hooray, a Piñata!* pp. 111–113
Outdoor Play 35 Minutes	**Conversations:** Observe for times children are looking at bugs, rocks, etc. Join them; coach use of words to describe size, color, and texture.	**Conversations:** Observe for children practicing motor skills. Comment on skill and persistence.	**Conversations:** Talk with a child who speaks a language you do not know. Ask him or her to teach you some words, such as *hello, thank you, jump,* or *run.*
Songs, Word Play, Letters 20 Minutes	**Songs:** "The Wheels on the Bus"; "The More We Get Together"; "Come On and Join In to the Game" **Poems:** "Mix a Pancake"; "Five Little Owls in an Old Elm Tree" **Literacy Skills:** Those Words Begin With the Same Sound!; I'm Thinking of ___ Clue Game pp. 100–101	**Songs:** "Clap Your Hands"; "What Are You Wearing?"; "Five Green and Speckled Frogs" **Predictable Book:** *Golden Bear* **Literacy Skills:** Those Words Rhyme!; If Your Name Starts With [first sound in a child's name], Raise Your Hand pp. 108–109	**Songs:** "Six Little Ducks"; "Down by the Bay"; Story-Character "Bingo" Song **Poems:** "Five Juicy Apples" **Literacy Skills:** Can You Think of Words That Rhyme With . . . .?; We Can Change It and Rearrange It; I'm Thinking of ___ Clue Game pp. 114–115
Handwashing/Toileting 10 Minutes			
Lunch/Quiet Time/ Center Time 90 Minutes	**Conversations:** *What words can you think of to describe food?* Use interesting words such as *delicious, scrumptious, crunchy,* and *salty.*	**Conversations:** *What is your favorite food? What does it do for your body?* Discuss nutrition and dangers of too many calories.	**Conversations:** *Can you teach us a few words about food?* Ask help from children who speak a language other than English.
Small Groups 25 Minutes pp. 91–93	**Mathematics:** Matching, Identifying, and Counting Coins/Making Play Money Bills **Language and Print Manipulatives:** Making Store Signs **Book Browsing:** Exploring Books	**Mathematics:** Matching, Identifying, and Counting Coins/Making Play Money Bills **Language and Print Manipulatives:** Making Store Signs **Book Browsing:** Exploring Books	**Mathematics:** Constructing a 3-D Shape (Piñata Body) **Language and Print Manipulatives:** Making Party Invitations **Writing:** Addressing Envelopes for Party Invitations
Let's Find Out About It/ Let's Talk About It 20 Minutes	Exploring Signs for Advertising p. 102	Social Skills Development p. 110	Exploring Piñatas p. 116
End-the-Day Centers 20 Minutes	Open selected Centers and prepare children to go home.		

Day 4	Day 5
2nd Reading – *Hooray, a Piñata!* pp. 117–119	**3rd Reading – *Matthew and Tilly*** p. 123 Read *A Cake All for Me!*, *The Doorbell Rang*, *Jamaica's Find*, or another book of your choice.
Conversations: Observe children who are running. Comment on speed; encourage jumping also.	**Conversations:** Observe a child who struggles to follow rules. If needed, restate rules clearly; explain reasons in terms of safety.
Songs: "Head and Shoulders, Knees and Toes"; "The More We Get Together"; "If You're Happy" **Poems:** "Three Little Monkeys" **Literacy Skills:** Can You Think of Words That Rhyme With ___?; If Your Name Starts With [name a letter], Raise Your Hand pp. 120–121	**Songs:** "Old MacDonald Had a Farm"; "Clap Your Hands"; "Come On And Join In to the Game" **Predictable Book:** *HUSH!* **Literacy Skills:** Can You Think of Words That Rhyme With ___? pp. 124–125
Conversations: *Have you been to a birthday party?* Discuss activities, including piñatas.	**Conversations:** *Which of the books that we have been reading do you like best?* Support recall of favorite parts.
Mathematics: Constructing a 3-D Shape (Piñata Body) **Language and Print Manipulatives:** Making Party Invitations **Writing:** Addressing Envelopes for Party Invitations	**Mathematics:** Constructing a 3-D Shape (Piñata Body) **Language & Print Manipulatives:** Making Party Invitations **Writing:** Addressing Envelopes for Party Invitations
Invitations to the Stuffed Animal Party p. 122	**Resolving Conflicts and Developing Self-Control** p. 126

Half-Day Program Schedule

2 hours 45 minutes
A half-day program includes two literacy circles.

10 min.	Start-the-Day Centers Writing Center, Book Area, Puzzles and Manipulatives
10 min.	Morning Meeting
60 min.	Center Time Include mathematics and science activities from Small Groups. Incorporate Small Groups writing activities at Writing Centers.
20 min.	Story Time Use discussion questions from Let's Talk About It to address social-emotional issues and topics from Let's Find Out About It to address concept development.
35 min.	Outdoor Play
20 min.	Songs, Word Play, Letters
10 min.	End-the-Day Centers Writing Center, Book Area, Puzzles and Manipulatives

Connect With Families

- Families can help children understand that written words have meaning. Suggest that parents read signs to children—store signs and street signs—and talk about what they mean. Some parents may also enjoy helping their child make a sign for the door of his or her room, with the child's name printed on it.

- Tell parents about the grocery store play area, and show it to parents. Suggest that they show children their shopping lists and name the items they buy.

- Most children enjoy teaching others what they've learned. Encourage children to sing "Clap Your Hands" and "Five Little Ducks" at home, and teach the words to their families. Suggest that parents ask their children to show them the motions done with these songs.

Start-the-Day Centers

- Open two to three Centers (e.g., Writing Center, Puzzles and Manipulatives, Book Area) for children to go to upon their arrival.

Morning Meeting

- Introduce children to Centers by showing some selected objects from each Center and briefly demonstrating activities to help them make a first choice. You might want to modify or substitute an activity to meet your children's needs. See page 127 for tips on managing the Centers.

- For example, **Monday:** Show children some road vehicles from the sand table. Remind children about the book *Road Builders* and tell them they can pretend they are members of a work crew. Demonstrate using a rolling pin and a cookie cutter to make clay dough cookies. Place cookies on a tray to bake in the play oven. **Thursday:** Show new clay dough props and demonstrate pushing clay dough inside a circular plastic lid to make pizza crusts, then sprinkling colored paper for toppings to make clay dough pizza. Show nametags and shopping lists and assign roles to children for grocery store play: bagger, stock person, cashier, and shopper in the Blocks and Dramatic Play areas. Demonstrate use of the tape recorder in the Writing Center for recording captions for the class photo album. Select other items to show and demonstrate on all mornings.

- Use suggested vocabulary for each Center as you demonstrate activities.

▲ Road Construction Vehicles

SAND AND WATER

Road Construction Vehicles

SCIENCE

Purposes: Explores simple machines. Becomes aware of the roles, responsibilities, and services provided by community workers.

Materials: clean sand, small quantity of small rock/gravel, small and sturdy plastic construction vehicles (2 dump trucks, 2 bulldozers, back hoe, roller, cement mixer, front loader), tag board, markers, small shovels or metal spoons, short lengths of thin-diameter dowel rods

Preparation: Fill table half full with sand. Color tag board pieces with orange marker or crayon, and fashion into cones for work site props. Use dowel rods and colored tag board to make flags for workers.

Suggested Vocabulary: back hoe, bulldozer, cement mixer, front loader, dump truck, construction, vehicle, cones, surface, smooth, dump, remove, roll

- Prompt children to talk about what they are doing. You might ask, *What kind of construction vehicle is that? What job does it do?*

- Comment on children's play. You might say, *I see you put cones around the big hole to warn people of the danger. That's a very important thing to do at a construction site.*

- Encourage children to work together. You might say, *Tina, tell Antonio that you need more gravel to finish your road. The storage pile is near him, and maybe he can bring you a load in his dump truck.*

- Take photos of the activity if time permits.

BOOK AREA

Exploring Books

Purposes: Independently chooses to read or to pretend to read books. Seeks out non-fiction texts to find information.

Materials: Add *Road Builders* and other books about road construction and vehicles.

- Join children for brief periods. Talk with children about books. You might say, *What kind of truck is that? Oh, a cement mixer. Yes, I see the cement coming out, right down here. I think the book says it's for the gutters on the side of the road. Do you know what a gutter is?*

- Help children compare books about trucks and road construction vehicles. You might say, *I don't remember seeing a tow truck in the* Road Builders *book. I think this book is about all kinds of trucks, not just trucks that build roads.*

ART AREA: TABLE

Making Clay Dough Cookies

Purposes: Uses a variety of tools and materials to strengthen hand grasp, flexibility, and coordination. Explores materials and transformations.

Materials: 2 batches of clay dough, small plates, hot pads, kitchen timer, cookie cutters, rolling pins, cookie sheets, pancake turners, play oven

Preparation: To make clay dough, mix and stir over medium heat: 2 c flour, 2 c water, 1 c table salt, 4 T cream of tartar, 2 T oil. When thick, turn out from pan. Cool and knead. Store in closed plastic bag in refrigerator. Make cookie sheets by covering pieces of cardboard with heavy aluminum foil. Create a play oven out of a small cardboard box.

Suggested Vocabulary: butter, eggs, flour, sugar,

water, dough, cookie cutter, cookie sheet, oven, recipe; bake, cook, cool, mix, stir

- Observe and talk with children as they experiment with the materials. You might say, *Oh, I see you are rolling the dough very thin. You'll have nice crisp cookies. You might want to use the timer to make sure your cookies don't bake too long. Thin cookies burn easily.*

Making Clay Dough Pizza

Purposes: Uses a variety of tools and materials to strengthen hand grasp, flexibility, and coordination. Explores materials and transformations.

Materials: cardboard play oven, plastic food container lids, plastic pizza slicers, empty shaker top jars (e.g., grated cheese containers), colored acetate term paper covers, small dishes, small plates, spatula, glue, hole puncher, paper

Preparation: Fill plastic shaker top jars with paper holes from hole-puncher for grated "cheese" to shake on pizza. Cut small circles and strips of colored acetate term paper covers to create pepperoni, green pepper, and other pizza toppings.

Suggested Vocabulary: dough, cheese, mushrooms, pepperoni, peppers, sauce, pizza, slices, toppings, pan; cold, hot; cook, roll

- Comment that the Little Red Hen made pizza, as children play creatively with the materials.

- Talk to children about pizzas. You might say, *What toppings are you putting on your pizza? Oh, cheese. I like that too, and I also like pepperoni.*

ART AREA: EASEL

Easel Painting With a Basic Set of Colors

Purposes: Creates two-dimensional artwork. Explores and experiments with wet media to create artwork.

Materials: easel, easel brushes, easel paper, markers, paint cups, smocks, tempera paint (yellow, orange, red, purple, blue, green)

Suggested Vocabulary: bristles, color names, easel, paintbrush, smock; dab, drip, mix, rinse, spread

- Observe and comment about their paintings. You might say, *Chris, you covered your whole paper with paint! I see that you created a new color here when you mixed blue and yellow—green.* Or, *Tell me about your painting.*

- Provide help as needed. For example, if a child's paint brush has too much paint on it and the child is unhappy with the drips, show how to dab it against the side of the paint cup.

- Ask children to write their names on their paintings. Provide help if asked.

BLOCKS

Materials for Making a Playground

Continue activity from Week 2 (page 53).

Setting Up and Shopping at the Grocery Store

SOCIAL STUDIES

Purposes: Sorts objects into subgroups that vary by one or more attributes. Engages in socio-dramatic play. Locates objects in a familiar environment. Creates simple representations of home, school, or community.

Continued on next page

Materials: plastic fruits and vegetables, empty cardboard food boxes (e.g., cereal), cash register, box lids/boxes to hold items on shelves, paper receipts, badges, roll of masking tape, plastic crates, 3–4 baskets or play shopping carts, brown paper bags or plastic bags with grocery logos, white stickers or masking tape, tag board, "open" and "closed" signs, empty food containers (e.g., cereal, crackers, pasta, dairy products) including containers seen in *Little Red Hen*.

Preparation: Prepare price stickers by writing small numbers, from 5 to 10, on small pieces of masking tape or the white stickers. Prepare tag board name badges for "Bagger," "Stock Person," and "Cashier." Laminate if possible. Make shopping baskets by attaching yarn handles to small cardboard boxes.

Suggested Vocabulary: bagger, cashier, stock person; bread, butter, can, cereal, cheese, crackers, dairy, fruits, groceries, juice, milk, vegetables; price, produce, shelves, boxes; purchase, shop

- Post a "Closed" sign on Wednesday as the store is set up by a group of children and a teacher. Give turns (in rotating groups) to all who wish to help. Open the store on Thursday.

- Select a child for each grocery store role on Thursday from those who indicate interest at Morning Meeting. Keep a turns list. Assure children that the grocery store will be open for many days so they will all get a turn.

- Model behavior for a role or coach children as they play a role. You might say, *I see you have cereal and rice in your shopping basket. I do too. I have more things on my list. Do you?*

- Remind children to return items to store shelves when they are finished. Return shopping items from house to store for the next group.

PUZZLES AND MANIPULATIVES

Beginning Sound Pictures, and Letter Font Matching

Purposes: Identifies words with the same beginning sound. Names many uppercase letters.

Materials: Add to materials from Week 2 (page 54): uppercase alphabet letter tiles in a variety of fonts, and picture cards for Unit 2 storybook words.

Preparation: Print 5–6 alphabet letters in 3–4 distinctive fonts to make laminated tag board tiles to sort into piles, or to match with a target mounted on a background board. Prepare simple drawings of items from Unit 2 storybook words (e.g., *parrot/pizza; crayon/candle; bouquet/bike; mailbox/money*) on tag board squares.

- As children sort or match letters, provide letter names. You might say, *Yes, that's another* F. *They are a little different from one another, but both have a long line here and two shorter ones up here.*

- As children match pictures, remind them of items' names. Isolate the first sound in picture names if a child needs help. You might say, *Yes, those are flowers, and a bunch of them is called a bouquet. Bouquet, /b/. Bouquet starts with /b/. Is there a picture of something else with a name that starts with /b/?*

DRAMATIC PLAY

Grocery Store Play

SOCIAL STUDIES

Purposes: Locates objects in a familiar environment. Creates simple representations of home, school, or community.

Materials: Add to materials from Week 2 (page 54): play money, coupons, new supply of grocery list paper, and new supermarket ads

Suggested Vocabulary: Add these words to those introduced in Week 2 (page 54): dairy, groceries, ingredients, recipes, shelves; cook

- Prompt children to make a shopping list. You might say, *I think I'll look through this ad to see what I might buy.* Or, *I'm going to check in the refrigerator to see if I am out of milk or yogurt.*

- Observe and comment as children play. For example, *You did a lot of shopping. Maybe I can help you put things away.*

WRITING CENTER

Recording Captions for Class Photo Album

Purposes: Composes and dictates or writes messages. Uses speech to communicate needs, wants, or thoughts. Tells a personal narrative.

Materials: Add to materials from Week 2 (page 54): audiotape recorder and blank audiocassette tape

Preparation: Put pieces of tape on the record and stop buttons on the audiotape recorder that say "RECORD" and "STOP".

Suggested Vocabulary: Add these words to those introduced in Week 2 (page 54): audiotape recorder, tape; record, stop, play, listen, talk

- Observe and monitor children as they record captions for photos. Help children take turns, using a turns list or a kitchen timer.

- Provide help as needed. For example, *I see Amy and Ted in this picture looking at books. Okay, press the record button like this to tape a caption. Do you want to say, "This is Amy and Ted looking at books," or something else?*

Overview of Small Groups

- Each day there are three different Small Groups activities. The same three activities are made available for three days, and each group of five or six children spends one of the three days in each activity.

- On Days 1 and 2, complete the rotation of children through the three groups started on Day 5 of Week 2.

- On Days 3, 4, and 5, children assemble the body frame for a piñata, make piñata party invitations, and address envelopes for them to deliver to their stuffed animals or dolls at home.

- Model suggested vocabulary words and phrases in a manner that clarifies their meaning for children.

▲ Constructing a 3-D Shape (Piñata Body)

MATHEMATICS
High support

Matching, Identifying and Counting Coins/Making Play Money Bills: Days 1, 2

- Continue with activity from Day 5 of Week 2 (page 58). You might say, *If you didn't play with the cash register and play money last week, today is your turn.*

LANGUAGE AND PRINT MANIPULATIVES
Medium support

Making Store Signs: Days 1, 2

- Continue with activity from Day 5 of Week 2 (page 58). Tell children it is their turn to make signs for the grocery store.

BOOK BROWSING
Low support

Exploring Books: Days 1, 2

- Continue with activity from Day 5 of Week 2 (page 57). You might say, *Today it is your turn to look at* Golden Bear, Hush! *or other books in the book area.*

MATHEMATICS

Constructing a 3-D Shape (Piñata Body): Days 3, 4, 5

Purposes: Uses a variety of age appropriate materials and media to create three-dimensional artwork. Performs fine motor tasks that require small muscle strength and control. Interacts appropriately with other children by cooperating, helping, sharing, and expressing interest.

Materials: 2 paper towel tubes, 2 empty tissue boxes, 1 shoebox with lid (for each piñata); tag board or construction paper, masking tape, paper ribbon, polystyrene foam trays, scissors, screwdriver, calendar

Preparation: Cut both paper towel tubes in half to make piñata's legs. At each end of the tubes cut 4 straight lines, 1" to 2" deep. (These will be tabs to attach the legs to the shoebox.) Cut one tissue box so that only half of its top remains. The second tissue box will be inserted at a right angle inside the other one. Use a screwdriver to make 6 holes on each side of the shoebox near the bottom. Cut 6 pieces of paper ribbon, 4' long each. Tear off multiple pieces of masking tape and stick them one the edge of the foam trays for easy access. Cut out ears from tag board.

Suggested Vocabulary: body, head, legs, neck, seam; attach, build, construct

Procedure

- Remind children about the piñatas in *Hooray, a Piñata!* and the Let's Find Out About It activity (page 116). Tell them that each group will make a piñata for the party they're having at the end of next week, but that it will take a few days to make them. You might say, *First, we will make the*

Continued on next page

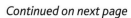

piñata. Next, we will decorate it. Third, we will celebrate by opening the piñatas. Show children a calendar to point out today's activity, the decorating activity early next week, and the party at the end of next week.

- Tell children they are going to make dog piñatas. Show children the materials that will be used for the dogs' body parts: the shoebox for the body, the tissue boxes for the head and neck, and the tubes for the legs.

- Begin with the shoebox. Show children how to thread the paper ribbon through the holes all the way around the box. Explain that the ribbon will be pulled at the party to break the bottom of the piñata and let the toys fall out.

- Tape the lid of the shoebox onto the box and turn it upside down. Help children fold down the tabs on each cardboard tube, flatten them against the box, and affix them with tape to the four corners of the box for the legs. As you hold the box, have children take turns adding tape to legs until they are secure. You might say, *John, you hold the leg steady while Emma tapes it to the box.*

- Demonstrate how the tissue boxes fit together at a right angle. Have children take turns taping the tissue boxes together at the seams.

- Show children how to fold a piece of masking tape so that it is sticky on two sides. They will need two-sided tape to affix the head and neck to the shoebox while you hold it still.

- Give children more tape to attach the ears to the dog's head.

- Remind children that they will be able to decorate them next week.

Copy pages 158–159 to use as you observe children's progress. Note if children worked together well. Note which children struggled with the fine motor tasks.

LANGUAGE AND PRINT MANIPULATIVES

Medium support

Making Party Invitations:
Days 3, 4, 5

Purposes: Writes for many purposes. Writes their own name, using good approximations of letters needed. Uses a variety of age-appropriate materials and media to create three-dimensional artwork.

Materials: *Dandelion*, colored paper (regular or light card weight), white paper, glue sticks, stickers, markers, poster board, sets of children's name cards (from Writing Center)

Suggested Vocabulary: card, date, invitation, signature, time; front, back, inside

Preparation: Print "PLEASE COME TO OUR PIÑATA PARTY" on both the top and bottom right-side quadrants of colored paper. Make enough to have one per child. Cut the colored sheets in half and fold the cards, so "PLEASE COME . . . ." Is on the front of each card, and the inside and back are blank. On paper sized to fit inside the card, print the following for each child, in a large font:

DEAR: _____

PLEASE COME TO OUR PARTY

WHERE: My School

WHEN: (print specific day of the week and date, not year)

WHAT TIME: (print specific time)

DRESS: Come as you are.

FROM, YOUR FRIEND: _____

Make a large model of the invitation with the poster board.

Procedure

- Tell children that they will be having a piñata party soon and that they are going to make invitations for their favorites dolls or stuffed animals to come to the party. Show children the page from *Dandelion* that shows the invitation Jennifer Giraffe sent to Dandelion for her tea and taffy party.

- Show children the large poster board model of the invitation that will be printed inside the cards they will make, and read it to them. Explain what to do when you come to the blanks. For example, *This is where you will write the name of your toy. This is where you will write your name.*

- Encourage children to decorate the invitation with stickers, pictures, or designs, to write their name and the name of their toy on the card, and to sign their name at the end. Accept pictures or other marks. As you go from child to child, ask children about the toys they are inviting. For example, *I see you are inviting Sammy. Tell me about him.*

- *EXTRA SUPPORT* Assist children who need help pasting the printed invitation inside the colored cards. Also assist those having trouble writing their names by naming the letters in their name, while referring to their name card, and offering to write some of the letters for them. Point to one letter at a time, to help children keep track.

- *ELL* Tell children that piñatas are big colorful paper animals filled with treats. Some children break a piñata open at parties and share the treats with their friends. Repeat the word slowly and show a picture, if possible. Have children repeat the word *piñata* with you several times.

- *SOCIAL-EMOTIONAL SUPPORT* Offer to let children who may not have a stuffed animal or doll invite another toy from home. Other children may not have named their toys. Allow them to invite "teddy bear" or "my doll." Be sensitive to children who do not have many toys.

WRITING

Addressing Envelopes for Party Invitations: Days 3, 4, 5

Medium support

Purpose: Follows two-step directions. Writes for many purposes. Writes their own name, using good approximations of letters needed.

Materials: children's piñata party invitations (made in small group session), list of children's addresses, markers, paper, stickers (round and square), 12–15 large paper clips

Preparation: Create a template envelope. Place an invitation lengthwise at the center of a vertical sheet of paper. Fold the top and bottom of the sheet over the invitation, and then the sides. Mark the front of the envelope with "FROM:" in the upper left corner, place a square box in the upper right corner, and four lines in the center of the envelope. Photocopy the template to make one for each child. Fold each copy as you did the template, creating crease lines to make it easier for the children to fold them.

Suggested Vocabulary: address, envelope, invitation, flap, postage, return address, stamp; deliver, enclose, fold, secure

Procedure

- Tell children they are going to make envelopes for their party invitations.

- Show them one of the envelope templates on which you have filled in return address, and address, and have placed a stamp.

- Give each child an envelope template, and point to the upper left corner to show children where they should write their names, and to the center of the envelope to show where their stuffed animal's name and address should go.

- Circulate the lists of children's addresses. Let them find their address on a list and offer help as needed in copying the information. Tell children that any way they write is fine. Give children square stickers to attach to the upper right corner as postage.

- Demonstrate with your own invitation and envelope template how to place the template face down and put the invitation inside the fold lines, and then how to fold the flaps around the invitation and press the folds to make them more permanent.

- Distribute the invitations children made in small groups (one group will have blank cards, and will do their invitations after making their envelopes). Help children place their invitations inside the fold lines on their envelope template, bend the paper around it, and crease the folds. Provide round stickers to use in securing flaps. (The group

making envelopes before invitations can secure the flaps the next day after they finish their invitations. Provide some large paper clips and help them attach to keep their envelope folded around their invitation.)

- Provide encouragement. For example, *Your card fits inside your envelope nicely because you folded it so carefully.* Ask children to take the invitations home and give them to their toys.

- *SOCIAL-EMOTIONAL SUPPORT, EXTRA SUPPORT* Help children who need it, and stress that any kind of writing is okay. Tell children that their stuffed animals don't know how to read yet, so the child will need to tell them what the writing says, anyway.

- *EXTENDING THE ACTIVITY* Prepare RSVP cards to insert in the invitations that read "Can you come to our party?" and have two boxes marked "YES" and "NO". Have children take the invitations home, ask their toy if it will attend, fill out the RSVP card, and bring it back. Guests can be counted during Songs, Word Play, Letters the day before the party.

SUGGESTED RESOURCES

Books

Barton, Byron. *Trucks.* New York: Greenwillow Books HarperCollins, 1986.

Mitton, Tony (author) and Ant Parker (illustrator). *Dazzling Diggers.* New York: Houghton Mifflin Company, 1997.

Rockwell, Anne. *Big Wheels.* New York: Walker & Company, 2003.

Developing Children's Language Through Conversation

Children's ability to use language to sustain dramatic play is an important area of language development. Many children benefit from help with this. This week you and the children will set up a grocery store. Children will play roles (shelf stocker, cashier) in the store. Help children by modeling and coaching the appropriate actions and dialogue.

Conversations About Friends

Preschool-aged children think of friendship in terms of playing together. When outdoors, watch children to see what they like to do. Later you can have conversations about children's favorite activities. Mention activities that several children enjoy and encourage them to talk about them. Seeing shared interests can help children find others to play with.

Center Time: Model Dialogue and Play Behaviors for Dramatic Play

Observe children during dramatic play to see what they are doing. Then enter into the play by taking an appropriate role. In this role, model behaviors and dialogue that children can use. Encourage children who are quiet or unaware of what to say by prompting them and engaging them in dialogue. Be careful not to take over the play. Leave after a few minutes.

A Model for Conversation

Dramatic Play: Dialogue and Play Behaviors

Teacher: (puts two boxes of food in front of cashier, who seems a little confused) *Good morning. I would like to buy these. Can you tell me how to find out how much they cost?*

Cashier: Umm. I don't know.

Teacher: (picks up box and looks for price) *Hmm. Let's see. I think this is the price sticker. What do you think?*

Cashier: Yeah, I forgot.

Teacher: *OK, I guess I can buy these. Oh, I see your scanner here. Do you drag items across like this?*

Cashier: Yes.

Teacher: *OK. Let me know how much I need to pay.*

Cashier: OK, here's your money.

Teacher: *Oh, let me pay you first. Here are two dollars. You are right. It's a little too much. I do need some change.* (You may need to coach some children about the fact that the cashier takes money in exchange for the things being purchased.)

Good Conversations

The Weekly Planners suggest topics of conversation for mealtimes and outdoors. On some days, similar suggestions are offered for both times, to help reinforce the skill or topic discussed. You may also want to use these ideas as a starting point to set your own goals for the week.

Social Skills Development: Encouraging Cooperation

You can help children learn to cooperate by having children perform chores best done by two children. One such task is sweeping (after lunch, around art table). Model the two roles (sweeper, dustpan holder) and encourage use of language to make clear what each child expects the other to do (where to sweep, where to hold the dustpan).

▶ **Start-the-Day Centers** (see pages 88–90)

Make two to three Centers available as you greet children and their families.

▶ **Morning Meeting** (see page 88)

Gather children and review plans for the day. Orient children to center activities and help them make a first choice. Create a turns list for Centers if necessary.

▶ **Center Time** (see pages 88–90)

Children spend time in Centers of their choice.

▶ **Story Time: 1st Reading**

Dandelion

Author: Don Freeman

Summary: Dandelion is invited to a come-as-you-are party. He arrives so dressed up that the hostess doesn't recognize him and shuts the door in his face. A sudden rainstorm ruins Dandelion's fancy clothing and hairdo. When he returns to the party looking like his usual self, his friends welcome him, and he decides never again to try to be someone he isn't.

Theme Link: Friends—When we are among friends we can just be ourselves because friends like us just the way we are.

Purposes

Listens to stories read aloud. Demonstrates increasing levels of sustained and focused engagement. Shows a steady increase in the number of words in listening vocabulary. Develops understanding of main events in a story.

Read the Story

Dandelion contains many words and phrases that will be new to children. Don't try to explain them all in this first reading, given the book's length. Decide which are most important for comprehension of the story. Read with lots of expression and keep the story moving.

Suggested Vocabulary

Use these words often in Story Time and throughout the day.

barbershop a place to go to get a haircut
blushing turning pink or red in the face because you are embarrassed
bouquet a bunch of picked flowers
cane a stick used when walking
cloudburst a sudden, heavy rain shower
fancy very nice; special
flustered feeling nervous and confused
gust a sudden blast of wind
hostess a woman who has guests or a party
mane the long, thick fur on the neck of a lion
pace to walk back and forth
protect to keep from harm or danger
shampoo a liquid soap used to wash hair

Extending the Book

Children who are ready for a challenge can help you read the title of the book as you underline the word with your finger, letter by letter. Tell children that this word contains a smaller word that names an animal. Say *Dan-de-lion* again, breaking apart the syllables, and ask children to name the animal. (lion)

English Language Learners

Explain that the phrase *laughed uproariously* means to laugh very hard. Demonstrate and invite children to say the phrase and laugh uproariously with you.

Progress Monitoring

Note children's level of interest in this new storybook. Do they show curiosity about the contents? Do they focus on the story from beginning to end, or does their attention waver? Record your observations on copies of pages 158–159.

A MODEL FOR READING: *Use the following model to help you plan your book reading.*

Cover

*The name or **title** of this book is* Dandelion. *The author of this book, the person who wrote the words, is Don Freeman. He is also the illustrator—the one who drew the pictures.*

*Look at this lion. He's all dressed up, and he's holding a **bouquet**—a bunch of flowers. I wonder why. Let's read the story to find out what the lion does.*

p. 1 (Read page 1.)

Stretch and yawn as you read those words.

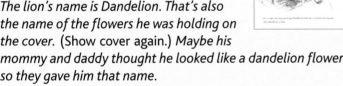

The lion's name is Dandelion. That's also the name of the flowers he was holding on the cover. (Show cover again.) *Maybe his mommy and daddy thought he looked like a dandelion flower, so they gave him that name.*

pp. 2–3 (Read pages 2 and 3.)

Read page 3 with enthusiasm to show Dandelion's curiosity and excitement about the letter.

*Oh, my, the letter was written in **fancy** gold ink. **Fancy** means special and very nice. I wonder who sent it.* Quickly turn the page.

pp. 4–5 (Read page 4.)

*Oh, here's the letter written in **fancy** gold ink. This letter is **fancier** than the one Peter sent to Amy, isn't it? Let's see what it says.*

Read page 4 slowly, one chunk at a time, to give children time to process the information.

Jennifer Giraffe wants Dandelion to come to her party. So this letter is an invitation, just like Peter's letter to Amy. But is Jennifer Giraffe's party for a birthday? (Children respond.) *Apparently not. At Jennifer's party, they're going to have tea and taffy. Tea is a hot drink, and taffy is candy. Sounds yummy, doesn't it?*

Now read page 5.

*Dandelion's **mane**, the hair on his head, looks shaggy and uneven. He had already planned to get his hair cut before he knew about this party.*

pp. 6–7 (Read page 6.)

Briefly define **barbershop** as a place where people go to get their hair cut.

*Lou the Kangaroo is the barber, the person who cuts hair at the **barbershop**. Dandelion must have made an appointment so the barber knew he was coming.*

Go back and read the text on page 7; then complete the sentence on page 8.

pp. 8–9 (Read page 8.)

*Lou used a lot of **shampoo**, the liquid soap we use to wash our hair. Look at all the soap bubbles on Dandelion's **mane**!* (Point.)

Now read page 9.

Point to Dandelion's extended paw.
Dandelion wants his claws to look nice. He is getting his claws cleaned and trimmed. He's getting a manicure.

pp. 10–11 (Read pages 10 and 11.)

Point to the lion's mane as you read page 10. Point to the fashion magazine when reading those words on page 11.

A wave is a way to put curls into hair so it's not so straight. If someone has straight hair and wants waves or curls, the hairdresser or barber can put them in. Of course, lions don't really go to barbers. (Say as though tipping children off.) *This is a pretend story about a lion.*

pp. 12–13 (Read page 12.)

Oh, here's the picture in the magazine the barber was holding up. Dandelion wants to look as beautiful as the lion in the picture.

Read page 13, pointing to the curls.
*Lou is putting curls in Dandelion's **mane**.*

pp. 14–15 (Read page 14.)

*He looked very, very good—absolutely wonderful. Just look at his beautiful curly **mane**.*

Now read page 15.

*Elegant clothes are very dressy—**fancy** clothes we wear on special occasions.*

pp. 16–17 (Read pages 16 and 17.)

Point to the jacket on page 16.
*Dandelion has already had his **mane** curled and his claws manicured, and he has a new jacket. Now he's going to get a cap and a **cane**. A **cane** is a special walking stick.*

pp. 18–19 (Read page 18.)

Explain that *dapper* means very stylish.
*I think Dandelion just bought a **cane*** (point) *from Happy the Crane.* (Point to bird.)

Then read page 19 with a tone of urgency. *Dandelion knows what time it is because he just looked at his watch. See?* (Point.) *The **hostess** is Jennifer Giraffe. She's giving the party. It's nice to take a little gift to the **hostess**, the lady giving the party.*

pp. 20–21 (Read page 20.)

Point to the **bouquet** of dandelions as you read page 20.

Now read page 21, pointing to the door, and emphasizing the word *many*.

Who do you think lives at this house?
(Jennifer Giraffe.) *Yes, Jennifer is the **hostess**, the one giving the party. She's a giraffe and that's why her house has such a tall door—giraffes are very tall. Dandelion looks happy and excited, doesn't he?*

pp. 22–23 (Read page 22.)

He rang the bell (point) *with the tip of his* **cane.**

Read page 23. Adopt an indifferent tone for the last sentence to show that Jennifer doesn't recognize Dandelion. Look at children with a surprised expression.

pp. 24–25 (Read pages 24 and 25.)

Hmmm. That's not usually how someone talks to a friend. Give a quizzical look. *Let's see what happens next.*

pp. 26–27 (Read page 26.)

That's not a nice way to talk to or treat a friend, is it? There must be some misunderstanding here. Move on quickly.

Read page 27 with great expression and slow down on the last two sentences to to show Dandelion's disappointment.

Oh, dear—I don't think Jennifer recognized Dandelion with that new curly **mane** *and those new* **fancy** *clothes. Do you think that's why she didn't let him in?*

pp. 28–30 (Read page 28.)

Paced *means that Dandelion walked back and forth. Maybe he was thinking or upset.* Move finger back and forth on page.

Read pages 29 and 30.

Oh, dear. The **gust** *of wind must have been very strong. His cap is flying through the air.*

pp. 30–31 (Read page 31.)

It's raining very, very hard. Poor Dandelion!

pp. 32–33 (Read pages 32 and 33.)

Dandelion must be feeling pretty unhappy. His cap and **bouquet** *blew away, his* **fancy** *clothes got all wet, and his lovely* **mane** *got soaked. And before that, his friend Jennifer wouldn't let him into her party. He must be feeling very sad and disappointed.*

pp. 34–35 (Read pages 34 and 35.)

pp. 36–37 (Read page 36.)

When reading, say *spied* slowly. *Dandelion spied these flowers right here.* (Point.) *He saw them. They had been* **protected**—*kept safe—from the rain and wind by the bottom step here.* (Point.)

Now read page 37.

Hmmm. I wonder what Dandelion meant when he said, "I think I will try again." Do not wait for children to respond; read on.

pp. 38-39 **(Read page 38.)**

Oh, Dandelion meant that he'd ring Jennifer's doorbell again.

Read page 39.

A **cloudburst** *is a heavy rain shower.*

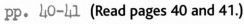

Jennifer Giraffe doesn't know that Dandelion was at her door earlier, trying to come to the party, does she? Why did she recognize him this time but not before? Guide children toward understanding that the lion looks more like himself this time.

pp. 40-41 **(Read pages 40 and 41.)**

Heartily *means that the other animals were very glad to see him. Now he looks happy.*

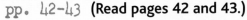

Who was that silly-looking lion that Jennifer Giraffe told Dandelion about? (Dandelion)

pp. 42-43 **(Read pages 42 and 43.)**

Point to Dandelion as you read "laughed uproariously."

Jennifer got **flustered**—*all confused and upset—when she found out she had made such a mistake.*

Do you think that Jennifer Giraffe felt a little embarrassed because she didn't recognize Dandelion earlier? (yes) *Yes, our faces get red—we* **blush**—*when we are embarrassed. And Jennifer was* **blushing**.

p. 44 **(Read page 44.)**

That's probably a good idea, isn't it? What can happen when we change ourselves too much all at once? (People might not recognize us.)

Story Discussion

Now let's go back to the letter—the party invitation. (Reread it.) *What did Jennifer mean when she said "Come as you are"? What if Jennifer's invitation had said, "Come all dressed up"? Do you think she would have recognized Dandelion the first time?* Guide children toward understanding that Jennifer probably would have tried to guess who it was.

That's the story of Dandelion. We'll read the book again another day.

▶ **Outdoor Play**

Say something like, *It's sunny outside today. If your name begins with /s/, like* sunny, *you may go to your cubby and then outside.* Use first sounds in other story words (*gust, bouquet*) to dismiss other children. See pages 86–87 for suggested conversation topics during this time.

▶ Songs, Word Play, Letters

Today children will be playing word games, singing songs, and reciting poems. Add your favorite game, song, or poem to this collection.

Songs

"The Wheels on the Bus," "The More We Get Together," "Come On and Join In to the Game"

Poems

"Mix a Pancake," "Five Little Owls in an Old Elm Tree"

Literacy Skills

Those Words Begin With the Same Sound!, I'm Thinking of ____ Clue Game

Purposes

Recites songs, rhymes, chants, and poems, and engages in language and word play. Listens with increasing attention. Discriminates between sounds that are the same and sounds that are different.

Suggested Sequence for Today's Circle

1. "The Wheels on the Bus"
2. "Mix a Pancake" (and Those Words Begin With the Same Sound!)
3. "The More We Get Together"
4. "Come On and Join In to the Game"
5. I'm Thinking of ____ Clue Game (and *A Letter to Amy*)
6. "Five Little Owls in an Old Elm Tree"

Materials and Instructional Procedures

THE WHEELS ON THE BUS

Materials: CD Track 7, Song Lyrics page 163

Vocabulary: wheels, bus, round, town, up, down, horn, box, wiper, glass, driver, back, daddies, children

Procedure

- Sing some verses that children already know well, leading them in the appropriate actions.

- Introduce some new verses and model the motions. You might try, *Daddies on the bus say sh-sh-sh-sh,* and *Children on the bus say 'look at that'!* (Place hand above eyes as if looking into the distance.)

MIX A PANCAKE (AND THOSE WORDS BEGIN WITH THE SAME SOUND!)

Materials: *Big Book of Poetry:* Poem 8, CD Track 33

Vocabulary: mix, pancake, stir, pan, toss

Procedure

- Show children the *Big Book of Poetry* illustration and ask them what poem they think you are going to do next.

- Present the poem orally to children. Linger on the first sounds of the first words in lines to help children chime in with you.

- When finished reciting the poem, say something like, *I noticed that some of the words in that poem have the same sound at the beginning, like* pop *and* pan: /p/ pot *and* /p/ pan. *The words* catch *and* can *also begin with the same sound:* /k/ catch *and* /k/ can. *That's interesting, isn't it? Some words start with the same sounds.*

THE MORE WE GET TOGETHER

Materials: CD Track 13, Song Lyrics page 163

Vocabulary: together, happier, friends

Procedure

- Tell children that next, they are going to sing the song about friends.

- Sing the song as usual.

- Say, *You can have more than one friend, can't you? And you can have friends at school and friends at home.*

- Sing "Shake My Sillies Out" for a more active alternative. Sources for this song are listed on page 101.

COME ON AND JOIN IN TO THE GAME

Materials: CD Track 20, Song Lyrics page 163

Vocabulary: clap, come, join, game, sneeze, yawn, jump, laugh, clasp

Procedure

- Tell children they haven't sung "Come On and Join In to the Game" in a while. Sing four familiar verses ("clapping", "sneezing", "yawning", "jumping") and model the motions.

- Sing a fifth verse with a new word and motion. For example, *Clasp your hands like me.* (Weave fingers of two hands together.)

- When you're done, you might sing "Willoughby, Wallaby, Woo," before moving on to the word clue game. A source for this song is listed below.

I'm Thinking of ____ Clue Game (and *A Letter to Amy*)

Materials: book: *A Letter to Amy,* Picture Cards: candles, envelope, parrot

Vocabulary: envelope, candles, parrot

Procedure

- Show children the book cover and tell them you will be playing a clue game with words from *A Letter to Amy.* Remind them to raise their hands when they have an idea.

- For *candles,* use these clues: *Peter had some of these on his birthday cake. Peter made a wish and blew them out.* If children need another clue, say, *The name of these things begins with /k/.*

- For *envelope,* use these clues: *Peter put the letter to Amy inside one of these. We lick its flap to seal it. When we say this word, we hear three parts* (clap three times).

- For *parrot,* use these clues: *This is Amy's pet animal. When we say name of this animal, we hear two parts* (clap two times). If children need another clue, say, *The name of this animal begins with /p/.*

- After they guess, show the picture card to reinforce the word.

Five Little Owls in an Old Elm Tree

Materials: *Big Book of Poetry:* Poem 7, CD Track 32

Vocabulary: big, elm, owls, round, tree

Procedure

- Ask children if they remember the poem called "Five Little Owls in an Old Elm Tree."

- Show the *Big Book of Poetry* illustration to the children.

- Recite the poem, pointing to the appropriate pictures on the illustration.

SUGGESTED RESOURCES

Books

Raffi. "Shake My Sillies Out." In *Raffi's Singable Songbook,* (New York: Crown Publishers Inc., 1980).

Raffi. "Willoughby, Wallaby, Woo." In *Raffi's Singable Songbook* (New York: Crown Publishers Inc., 1980).

CDs

Raffi. "Shake My Sillies Out." *More Singable Songs.* Raffi. Rounder Records, 1996.

Raffi. "Willoughby, Wallaby, Woo." *Singable Songs for the Very Young.* Raffi. Rounder Records, 1996.

▶ Lunch/Quiet Time/Centers

This time is set aside for lunch, quiet time, and center activities. See pages 86–87 for suggested conversation topics during this time.

▶ Small Groups

Refer to page 91–93 for information about Small Groups.

▶ Let's Find Out About It

Exploring Signs for Advertising

Purposes

Develops an understanding of different kinds of texts. Scans text from left to right. Develops background knowledge. Develops understanding of relationship to buying/selling.

Materials

book: *Matthew and Tilly;* coins (quarters, dimes, nickels), advertising signs from local businesses

Preparation

Copy Matthew and Tilly's lemonade stand sign onto easel paper and hang it where children can see it clearly.

Suggested Vocabulary

Use these words in context in this discussion: advertisement, dime, nickel, post, price, quarter, sign

Procedure

- Show the page in *Matthew and Tilly* where it says, "They sold lemonade together." Point out the pitcher of lemonade, the glasses, and the sign hung on the railing. Point to the sign you have copied onto the easel paper, and tell children that you have copied it from the sign in the book. Read the sign, underlining with your finger as you go. Explain that the sign tells what is for sale, and the price—how much the lemonade costs.

- If you've been able to acquire signs from local businesses that have the names and the prices printed on them, such as bakeries or restaurants, read a couple of signs to the children.

> **English Language Learners**
>
> Say the names of the different coins you brought in slowly and clearly, and have children repeat the names.

- Tell children they will be making signs for their play grocery store, and that one of the signs will advertise—let people know about—the opening of the store. Tell children they can post this sign in the hall—put it on the wall for all to see.

Small Groups Connections

Children will assemble and decorate signs for the grocery store.

Center Time Connections

Children can choose to work on special signs at the Writing Center.

> **Extending the Activity**
>
> For children who are ready for a challenge, help them sound out and read with you some of the store signs.

▶ End-the-Day Centers

Children choose among the open Centers. As children leave for home, you might remind them that the construction equipment will still be at the sand table tomorrow, and that children also can choose to decorate signs for the grocery store.

▶ **Start-the-Day Centers** (see pages 88–90)
As you greet children and family members, make two to three Centers available.

▶ **Morning Meeting** (see page 88)
Teachers orient children to center activities.

▶ **Center Time** (see pages 88–90)
Children spend time in Centers of their choice.

▶ **Story Time: 2nd Reading**

Dandelion

Author: Don Freeman

Purposes

Recalls some main events when asked, "What is happening in this story?" Begins to link characters' basic emotions to their actions. Uses own experiences to understand characters' feelings and motivations. Recalls story events in a way that shows increasing understanding.

Read the Story Again

This time reconstruct the story with children. Prompt children's recall of events and characters' actions by asking questions like *What is happening here?* and *What did Dandelion do next?* Help children recall the story by using pictures and reading major portions of text. Use key vocabulary words as you reconstruct the story, and encourage children to use them.

Suggested Vocabulary

Use these words often during Story Time and throughout the day.

barbershop a place to go to get a haircut
blushing turning pink or red in the face because you are embarrassed
bouquet a bunch of picked flowers
cane a stick used when walking
cloudburst a sudden, heavy rain shower
fancy very nice; special
flustered feeling nervous and confused
gust a sudden blast of wind
hostess a woman who has guests or a party
mane the long, thick fur on the neck of a lion
pace to walk back and forth
protect to keep from harm or danger
shampoo a liquid soap used to wash hair

Extending the Book

Tell children who are ready for a challenge that letters often begin with the word *Dear* and end with *Sincerely* and a name. Invite them to read these words from the fancy invitation with you as you underline them with your finger, letter by letter.

English Language Learners

On page 28, demonstrate the meaning of *paced,* by moving your finger back and forth on the sidewalk in the illustration. Say, *Dandelion walked back and forth, back and forth—he* paced. Explain that people sometimes pace if they are anxious or trying to think.

Progress Monitoring

Notice which children respond to events in the story with smiles, frowns, giggles, and shaking heads. Notice any quizzical looks as well. All are cues to children's understanding. Which children join in the story discussion? Record your observations on copies of pages 158–159.

A MODEL FOR READING: *Read all the text on each page. When you read it will vary, depending on the flow of your conversations with children.*

Cover

You know the title of this book because we read it the other day. The title is . . . (Dandelion). *Right.* Underline title with your finger as you read it.

We're going to read the story again today and talk about the things that happened.

p. 1

Read page 1. Point to Dandelion waking up.

This story begins on a Saturday, not Monday or Tuesday, like today. Saturday is a weekend day. We don't have school, and a lot of people don't go to work on Saturday.

pp. 2–3

Point to the picture on page 2. *Dandelion got up. Then he was thinking about something as he looked out his window. Do you remember what it was?* (Children respond.) *Yes, he was wondering if the mail had come.*

What did he find in the mailbox? (a letter) *Yes, a letter! Was the ink special?* (Children respond.) *Right, not ordinary blue or black ink.*

Read pages 2 and 3.

pp. 4–5

Let's read the letter again. How does it start? Prompt by pointing to *D* in *Dear*, and sounding it out.

Read the letter slowly, one chunk at a time, and then ask questions to review details of the invitation, including when the party is scheduled, what will be served there, and who signed the letter. *What part of the invitation did Dandelion misunderstand?* Guide children toward realizing that Dandelion missed the instruction to "Come as you are."

Read page 5.

The invitation arrived on the same day as the party, Saturday. Dandelion didn't have much time to get ready, did he?

pp. 6–7

Point to the picture on page 6. *What is happening here?* (Dandelion is hurrying to the **barbershop**.)

Read page 6.

Point to the picture on page 7. *Now what is happening?* (Dandelion is getting his **mane** cut.) *Yes.*

Read page 7.

pp. 8–9

Point to the picture on page 8. *What is happening here?* (Children comment.) *Yes, Dandelion is getting a **shampoo**. He's getting his **mane** washed.*

Point to the picture on page 9. *What's going on here?* (Children respond.) *Yes, Dandelion is getting a **manicure**. He's getting his claws made neat and clean.*

Now read pages 8 and 9, going back to page 7 to begin the sentence that continues on page 8. Doing this provides the full sentence. Before you turn the page ask, *Do you remember what happened next?* (Children respond.)

pp. 10-11

Affirm what children recalled and comment. *Dandelion was not very happy with how his **mane** looked.* (Point.) *It was too frizzy and fuzzy, and it was sticking out all over.*

Read page 10.

Point to the kangaroo on page 11.

Do you remember the suggestion that Lou the Barber made? Guide children to recall that he thought Dandelion's mane would look better if it were curly—if it had a wave.

Read page 11. Read text in the book the barber is holding. Turn to the next page to show the picture.

pp. 12-13

Here's a close-up of the picture in the magazine.

Read page 12.

Point to the picture on page 13. *What's happening here?* (Children respond.)

Read page 13. You may want to comment on the process—using rollers to make curls, etc.

pp. 14-15

Read page 14.

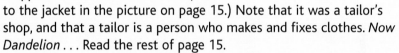

Dandelion looks absolutely wonderful.

After he left the barbershop, what did he do? Guide children to recall that he stopped at a window of a store. (Point to the jacket in the picture on page 15.) Note that it was a tailor's shop, and that a tailor is a person who makes and fixes clothes. *Now Dandelion . . .* Read the rest of page 15.

*He thought his sweater wasn't dressy enough for the party, not **fancy** enough.*

pp. 16-17

Read the first sentence on page 16.

And then what did Theodore the Tailor suggest? (Dandelion needed a cap and cane.) Support children's efforts to remember.

Read the last line on page 16 and read page 17.

pp. 18-19

Read page 18.

Here he is in the cap and cane shop with Happy Crane, who has helped him find a cap and cane for himself.

Point to the picture on page 19. Ask children what Dandelion is doing here. (checking the time on his watch) Read page 19.

*What did Dandelion decide to get for the party **hostess**, Jennifer Giraffe?* (flowers)

Continued on next page

pp. 20–21

Read page 20 to confirm children's recall. Then read page 21.

pp. 22–23

Read page 22; then point to the illustration on page 23.

Did Jennifer Giraffe say, "Oh, hi, I'm so glad you're here"? (Children respond. Lead them to recall what Jennifer said.)

Read page 23.

pp. 24–25

Read page 24. Then read page 25 in a way that shows Jennifer's utter rejection of this "stranger."

pp. 26–27

Read pages 26 and 27. *What happened?* Guide children to state that there was a big misunderstanding because Jennifer didn't recognize her friend Dandelion.

pp. 28–29

Read pages 28 and 29. Explain **gust** and *bouquet* using the picture and words.

pp. 30–31

Read pages 30 and 31.

Explain *torrents* using the picture and words.

pp. 32–33

Comment that things are not going well for Dandelion.

Read pages 32 and 33.

pp. 34–35

Read page 35.

pp. 36–37

*What did Dandelion **spy** when he was sitting on the steps drying himself in the sun?* (Point to the dandelions while children respond.) *Yes, he noticed a clump of dandelions. What did Dandelion decide to do?* Guide children to recall that he picked flowers to make a new bouquet.

Read page 37.

pp. 38–39

Read page 38.

Here's Jennifer, answering the door. What did she say this time? Help children to recall, "We've been waiting for you . . ."

Read page 39.

So did Jennifer know that he had rung her doorbell before? Support recognition of the misunderstanding. Jennifer did not know he was there before.

pp. 40–41

Read page 40.

Look how Dandelion's friends smiled at him and shook his paws hello and welcomed him.

Now read page 41.

pp. 42–43

Read pages 42 and 43.

And how did Jennifer Giraffe feel when she realized there had been a misunderstanding?

p. 44

Read page 44. *Jennifer Giraffe was a little upset and embarrassed about what she'd done.*

Story Discussion

Prompt discussion with questions. For example, *Do you remember what Jennifer and Dandelion promised?* Read pages 43 and 44 to confirm or clarify children's recall.

In another story we read recently, someone else sent a letter to invite a friend to a party. Do you remember what that story was? (A Letter to Amy) Show book cover if necessary to prompt recall. *Someone in this story was also disappointed for a while, and then everything turned out okay. Who was it?* Support recall of Peter. *Who do you think felt disappointed longer, Peter or Dandelion?* Support comparison by flipping through pages in *Dandelion* to show all that he did, in between first and second attempts.

That's the end of Story Time for today. We'll read Dandelion *again another day.*

▶ Outdoor Play

Practice initial sounds. For example, *If your name starts with the same sound as tea and taffy, you may go to your cubby . . . /t/, like tea or taffy.* Continue with *giraffe* and *Jennifer, cane* and *candy, doorbell* and *Dandelion,* or other word pairs that work for names in your class. See pages 86–87 for suggested conversation topics during this time.

▶ Songs, Word Play, Letters

Today children will be playing word games, singing songs, and reciting poems. Add your favorite game, song, or poem to this collection.

Songs

"Clap Your Hands", "What Are You Wearing?", "Five Green and Speckled Frogs"

Predictable Book

Golden Bear

Literacy Skills

Those Words Rhyme!; If Your Name Starts With [first sound in a child's name], Raise Your Hand

Purposes

Recites songs, rhymes, chants, and poems, and engages in language and word play. Recognizes words that complete rhymes, in a group. Listens with increasing attention. Listens to a variety of genres read aloud: stories, songs, rhymes, poems. Moves body with balance and control. Segments the beginning sounds in words. Participates successfully as a member of a group.

Suggested Sequence for Today's Circle

1. "Clap Your Hands"
2. "What Are You Wearing?"
3. *Golden Bear* (and Those Words Rhyme!)
4. "Five Green and Speckled Frogs"
5. If Your Name Starts With [first sound in a child's name], Raise Your Hand

Materials and Instructional Procedures

CLAP YOUR HANDS

Materials: CD Track 12, Song Lyrics page 163

Vocabulary: clap, hands, stamp, jump

Procedure

- Tell children that the first song today is "Clap Your Hands".

- Start by asking children to stand up, and guess the first verse you are going to sing. Sing the first verse (stamping feet). Follow with "jump with me."

- Follow this with another verse that requires standing up (e.g., "bend your knees" or "touch your toes"). Tell children that for the last verse, you want children to blink their eyes. Ask children if they need to stand up to do that one, or if it would work sitting down. Sit down with the children to do the last verse.

WHAT ARE YOU WEARING?

Materials: CD Track 14, Song Lyrics page 163

Vocabulary: day, long, pants, shirt, wearing

Procedure

- Tell children, *You sang this song last week. It is about what you're wearing.*

- Go around the circle singing about each child's name and the color of an article of clothing he or she is wearing.

GOLDEN BEAR (AND THOSE WORDS RHYME!)

Materials: book: *Golden Bear*

Vocabulary: bear, dancing, everywhere, golden, rocking, stair

Procedure

- Show children the cover of *Golden Bear* and underline the title with your finger as you read it with children.

- Read *Golden Bear,* keeping the natural rhythm of the verse.

- Go back to pages with rhyming words (e.g., *tub/scrub, fish/wish, night/tight*) and reread some of those verses. You might say, tub *and* scrub *have the same sound at the end. They rhyme.* Say *tub* and *fish,* and ask if they rhyme. Agree that they don't because they don't have the same sound at the end. Then comment that *fish* and *dish* rhyme.

- If you would like to read a different predictable text book about road construction to go along with the construction vehicle play at the Sand Table this week, you might try *Dazzling Diggers.* (A source for this book is provided on page 109.) Read it naturally as you would any predictable text book and comment on rhyming words (e.g., *ground/pound, soil/oil, break/shake*).

FIVE GREEN AND SPECKLED FROGS

Materials: CD Track 10, Song Lyrics page 163, flannel board and flannel pieces

Vocabulary: cool, delicious, green, log, pool, speckled

Preparation: Make two more flannel frogs.

Procedure

- Perform the song as usual. After putting up the usual five frogs, say that two friends have come to visit, and they want to play in the pool too. Ask what number you should use in the first verse, now that two more frogs are here. Count to confirm by gesturing to the group of five, and say, *5...then, 6, 7,* as you point to the new frogs.

- When you are down to four frogs, remove two at once in the next verse, and then remove the last two together to make the song go a bit faster.

IF YOUR NAME STARTS WITH [FIRST SOUND IN A CHILD'S NAME], RAISE YOUR HAND

Vocabulary: letter, name, raise

Procedure

- Tell children you are going to play a game again with their names, but that, this time, you are going to say sounds, not hold up letter cards.

- Play one round of the game, as you did when you played it earlier. If a child does not respond to the sound that is the first one in their name, say, *Nancy, your name begins /n/, so you raise your hand. Nancy begins with /n/.* Emphasize */n/* in the name. Be sure to say sounds and do not say letter names.

- You might want to do the "Five Little Monkeys" chant if you have enough time today. A source for this song is listed below.

Progress Monitoring

Make copies of pages 158–159 to use as you take notes on children's progress. Notice which children engage quickly with known songs and which ones need prompting to remember words or motions. Which children recognize the first sound in their names and which ones need prompting?

SUGGESTED RESOURCES

Book

Mitton, Tony (author) and Ant Parker (illustrator). *Dazzling Diggers.* New York: Kingfisher (Houghton Mifflin Company), 1997.

CD

Tilsen, Barb. "Five Little Monkeys." *Make a Circle Like the Sun.* Barb Tilsen. The Orchard, 2001.

▶ Lunch/Quiet Time/Centers

This time is set aside for lunch, quiet time, and center activities. See pages 86–87 for suggested conversation topics during this time.

▶ Small Groups

For information about Small Groups, refer to pages 91–93.

▶ Let's Talk About It

Social Skills Development

Purposes

Discusses interacting appropriately with other children. Talks about understanding of relationships among objects and people.

Procedure

- Use photos of children playing together at school. Select some that show children sharing or using materials together. Ask the children who are shown in the pictures to tell what they were playing.

- If there is time, ask several children, *Can you remember a time when you wanted to keep a toy or something else all to yourself and not share, but then changed your mind and had a good time playing with others?*

- Give interested children turns to tell about times that they were able to share toys and had a good time playing with a friend. As children tell about these times, point out that sharing toys or materials helps everyone have a better time. For example:

  Julia, I saw that you and Hank were drawing together today and sharing the markers. The two of you seemed to have a good time drawing together.

▶ End-the-Day Centers

Place some of the recent photos in the Writing Center for children to look at. Invite them to think of captions. You may wish to comment specifically to individual children about something that happened on this day, or about something to expect or look forward to on the next day. It is important to personalize your goodbye comments.

▶ **Start-the-Day Centers** (see pages 88–90)
Provide two to three open Centers.

▶ **Morning Meeting** (see page 84)
Teachers orient children to center activities.

▶ **Center Time** (see pages 88–90)
Children spend time in Centers of their choice.

▶ **Story Time: 1st Reading**

Hooray, a Piñata!

Author: Elisa Kleven

Summary: Clara buys a little dog-shaped piñata for her birthday party. She plays with the piñata as if it were a pet, and it becomes so real to her that the thought of breaking it makes her sad. Her friend Samson solves the problem by buying a different piñata for Clara's party.

Theme Link: Friends—Friends care about each other's feelings and try to help each other solve their problems.

Purposes

Listens to stories read aloud. Demonstrates increasing levels of sustained and focused engagement during read aloud times. Shows a steady increase in the number of words in listening vocabulary. Develops understanding of the main story events.

Read the Story

As you read *Hooray, a Piñata!,* draw children in by reading with expression. Say words such as *whack, smack,* and *crack* with gusto. Use voice, gestures, and pantomime or provide brief explanations. As you read, point out important objects, people, and facial expressions in the illustrations.

Suggested Vocabulary

Use these words often to discuss the story and throughout the day.

collar a leather or cloth band for a dog's neck

crack to break or split with a sharp sound

dreams pictures, thoughts, and emotions that happen during sleep

flapped moved back and forth

hooray a cheer; a word used to show excitement or approval

leash a line for leading an animal

mash to crush or grind

merry-go-round a ride with seats shaped like horses that go around in a circle

monster a frightening make-believe creature

pretended made believe

smash to break into pieces

sniffed smelled by drawing short breaths into the nose

thundercloud a cloud that goes with a thunderstorm

wrecked ruined, spoiled so it cannot be used

Extending the Book

After reading the book, go back to pages 6 and 7. Ask children what other kinds of piñatas they might see in a store that they don't see in the book.

English Language Learners

Explain that *hooray* is a kind of cheer that people shout when they are happy about something. Read the title several times, saying *Hooray!* in a cheering fashion. Have children join in with you.

Progress Monitoring

Note how individual children react to this new story (curiosity, enthusiasm, little interest). Which children focus on the story throughout the reading? Notice facial expressions that indicate understanding, as well as verbal answers to discussion questions. Record your observations on copies of pages 158–159.

A MODEL FOR READING: *Use the following model to help you plan your book reading.*

Cover

The title of this book is . . . (Pause; then read enthusiastically.) *Hooray, a Piñata!* [pronounced pin-YAH-tah] *Let's say it together— Hooray, a Piñata! I wonder what a piñata is?*

p. 3 (Read page 3.)

Samson must be Clara's friend. We like to do things with our friends, and Clara wants her friend Samson to come shopping with her for a piñata, something very special for her party.

pp. 4–5 (Read pages 4 and 5.)

Read *whack, smack,* **crack,** **mash,** **smash** to convey meaning, adding gestures.

Oh, so now we know something about a piñata. It sounds like it's something that you fill up with candy or toys, then hit and whack and smack it to crack it open. Then the treats fall out.

pp. 6–7 (Read pages 6 and 7.)

As you read, point to pictures to help children understand *paper curls,* **monster,** *jagged,* and **thundercloud.**

So piñatas are made to look like different kinds of animals and things, and they're made out of colorful paper with curly paper decoration. Samson wanted Clara to get the big, scary piñata that looks like a cloud in a thunderstorm (point), *but she shook her head "no."* (Shake your head.) *Which piñata did Clara want?* (the dog) *Yes, she wanted to buy the little dog.*

pp. 8–9 (Read page 8.)

Say *vendor* slowly and point to him. *What bothered Samson about the dog piñata? Yes, he thought it was too little to hold a lot of candy.*

Read page 9. Define **wrecked** briefly as you read.

Clara wanted to play with Lucky as if he were a real little dog. Samson was worried that the paper dog piñata might break and then they wouldn't have a piñata at the party. She told him not to worry, that it wouldn't get **wrecked.**

pp. 10–11 (Read page 10.)

Point to **collar** and **leash** as you read. *Clara found fun ways to play with Lucky.*

Read page 11.

They greeted people—said hello to them. Clara was **pretending.** *She was making believe that Lucky was a real dog.*

pp. 12–13 (Read page 12.)

As you read page 13, sniff to demonstrate that word. *The car was going fast, and Lucky's ears* **flapped** (flap hands to demonstrate) *back and forth in the wind.*

pp. 14–15 (Read page 14.)

Clara's grandmother gave Clara a nice blanket that she may have crocheted herself using yarn and a needle. Clara's grandmother also gave her some money. Hmm. I wonder how she'll spend it.

Read page 15. *So Clara and Lucky went fast around and around on the* **merry-go-round** (point).

pp. 16-17 (Read page 16.)

Clara dreamed while she was sleeping that she and Lucky could fly. Dreams are pictures in your head, sounds and feelings that you experience when you are sleeping.

pp. 18-19 (Read pages 18 and 19.)

Neither Clara nor Samson wanted Lucky to be **wrecked***, did they?*

pp. 20-21 (Read page 20.)

Read the first three paragraphs. *I think Clara started to cry when she thought about Lucky getting broken. I wonder what Samson is going to do?*

Now read the rest of page 20.
I wonder what Samson will give her. (Give children a wide-eyed questioning look.)

pp. 22-23 (Read page 22.)

Say **jagged** with expression and point to the picture. *Samson's first present was a bone for Lucky. Let's look at the second present. Have you seen it before?* (Children respond.)

Now read page 23.

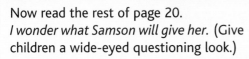

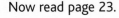

pp. 24-25 (Read pages 24 and 25.)

The boy's eyes are covered (point) *so that he can't see where the piñata is. Clara and her mother* (point) *are pulling on this rope to make the piñata go up and down. That makes it hard to hit. Each child takes a turn trying to break it.*

pp. 26-27 (Read pages 26 and 27.)

When Clara hit the piñata hard, there was a loud sound like thunder and it broke. Then, all of the candies came pouring down, like rain.

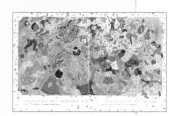

p. 28 (Read page 28.)

Once the thundercloud was broken, the children and Lucky found other ways to play with it.

Story Discussion

You probably remember that Clara didn't like the thundercloud piñata at first (show pages 6–7), *but then changed her mind* (show page 23). *Why?* Guide children toward seeing that she could keep her dog and make her friend happy too.

That's all the time we have for stories today.

▶ Outdoor Play

Use first sounds of story characters' names to dismiss children. For example, *If your name starts with /l/ like Lucky . . . If your name starts with /k/ like Clara . . . and so on.* See pages 86–87 for suggested conversation topics during this time.

▶ Songs, Word Play, Letters

Today children will be playing word games, singing songs, and reciting poems. Add your favorite game, song, or poem to this collection.

Songs

"Six Little Ducks", "Down by the Bay", Story-Character "Bingo" Song

Poem

"Five Juicy Apples"

Literacy Skills

Can You Think of Words That Rhyme With ____?, I'm Thinking of ____ Clue Game, We Can Change It and Rearrange It

Purposes

Recites songs, rhymes, chants, and poems, and engages in language and word play. Follows two-step directions building up to following multi-step directions. Produces words that rhyme. Names many uppercase letters.

Suggested Sequence for Today's Circle

1. Can You Think of Words That Rhyme With ____? (and "Six Little Ducks")
2. "Down by the Bay"
3. I'm Thinking of ____ Clue Game (and *Matthew and Tilly* and *Dandelion*)
4. "Five Juicy Apples"
5. Story-Character "Bingo" Song and We Can Change It and Rearrange It (and *Matthew and Tilly*)

Materials and Instructional Procedures

CAN YOU THINK OF WORDS THAT RHYME WITH ____? AND SIX LITTLE DUCKS

Materials: CD Track 19, Song Lyrics page 164

Vocabulary: back, down, feather, led, river

Procedure

- Tell children that you are going to sing a new song about ducks. This song has one more duck than the song they already know ("Five Little Ducks"). See if they can guess the name of the song. Provide a hint by reciting numbers up through five, and pausing, *1, 2, 3, 4, 5 . . .*

- Sing the song to teach it to children. Put palms of your hands together, wiggling them back and forth, every time you sing "wibble-wobble, wibble-wobble".

- Tell children that some of the words in this song rhyme. Ask them if they can think of other words that rhyme with *back* and *quack*. Be ready to offer ideas yourself (e.g., *smack, crack, sack, whack*), given that thinking up rhymes is new for children.

DOWN BY THE BAY

Materials: CD Track 3, Song Lyrics page 162, flannel board and pieces for the song

Vocabulary: cake, dog, frog, go, grow, house, mouse, snake

Procedure

- Sing the song, as usual.
- Add a new verse or two. Be creative!

I'M THINKING OF ____ CLUE GAME (AND *MATTHEW AND TILLY* AND *DANDELION*)

Materials: books: *Matthew and Tilly*, *Dandelion*, Picture Cards: bike, crayon, giraffe, zebra

Vocabulary: bike, crayon, giraffe, zebra

Procedure

- Show children *Matthew and Tilly* and *Dandelion*, and tell them they are going to play a clue game with words from these two books. Remind them to listen to the clues, think about them, and then raise their hands without calling out their idea because other children might still be thinking.

- Start with *Matthew and Tilly*. Clues for *bike: This is something you ride on that has two wheels. It also has handlebars. It begins with /b/.* Clues for *crayon: You use these to color. In the story, Matthew broke a purple one that belonged to Tilly.* If children need another clue, say, *It begins with /k/.*

- After they guess each answer, show the picture card to reinforce the words.

- If children are engaged, play the same game with words from *Dandelion*. Clues for *zebra: This is the name of an animal that has black and white stripes. This animal's name begins with /z/.* Clues for *giraffe: This kind of animal has a very long neck and brown spots. Its name begins with /j/.*

FIVE JUICY APPLES

Materials: *Big Book of Poetry:* Poem 5, CD Track 30

Vocabulary: apples, juicy, sitting, store

Procedure

- Proceed as usual with the poem.

- Say the poem enough times to do everyone's name. Comment that you can do only five names each time you do the poem, and that it took [number] times to include everyone's name.

STORY-CHARACTER "BINGO" SONG, WE CAN CHANGE IT AND REARRANGE IT (AND *MATTHEW AND TILLY*)

Materials: *Matthew and Tilly,* "TILLY" printed on a piece of paper or tagboard. CD Track 2 (for "Bingo" melody), flannel board and flannel letter pieces: T, I, L, L, Y, M, B, S

Vocabulary: change, rearrange, remove, replace

Procedure

- Show the cover of *Matthew and Tilly,* and have children identify the characters. Tell children that they are going to sing the "Bingo" song, but are going to sing about Tilly, and not the farmer's dog. Show the children the card with "TILLY" printed on it.

- Point to the first letter in Tilly's name. You might say, *Tilly's name begins with the letter T, so I'll put that letter up first.* Point to the second letter and ask, *What is the second letter in TILLY's name?* Say *I* if children don't

name it, and put the flannel letter *I* up on the board. Point to *L* and ask what the third letter is. Continue similarly with the last two letters, *L* and *Y.*

- Use the melody from "Bingo" and sing, *There was a boy who had a friend and Tilly was her name-o.* T-I-L-L-Y (three times), *and Tilly was her name-o.*

- Invite children to sing along. Each time you sing a verse substitute a clap for the missing letter, as you usually do with "Bingo".

- After removing all the letters to finish the song, put the letters back up to spell "TILLY" again. Then, remove the letter *T* and replace it with the letter *M.* Ask children what letter you have put there, and then sound it out to help them guess the new name (Milly). Next, replace *M* with *S,* and ask children what they think the new word says (Silly). Sound out *S* if needed, to help children figure out the new word, and then comment that the word really is silly, because that's not anyone's name.

- As you remove letters to put them away, you might say, *We can make a lot of different words by changing one letter. We can change and rearrange them in many different ways.*

▶ Lunch/Quiet Time/Centers

This time is set aside for lunch, quiet time, and center activities. See pages 86–87 for suggested conversation topics during this time.

▶ **Small Groups**

See pages 91–93 for information about Small Groups.

▶ **Let's Find Out About It**

Exploring Piñatas

Purposes

Develops understanding that nonfiction texts are used to find information. Develops background knowledge. Uses comparative terms to describe weight. Demonstrates an emerging awareness and respect for culture and ethnicity.

Materials

book: *Hooray, a Piñata!;* a real piñata, small toys to stuff inside the piñata, library books with pictures and information about piñatas

Suggested Vocabulary

Use these words in sentences to make their meanings clear: piñata; filled, heavier, lighter, stuffed

Procedure

- If possible, bring in a real piñata for children to look at. Give children quick turns to hold the piñata. Then fill the piñata with small toys. Invite children to hold the piñata again. Help them contrast how it feels when it's empty and how it feels when it's full. Use terms *heavier* and *lighter*.

- Find the pages in *Hooray, a Piñata!* that show Clara and Samson looking at piñatas. Remind children that Clara and Samson talked about filling a piñata with candy or toys, and then whacking and smashing the piñata.

- Obtain books about piñatas from the library. Show pictures of different types of piñatas being made or used, and read any appropriate information about them.

> **English Language Learners**
>
> As you talk about piñatas, mention that this word and many others we use (*tortilla, quesadilla*) come from other languages, such as Spanish. Invite children to practice saying *piñata*.

- Tell children that they will be making a piñata very soon and that they will also have a piñata party next week. At the party they will get to pull open a filled piñata to let the toys fall out.

Small Groups Connections

Children help assemble a piñata.

Center Time Connections

Children can choose to decorate a piñata.

> **Extending the Activity**
>
> Invite children to name the toys as you put them inside the piñata.

▶ **End-the-Day Centers**

Children spend time in open Centers of their choice. As children leave for home, say something such as, *Tomorrow we will be reading* Hooray, a Piñata! *again and more children will have a turn to make invitations for their stuffed animals.*

▶ **Start-the-Day Centers** (see pages 88–90)

Direct children to choose among two to three open Centers as the day begins.

▶ **Morning Meeting** (see page 88)

Gather children, review plans for the day, and update the turns list.

▶ **Center Time** (see pages 88–90)

Children spend time in Centers of their choice.

▶ **Story Time: 2nd Reading**

Hooray, a Piñata!

Author: Elisa Kleven

Purposes

Recalls some main events when asked, "What is happening in this story?" Links characters' basic emotions to their actions. Uses own experiences to understand characters' feelings and motivations. Expresses the main idea of a story or other text in a way that shows increasing understanding.

Read the Story Again

This time help children understand events by talking about the story and revisiting the text. Ask questions before or after you read a page. For example, *What did Clara [or Samson] do next? What's happening here?* If children have difficulty answering questions you ask before reading a page, simply read the page and move on.

Suggested Vocabulary

Repeat these words often in context.

collar a leather or cloth band for a dog's neck

crack to break or split with a sharp sound

dreams pictures, thoughts, and emotions that happen during sleep

flapped moved back and forth

hooray a cheer; a word used to show excitement or approval

leash a line for leading an animal

mash to crush or grind

merry-go-round a ride with seats shaped like horses that goes around in a circle

monster a frightening make-believe creature

pretended made believe

smash to break into pieces

sniffed smelled by drawing short breaths into the nose

thundercloud a cloud that goes with a thunderstorm

wrecked ruined; spoiled so it cannot be used

Extending the Book

Invite children to read the words *whack, crack, mash,* and *smash* (pages 4 and 5) along with you, especially if you have children ready for a challenge.

English Language Learners

Shake your head from side to side to demonstrate the sentence "Clara shook her head" (page 7). Explain that *shaking your head* means *no*. Invite children to shake their heads for *no*.

Progress Monitoring

Notice which children respond to events in the story with smiles, frowns, giggles, and shaking heads. Note which children answer the discussion questions, who can identify characters' emotions, and who can relate story events to personal experiences. Record your observations on copies of pages 158–159.

A MODEL FOR READING: *Read all the text on each page. When you read it will vary, depending on the flow of your conversations with children.*

Cover

We read this book once before, so you know that the title is . . . (Pause, then read the title with enthusiasm.) *Hooray, a Piñata! We're going to read and talk more about the book today.*

What is happening here? (Point to cover. Children respond.)

p. 3

OK, so here are Clara and Samson (point). Pause to let children say their names. *Do you remember what they are talking about?* Guide recall that they are talking about the things Clara will have at her birthday party. Be sure children mention the piñata.

Read page 3.

pp. 4–5

Where are they going here? (Children respond.) Read pages 4 and 5.

pp. 6–7

What kinds of colorful piñatas did they see in the piñata store? Point to them while children name a few.

Did Clara and Samson want the same ones? Guide children to recall which ones each child wanted. If they struggle to recall, read both pages and move on.

Read pages 6 and 7.

pp. 8–9

Based on your children's level, pose the suggested question before or after you read page 8.

What did Samson think about the piñata Clara chose? Why? Guide children to note that the dog is so small, he won't hold very much candy.

Clara's mom bought her the dog piñata. Then Clara did some things that made it seem like a pet. See what clues you hear on this page.

Read page 9. Guide children to note: petting, giving the dog a name, planning to take it to the picnic, caring for it.

pp. 10–11

Clara had fun treating her dog piñata like a pet. Read the text.

pp. 12–13

Point to the picture on page 12. *What is happening here?* Guide children to recall that Clara played with Lucky in the sand and Samson was worried he would get ruined or **wrecked.** Read the text.

As you read page 13, use voice, actions, and the picture to clarify **sniffed,** *sped,* and **flapped.**

pp. 14–15

Point to Grandma on page 14. *Who is this?* (Children respond.) *Yes, it's Clara's Grandma.* Note smiling face and open arms and comment that she seems happy to see Clara.

Read pages 14 and 15.

pp. 16-17

Read page 16.

Who was flying in Clara's **dream?** (Point to some of the people in Clara's dream.)

pp. 18-19

Point to the pictures on page 18. *What is happening here?* Guide recall of some of the things Clara did with Lucky.

Then read pages 18 and 19. *Is Samson still worried?* Guide children to note that Samson is still worried. Clarify that he wants to be sure there is a piñata for the party.

pp. 20-21

Read page 20.

Does Samson realize how much Clara wants Lucky to be a real dog? (Children respond.) Note that he offers to get her one.

pp. 22-23

What's happening here? (Children respond.)

Read pages 22 and 23.

pp. 24-25

What's happening now? Guide discussion of the party, the scowling thundercloud piñata, and their efforts to break it. Try to use the words **thundercloud**, *whacked, smacked* as you speak.

Read pages 24 and 25. *Do you remember what happened next?* (Children respond.)

pp. 26-27

Read pages 26 and 27.

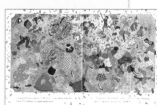

p. 28

Read page 28. Use voice to clarify meanings of *whooped* and *hollered*.

Story Discussion

Prompt discussion with questions. For example, *In this book, two friends had fun together. What are ways Clara showed she liked Samson? How did Samson show he was a friend?* You might want to return to pictures to help children recall events that showed Clara's and Samson's friendship.

That's all the time we have today. We'll read the story again another day.

▶ Outdoor Play

Point out that friends often compliment one another. Then dismiss each child with a compliment such as, *Danny, you did a great job sweeping up the sand at clean-up time.* See suggested conversation topics for Outdoor Play on pages 86–87.

▶ Songs, Word Play, Letters

Today children will be playing word games, singing songs, and reciting poems. Add your favorite game, song, or poem to this collection.

Songs

"Head and Shoulders, Knees and Toes", "The More We Get Together", "If You're Happy"

Poems

"Three Little Monkeys"

Literacy Skills

Can You Think of Words That Rhyme With ____?; If Your Name Starts With [name a letter], Raise Your Hand

Purposes

Responds to own name and requests for action or information. Recognizes many uppercase letters. Communicates using verbal and non-verbal cues. Scans text from left to right.

Suggested Sequence for Today's Circle

1. "Head and Shoulders, Knees and Toes"
2. "The More We Get Together"
3. "Three Little Monkeys" (and Can You Think of Words That Rhyme With ____?)
4. If Your Name Starts With [name a letter], Raise Your Hand
5. If You're Happy

Materials and Instructional Procedures

HEAD AND SHOULDERS, KNEES AND TOES

Materials: CD Track 4, Song Lyrics page 162

Vocabulary: ears, eyes, head, knees, mouth, nose, shoulders, toes

Procedure

- Sing the song as usual.

- Sing it a second time, very slowly, and then a third time, very fast.

THE MORE WE GET TOGETHER

Materials: CD Track 13, Song Lyrics page 163

Vocabulary: friends, happier, together

Procedure

- Sing the song as usual.

- Substitute a song about friends that you like.

THREE LITTLE MONKEYS (AND CAN YOU THINK OF WORDS THAT RHYME WITH ____?)

Materials: *Big Book of Poetry:* Poem 6, CD Track 31

Vocabulary: catch, crocodile, monkeys, swinging, tree

Procedure

- Tell children that you are going to recite the silly poem about the monkeys again. Point to the title of the poem in the *Big Book of Poetry,* and run your finger under the words as you read them.

- When you finish, say something like, *Some of the words in this poem have the same sound at the end. They rhyme.* Tree, be, *and* me *all rhyme. Can you think of any other words that rhyme with* tree, be, *and* me? If children cannot think of other words that rhyme with these, offer some. Ask, *Does* see *rhyme with* tree *and* me? *Does* we *rhyme with* be *and* me?

IF YOUR NAME STARTS WITH [NAME A LETTER], RAISE YOUR HAND

Procedure

- Play this game a different way this time, if you feel your children are ready for it. For example, tell children that this time you are going to hold up letters, but that no one should identify it as the one in their name. Instead, you will call on someone else, and he or she will identify all the children whose names start with the letter.

- Tell children not to shout out an answer. Tell them you will call on someone to tell whose name starts with the letter you are holding. Tell children that everyone will get a turn with a letter.

- Proceed with the game by holding letters up, one at a time, and calling on children.

- Try to give children who you think know fewer letters, the easier letters to identify.

IF YOU'RE HAPPY

Materials: CD Track 1, Song Lyrics page 162

Vocabulary: clap, feet, hands, stamp, tap, toes

Procedure

- Sing three verses using clapping hands, tapping toes, and stamping feet as motions. Sing some new verses with new motions, if you have time.

Progress Monitoring

Use copies of pages 158–159 to keep a record of your observations. Note which children were able to think of rhyming words. Which children knew the first letter in names you held up for them? Which children were able to sing all or most of "Head and Shoulders, Knees and Toes", "The More We Get Together", and "If You're Happy"?

▶ Lunch/Quiet Time/Centers

This time is set aside for lunch, quiet time, and center activities. See pages 86–87 for suggested conversation topics during this time.

▶ Small Groups

For information about Small Groups, refer to pages 91–93.

▶ Let's Find Out About It

Sharing Our Invitations to the Stuffed Animal Party

Purposes

Understands that print carries meaning. Demonstrates an awareness of different kinds of texts. Listens with increasing attention.

Materials

books: *A Letter to Amy* and *Dandelion;* sample printed invitations, invitations children have been making in Small Groups

Suggested Vocabulary

Use these words meaningfully during the discussion: date, invitation, place

Procedure

- Remind children that invitations are special cards that ask people to come to a party or special event. Remind children, too, about the kinds of information included in an invitation—time, place, date.

- Hold up the page in *A Letter to Amy* that shows Peter's invitation to Amy. Identify for children the kind of information Peter put on his invitation and envelope (kind of party, time, date).

- Then show the page in *Dandelion* with the invitation to Jennifer Giraffe's party. Read it to the children, and tell them that "half-past three" is the time of the party, and Saturday is the day. Point out that Peter and Jennifer Giraffe did not include place information, and ask children why they think they did not.

> **English Language Learners**
>
> As you review the children's invitations, have children repeat words like *to, from, date, time.*

- Remind children that they have been making invitations to invite their dolls and stuffed animals to a piñata party. Show a few of the children's invitations and talk about the information included and why the place of the party is on this invitation.

- See the Notes to Teachers on page 127 for suggestions on how to provide parents with information about this activity.

Small Groups Connections

Children continue to make invitations for the piñata party.

> **Extending the Activity**
>
> Invite children to talk about invitations they have sent or received. What was the invitation for?

Progress Monitoring

Note which children listen closely while you share information about invitations. Which children begin using the term *invitations* and terms such as *time* or *day/date?* Record your observations on copies of pages 158–159.

▶ End-the-Day Centers

Children spend time in Centers of their choice. As children leave for home, you might want to tell the children who are taking invitations home today to be sure to deliver them to their stuffed animals and to read them aloud.

▶ **Start-the-Day Centers** (see pages 88–90)
Make two to three Centers available as you greet children and their families.

▶ **Morning Meeting** (see page 88)
Review plans for the day with children and orient them to center activities.

▶ **Center Time** (see pages 88–90)
Children spend time in Centers of their choice.

▶ **Story Time: 3rd Reading**

Matthew and Tilly

Author: Rebecca C. Jones
Illustrator: Beth Peck

Read the Story Again

In this reading, pause as you read to invite children to chime in with short parts of the story. This gives children the opportunity to practice saying many of the new words. Prompt children's recall by lingering over the first sound of a word or by saying the first word in a phrase. If children are not quick to chime in, provide the words yourself so that the reading moves along.

If there is time to read a second book, read *A Cake All for Me!* or another of the books listed on page 7.

Story Discussion

Prompt discussion with questions. For example, *After Matthew and Tilly had a fight and didn't play with each other for a while, they decided to play together again. Maybe Tilly decided that Matthew broke the crayon by accident. Did you ever have a fight with a friend over something that was broken or ruined? And then, when you weren't so upset and had time to think about it, you decided it had happened by accident?*

Words and Phrases for Chiming In

(Vocabulary words appear in **dark** type.)

friends – p. 1
bikes together – p. 2
hide-and-seek together – p. 3
lemonade together – p. 4
ice-cream cones together – p. 6
rescued – p. 8
chewed, brave – p. 11
got sick of each other – p. 12
crayon – p. 12
old crayon – p. 15
break everything – p. 15
stomped up the stairs – p. 16
numbers and squares – p. 19
by herself – p. 19
store – p. 20
customer – p. 20
play with – p. 23
much fun – p. 23
Tilly was doing – p. 25
I'm sorry – p. 25
So am I – p. 25
together again – p. 28

Extending the Book

Ask children who are ready for a challenge to help you read Tilly's line "You broke my crayon" (page 15) in their "crabbiest voice" and Matthew's line "It was an old crayon" in their "grouchiest voice."

English Language Learners

If children do not chime in with you the first time, slow the pace a little, and repeat the word or phrase to give them a second chance. Repeat the key word: "Yes, they **rescued** a kitten. They saved it—they **rescued** it."

▶ **Outdoor Play**

Call children's names, three at a time: *I want these three children to stand up and walk to the cubby area together: Alex, Terrel, Joshua.* See suggested conversation topics for Outdoor Play on pages 86–87.

▶ Songs, Word Play, Letters

Today children will be playing word games, singing songs, and reciting poems. Add your favorite game, song, or poem to this collection.

Songs

"Old MacDonald Had a Farm", "Clap Your Hands", "Come On and Join In to the Game"

Predictable Book

HUSH!

Literacy Skills

Can You Think of Words That Rhyme With ____?

Purposes

Listens with increasing attention. Listens to a variety of genres read aloud: stories, songs, rhymes, poems, and expository text.

Suggested Sequence for Today's Circle

1. "Old MacDonald Had a Farm"
2. *HUSH!* (and Can You Think of Words That Rhyme With ____?)
3. "Clap Your Hands"
4. "Come On and Join In to the Game"

Materials and Instructional Procedures

OLD MACDONALD HAD A FARM

Materials: CD Track 6, Song Lyrics page 162, flannel board and flannel pieces

Vocabulary: chick, duck, farm, goat, horse, pig, sheep

Procedure

- If you want to do something different, tell children that, today, Old MacDonald has a zoo, not a farm. If you don't have flannel board pieces, use a book with zoo animals in it, and turn the pages to expose the ones you want to sing about (e.g. tiger, elephant, monkey). Use appropriate sounds (e.g., "grrr, grrr"; "bray, bray"; and "chee, chee").

HUSH! (AND CAN YOU THINK OF WORDS THAT RHYME WITH ____?)

Materials: book: *HUSH!*

Vocabulary: creeping, lizard, mosquito, sleeping, weeping, wind

Procedure

- Show children the cover of *HUSH!* and point to the title as you and the children read it.

- Read the book, expressively.

- After reading the book, tell children they are going to play a rhyming game with words from the story. Turn to the page with the lizard. Read the page aloud, and point to the illustration. Say something like, *The lizard is creeping. Creeping* and sleeping *rhyme— they have the same sound at the end.* Ask children if they can think of other words that rhyme with *creeping* and *sleeping.*

- Ask children to raise their hands if they have an idea. If anyone suggests a nonsense word, accept it. You might say, Jeeping *might not be a real word, but it does rhyme with* sleeping. Be ready to offer ideas of your own (e.g., *peeping, seeping, weeping, leaping*). When you've finished, review the list of rhyming words with children.

CLAP YOUR HANDS

Materials: CD Track 12, Song Lyrics page 163

Vocabulary: stamp, swing leg, feet, crook, finger, nod head

Procedure

- Stand up and ask children to stand up too. Sing the first two verses and model the motions for children ("stamp feet", "swing leg").

- Have children sit back down, and then do two more verses. Try "crook finger" or "nod head".

- If you'd rather do a new song instead, sing "Good Morning." A source for this song is listed on this page.

COME ON AND JOIN IN TO THE GAME

Materials: CD Track 20, Song Lyrics page 163

Vocabulary: clap, tap, touch, cheeks

Procedure

- Tell children that next you are going to sing "Come On and Join In to the Game" again, first with a familiar verse (clap), and then with some new verses.

- For new verses, try "tap noses" and "touch cheeks."

- If time permits, you may want to end today with the chant, "Five Little Monkeys." A source for this chant is listed on this page.

SUGGESTED RESOURCES

Book

Sipe, Muriel. "Good Morning." *Sing a Song of Popcorn.* B. Schenk de Regniers. New York: Scholastic, 1988.

CD

Tilsen, B. "Five Little Monkeys." *Make a Circle Like the Sun.* B. Tilsen. The Orchard, 2001.

▶ Lunch/Quiet Time/Centers

This time is set aside for lunch, quiet time, and center activities. See pages 86–87 for suggested conversation topics during this time.

▶ Small Groups

See pages 91–93 for information about Small Groups.

▶ Let's Talk About It

Resolving Conflicts and Developing Self-Control

Purposes

Discusses interacting appropriately with other children. Develops beginning understanding of using language to resolve conflicts.

Procedure

- Remind children that when Tilly and Matthew had a fight, they called each other mean names and got mad at each other.

- Tell children that instead of calling a person a name, we can say what we don't like. For example:

  Kim, instead of calling Pedro a mean name, say, "I don't like it when you take the blocks I need. It's not fair to take all of a certain kind, and it's not being a good friend!"

- Ask several children what they might say if someone accidentally knocks over their block building, if someone gets to use a tricycle first, or if some other situation occurs in your group. Add to the children's ideas, as appropriate.

- Sum up the discussion. Fox example, you might say, *Even good friends get mad at each other sometimes. But when friends are mad, it's better to tell a friend exactly what makes you mad instead of calling your friend a mean name.*

Connect With Families

Send a note home to families. Tell them that this week children have been making invitations. Suggest that parents look at any invitation that the child has brought home, read it with interest, and encourage the child to select a stuffed animal or doll to receive it. Tell parents to help the child remember to bring the stuffed animal to school on the day indicated in the invitation (Friday of the following week).

▶ End-the-Day Centers

Children play in the open Centers. As children leave for home, say something such as, *We won't be in school for two days, because it's the weekend, but when you come back next week, on Monday, we will make the covers for our photo albums.*

Notes to Teachers

Here are some tips and suggestions that might be helpful.

Center Time

Blocks Area—Setting Up the Grocery Store

- The grocery store is set up on Wednesday of Week 3. One teacher should plan to stay in the Blocks Area to assist with the store set up.

Dramatic Play—Grocery Store Roles

- When the store opens on Thursday, it will affect not only the Blocks Area, but the Dramatic Play area as well. One teacher should be available in this part of the classroom to coach children in their roles.

Sand and Water Table—Road Construction Vehicles

- The road construction vehicles start on Monday of Week 3. This area is likely to be very popular. Use a turns list and show children where their names are on the list when they say, "I want to play here. When do I get my turn?" Tell children that the vehicles will be available for many days, and that all children will have the opportunity to have many turns. Help children find another place to play while they wait, and reassure them that you will not forget to come find them when it is their turn.

Providing Information to Parents

Stuffed Animal Invitations

- This week, children will write invitations to one of their stuffed animals for a piñata party that will take place during Week 4. If you plan to do the party, write a note to parents explaining what this is about. If parents know what is going on, they will be able to help their child follow through at home with the invitation, and to remember to bring the stuffed animal to school on the day of the party.

- Think about the possibility that a child might not have a stuffed animal to bring. Will it be okay for the child to bring a doll instead? Some other toy?

Weekly Planner

	Day 1	Day 2	Day 3
Start-the-Day Centers 30 Minutes **Morning Meeting** 15 Minutes **Center Time** 60 Minutes pp. 130–132	Greet children and open selected Centers. Introduce Center Time activities. **Blocks:** Shopping at the Grocery Store; **Sand and Water:** Building and Playing With Roads; **Dramatic Play:** Grocery Store Play; **Book Area:** Exploring Books; **Art Area/Table:** Decorating Our Piñata; Crayon Resist and Watercolors; **Puzzles and Manipulatives:** Upper and Lowercase Letter Matching Materials and Picture-Word Matching Cards for *Matthew and Tilly*; **Writing Center:** Making Photo Album Covers and Signing Author Pages; Dandelion Word Cards and Fancy Ink Pens		
Toileting and Snack 15 Minutes			
Story Time 20 Minutes	**4th Reading – *Matthew and Tilly*** p. 137 Read *The Little Red Hen (Makes a Pizza)*, *A Cake All for Me!*, or another book of your choice.	**3rd Reading – *Dandelion*** p. 141 Read *A Letter to Amy*, *Matthew and Tilly*, *Jamaica's Find*, or another book of your choice.	**3rd Reading – *Hooray, a Piñata!*** p. 145 Read *Noisy Nora*, *Oonga Boonga*, *Corduroy*, *A Cake All for Me!*, or another book of your choice.
Outdoor Play 35 Minutes	**Conversations:** Observe for repeated actions. Count with children. After you finish counting, comment on how many times they did the action.	**Conversations:** Observe friends playing. Make specific comments about how they play together.	**Conversations:** Observe play and talk with available children. Use precise language, including terms to name the toys and actions.
Songs, Word Play, Letters 20 Minutes	**Songs:** "Five Green and Speckled Frogs"; Story-Character "Bingo" Song; "The More We Get Together" **Poems:** "Five Little Owls in an Old Elm Tree" **Literacy Skills:** We Can Change It and Rearrange It, Alphabet Letter Clue Game; Interesting-Sounding Words pp. 138–139	**Songs:** "Clap Your Hands"; "What Are You Wearing?"; "Down by the Bay" **Predictable Book:** *Golden Bear* **Literacy Skills:** Chiming In With Rhyming Words; Guess What Word I'm Saying pp. 142–143	**Songs:** "If You're Happy"; "Bingo"; "Come On and Join In to the Game" **Poems:** "Mix a Pancake"; "Five Juicy Apples" **Literacy Skills:** We Can Change It and Rearrange It; I'm Thinking of__ Clue Game; Interesting-Sounding Words pp. 146–147
Handwashing/Toileting 10 Minutes			
Lunch/Quiet Time/ Center Time 90 Minutes	**Conversations:** *How many peas are on your plate? If you eat two, how many will there be?* Guide talk about counting backwards.	**Conversations:** *Have you gotten a letter from someone?* Help child tell who the letter was from and how they felt about getting it.	**Conversations:** *How was our food made today?* Discuss cooking methods; what is eaten raw; need to wash raw foods.
Small Groups 25 Minutes pp. 133–135	**Science:** Making Lemonade **Language and Print Manipulatives:** Match Pictures and Words From Stories, Alphabet Puzzles, Uppercase and Lowercase Matching, Children's Name Card Matching **Book Browsing:** Exploring Books	**Science:** Making Lemonade **Language and Print Manipulatives:** Match Pictures and Words from Stories, Alphabet Puzzles, Uppercase and Lowercase Matching, Children's Name Card Matching **Book Browsing:** Exploring Books	**Science:** Making Lemonade **Language and Print Manipulatives:** Match Pictures and Words From Stories, Alphabet Puzzles, Uppercase and Lowercase Matching, Children's Name Card Matching **Book Browsing:** Exploring Books
Let's Find Out About It/ Let's Talk About It 20 Minutes	**Resolving Conflicts** p. 140	**Understanding Feelings** p. 144	**Social Skills Development: Why We Need Rules** p. 148
End-the-Day Centers 20 Minutes	Open selected Centers and prepare children to go home.		

Day 4	Day 5
4th Reading – *Dandelion* p. 149 Read *A Cake All for Me!, The Doorbell Rang, Jamaica's Find,* or another book of your choice.	**4th Reading – *Hooray, a Piñata!*** p. 153 If time allows, reread *Noisy Nora, Oonga Boonga, Jamaica's Find,* or another book of your choice.
Conversations: Watch for accidents; resolve resulting conflicts. Link events to books. Highlight the lack of intent to hurt.	**Conversations:** Observe a child who has struggled to find friends. Comment on any successes and growth in social skills.
Songs: "Head and Shoulders, Knees and Toes"; "The Wheels on the Bus"; "The More We Get Together"; "Clap Your Hands" **Poems:** "Five Little Owls in an Old Elm Tree"; "Ten Little Fingers" **Literacy Skills:** First Sound Matching Story Characters' and Children's Names pp. 150–151	**Songs:** "Head and Shoulders, Knees and Toes"; "Five Little Ducks"; "Five Green and Speckled Frogs" **Predictable Book:** *HUSH!* **Literacy Skills:** Can You Think of Words That Begin with the Same Sound as __?; Alphabet Memory Pocket Chart Game, Guess What Word I'm Saying pp. 154–155
Conversations: *In some of our books, friends had accidents that caused trouble. Has that happened to you?* Support recall; link to books.	**Conversations:** *What pictures in our photo albums do you like best?* Guide recall of Unit activities.
Mathematics: Let's Share With the Hungry Monkeys **Games:** Picture Card Memory **Book Browsing:** Exploring Books	**Mathematics:** Let's Share With the Hungry Monkeys **Games:** Picture Card Memory **Book Browsing:** Exploring Books
Discussing Rules for the Piñata Party p. 152	**The Piñata Party** p. 156

Half-Day Program Schedule

2 hours 45 minutes

A half-day program includes two literacy circles.

10 min.	**Start-the-Day Centers** Writing Center, Book Area, Puzzles and Manipulatives
10 min.	**Morning Meeting**
60 min.	**Center Time** Include mathematics and science activities from Small Groups. Incorporate Small Groups writing activities at Writing Centers.
20 min.	**Story Time** Use discussion questions from Let's Talk About It to address social-emotional issues and topics from Let's Find Out About It to address concept development.
35 min.	**Outdoor Play**
20 min.	**Songs, Word Play, Letters**
10 min.	**End-the-Day Centers** Writing Center, Book Area, Puzzles and Manipulatives

Connect With Families

- Tell parents you are talking about feelings in the classroom. Suggest they help children name feelings (happy, sad, angry, frustrated, and impatient) in situations that occur naturally at home.

- Send home a short list of classroom rules with parents. For each one, include the reason for it. For example, *Walk in the Classroom—If we run, we might bump into someone, and hurt them.*

- Take pictures of children at the piñata party on Day 5 and send them home with parents as soon as you can. Encourage them to talk with children about the pictures, what they did at the party, and what they liked best about it.

129

Start-the-Day Centers

- Open two or three Centers (e.g., Writing Center, Puzzles and Manipulatives, Book Area).

Morning Meeting

- Introduce children to Centers by showing some selected objects from each Center and briefly demonstrating activities to help them make a first choice.

- For example, **Monday:** Show the materials you made for the sand table: black strips of poster board for "pavement," road signs, a car and truck. Apply a few pieces of tissue paper and other materials from the Art Area to a piñata frame. **Tuesday:** Demonstrate ways to decorate class photo album covers with friendship words in the Writing Center. **Wednesday:** Mention the signs for the grocery store that need painting at the easel. **Thursday:** Demonstrate how to make a crayon resist picture in the Art Area using white crayons and watercolor paints. **Friday:** Tell children that a photo album is now in the Book Area.

- You might want to modify or substitute an activity to meet your children's needs. See the Notes to Teachers on page 157 for tips on managing and adapting the Centers to your classroom.

▲ Crayon Resist and Watercolors

SAND AND WATER

Building and Playing With Roads

SCIENCE

Purposes: Observes and discusses the various kinds of work people do outside their homes. Uses and responds to words to indicate relative distance. Recognizes highly familiar words in the environment.

Materials: Add to sand table materials from Week 3 (page 88): simple and sturdy small plastic cars and trucks, strips of black poster board, craft stick road signs, empty box for vehicles

Preparation: Cut pieces of black poster board into 8"–10" lengths wide enough for sand table road surfaces. Use masking tape to create broken lines

down the center of the road pieces. Laminate if possible. These serve as "paved road" pieces. Make road signs (e.g. "STOP", "ONE WAY", "CAUTION") and billboards from paper, laminate, and attach to craft sticks. Add these materials plus cars and trucks to sand table. Provide a box for construction vehicles.

Suggested Vocabulary: Add these words to those introduced in Week 3 (page 88): road, truck, car, billboard, cement, highway, gutters; pave, pour, sign

- Encourage children to work together. You might say, *Seth, I see that you just paved the surface for the road. Molly has the cement mixer. Maybe you can order a load to make the gutters for your road.* Or, *It looks like your roads are ready. Where are you going to put the road signs and billboards?*

BOOK AREA

Exploring Books

Purposes: Independently chooses to read or to pretend to read books in the Book Area and other settings. Understands that pictures, print, and other symbols carry meaning. Recalls some main events when asked, "What happens in this story?"

Materials: Add *Hooray, a Pinata!* and *Dandelion* to book collection.

- Join children for brief periods to read portions of books or listen to children's retellings and respond to their comments. You might say, *You're right. Jennifer Giraffe wasn't very nice when she shut the door in Dandelion's face. But, she didn't*

seem to realize that it was her friend Dandelion standing there. What do you think?

ART AREA: TABLE

Decorating Our Piñata

Purposes: Creates three-dimensional artwork. Participates successfully as a member of a group. Demonstrates an emerging awareness and respect for culture and ethnicity.

Materials: a variety of colorful paper, tissue paper, shiny materials, stickers, items for eyes, material for tail (e.g., ribbons, braided rope or string, yarn, cotton balls, pom-pom), pencils, small bottles of glue with squeeze top lids, tape, small trays or plates, bowls, polystyrene foam trays, piñata bodies children made in Small Groups, *Hooray, a Piñata!,* photos of piñatas from party store fliers, etc.

Preparation: Cut sheets of stickers into small strips with a few stickers each; cut squares of tissue paper; tear colored construction paper into small pieces; cut ribbon into small lengths. Tear strips of tape and attach to edges of polystyrene foam trays. Set up small bowls or plates, each with a different material in it and place them within reach of all children. Place two piñata bodies (from Small Groups) on the table at the same time. Children work in two small groups with one piñata body each.

Suggested Vocabulary: eyes, tail, thread, yarn, ribbon, piñata; attach, decorate

- Show *Hooray, a Piñata!* for inspiration and show other illustrations or photos of piñatas.

- Encourage children to cover entire piñata with decorations, so that box labels are hidden. You might say, *You've almost covered the whole box, but here's one more spot. What could you glue there to cover it?* Or, *Remember, the piñata needs eyes and a tail.*

Crayon Resist and Watercolors

Purposes: Creates two-dimensional artwork. Explores and experiments with wet and dry media to create artwork. Observes and explores materials, objects, or events in the environment.

Materials: watercolor paints for each child (dried blocks of tempera paint work best for preschoolers), 4–6 paint brushes, 6–8 white or lighter color (e.g., beige, yellow) crayons, 4–6 shallow dishes of water for rinsing paint brushes and trays to hold them, paper toweling for dabbing rinsed paint, sheets of 8 1/2" x 11" white paper, smocks, markers

Preparation: Fill rinse dishes with water about half full. Place folded dry toweling and paintbrushes on tray near rinse dishes. Set up 4–6 places at a table with the following: tray of tempera block paints, piece of paper, tray of rinse water with brush wiping towel folded on it, and 1–2 white or other light color crayons.

Suggested Vocabulary: bead, droplet; curved, squiggly, spiral; cover, repel, rinse, soak up,

- Ask children to write their names on the piece of paper with crayon, before they start painting. You might ask, *Do you think we'll still be able to see your name if you paint over it?*

- Engage children in conversation about their paintings. You might ask, *What happened when you painted blue over the white crayon marks? Did the paint cover it? If you paint along a crayon mark, what happens?*

BLOCKS

Shopping at the Grocery Store

Continue activity from Week 3 (page 90). For children who have consistently chosen one role (e.g., cashier or customer) in the store play, encourage them to try another role.

PUZZLES AND MANIPULATIVES

Upper and Lowercase Letter Matching Materials and Picture-Word Matching Cards for Matthew and Tilly

Purposes: Associates the name of a letter with its shape. Names many uppercase letters. Attempts to read words by sounding out individual aspects of print.

Materials: Picture Cards: bike, cash register, crayon, ice-cream cone, lemon; word matching cards for *Matthew and Tilly,* uppercase and lowercase letter matching materials

Preparation: Place materials you prepared for use in Small Groups in the Puzzles and Manipulatives center. You can make more picture-word card pairs, if you'd like.

Suggested Vocabulary: Add these words to those introduced in Week 3 (page 90): bikes, cash register, crayon, ice-cream cones

Continued on next page

- Interact as time permits, to help with letter matches and names. You might say, *Yes, that is an* F, *a big* F, *an uppercase* F. *Which of these letters is the little* f, *the lowercase* f?

- Help with picture-word matching. You might say, *I see you found a picture of an ice-cream cone.* Ice, /ī/. *What letter does* ice *start with? Yes, the letter* I, *so we need to find a word on one of these cards that starts with* I.

DRAMATIC PLAY

Grocery Store Play

Continue activity from Week 3 (page 90). When children write their shopping lists, ask what they plan to cook, and then suggest items needed for a cake, spaghetti, etc.

WRITING CENTER

Making Photo Album Covers and Signing Author Pages

Purposes: Writes own name. Attempts to read words by sounding out aspects of print. Identifies the cover of a book, and knows that title is on the cover.

Materials: markers, authors' page, glue sticks, printed friendship words

Preparation: Write or print friendship words on tag-board strips (e.g., *share, help, cooperate, invite to play, compliment*). Have children sign author pages on Monday, Tuesday, and Wednesday.

Suggested Vocabulary: Add these words to those introduced in Week 3 (page 90): author, cover; front, back

- As children work together to decorate covers for three photo albums, help them read the words available for gluing on the covers. You might say, *This word says* share. *It starts with the letters* sh *and has an* r *right here.*

- Encourage children to sign the authors' page in each photo album.

Dandelion Word Cards and Fancy Ink Pens

Materials: *Dandelion* word cards, Picture Cards: dandelions, cane, mailbox; tag board, fancy ink pens

Preparation: Print some words from the story (e.g., *dandelion, cane, mailbox, letter, pen*) and glue onto rectangular strips of tag board. Use Picture Cards to indicate the meanings of the words. Draw simple pictures on tag board to represent *letter* and *pen*. Laminate, if possible.

Suggested Vocabulary: cane, fancy, ink, letter, mailbox, pen

- Make connections to *Dandelion* in your conversation as children work. You might say, *This fancy pen reminds me of the one Jennifer Giraffe used to write her invitation to Dandelion. You can use the pens to write or draw with.*

Overview of Small Groups

- Each day there are three different Small Groups activities. The same three activities are made available for three days. Each group of five or six children spends one of the three days in each activity.

- On Days 1, 2, and 3, children make lemonade, use four kinds of Language and Print Manipulatives, and browse a collection of fiction and information books.

- On Days 4 and 5, children do a mathematics activity involving simple division, play a memory game, and continue to browse books. (On Day 5, Small Groups might not meet if the classroom is having a piñata party. In that case, complete the rotation of the children started this week on Monday and Tuesday of the following week.)

- Model suggested vocabulary words and phrases in a manner that clarifies their meaning for children.

▲ Making Lemonade

SCIENCE

Making Lemonade: Days 1, 2, 3

High support

Purposes: Observes, explores, and describes plants and other materials. Performs fine-motor tasks that require small-muscle strength and control. Uses concrete objects to understand the concepts of part and whole.

Materials: large bowl, large pitcher, 4 lemons, long handled spoon, one cup measuring cup (clear plastic), 6 plastic bowls, paper napkins, paper towels, craft sticks, small paper cups and plates, sweetener (1 c of honey, maple syrup, or sugar), 3 quarts water, plastic juice squeezer (optional)

Preparation: Thoroughly wash 3 lemons and slice in half crosswise. Have children wash their hands.

Suggested Vocabulary: fruit, lemon, lemonade, seeds, rinds; sour, sweet; blend, measure, mix, stir, sweeten, taste

Procedure

- Tell children they are going to make lemonade, like the lemonade Matthew and Tilly sold at their stand. Explain that the first thing they need to do is wash their hands because clean hands are important for preparing food.

- Show children the whole lemon and talk about it. You might say, *This lemon is a fruit. It grows on a lemon tree. What do you think is inside this lemon?* Then, cut the lemon in half, show children seeds, and explain that they need to be removed.

- Give each child half a lemon, a paper plate, and a craft stick. Demonstrate how to dig the seeds out with the stick and discard them onto paper plates. Show children how to squeeze out the juice over a bowl. If a plastic juice squeezer is available, let children take turns extracting extra juice using it. Have each child pour their juice into the pitcher and discard the lemon rinds.

- Tell children that next, you are going to make lemonade with the juice from their lemons. Add water to the pitcher and explain why you're doing that. For example, *The lemon juice is very, very sour by itself so we need to add water to make it less sour. Have you ever tasted something sour? It can make your mouth pucker like this.* Demonstrate. Set aside a small cup of the unsweetened juice, then add the sweetener to the pitcher. Stir the pitcher and give each child a turn to stir as well.

- Give children cups of the lemonade to taste. Let them taste a tiny sip of the unsweetened juice to compare its taste with the sweetened version. (Provide a napkin in case the child wants to spit it out.)

- *ELL* Use words, such as *lemon juice, stir, squeeze, taste,* that come up naturally many times in the activity. Encourage children to say them with you.

Continued on next page

LANGUAGE AND PRINT MANIPULATIVES

Children will have four different activities to choose during this time. They should have time to do at least two or three of them.

Purposes: Understands that pictures, print, and other symbols carry meaning. Recognizes their own names. Associates the name of a letter with its shape. Names many uppercase letters.

Materials: children's name cards, double sided tape (or other self-fastening material), letter charts from Week 2 (page 56), picture and word cards of story words from Unit 2, simple alphabet jigsaw puzzles, upper and lowercase letter tiles

Match Pictures and Words From Matthew and Tilly: Days 1, 2, 3 `Low support`

* Repeat activity from Week 2 (page 57). You might say, *Today we're going to match pictures and words from* Matthew and Tilly *like we did before.*

Alphabet Puzzles: Days 1, 2, 3 `Low support`

Procedure

* Explain that today they can play with puzzles that have alphabet letters for pieces, instead of pictures.

* *ELL* Join in occasionally and say letter names with children. You might say, *This letter has two lines that come together at the top in a point. It's the letter* A. *Can you say* A?

Uppercase and Lowercase Matching: Days 1, 2, 3 `Low support`

Procedure

* Repeat activity from Week 2 (page 56). Show children the materials and remind them that they have played with them before.

Children's Name Card Matching: Days 1, 2, 3 `Low support`

Preparation: Make two small charts with 5–6 children's names mounted on them (similar to the chart for Uppercase and Lowercase Matching). Print out a second set of names on small strips so that each name you mounted on a small chart has a match on one of the small name strips. Laminate the small charts and the name strips, if possible. Place name strips with the appropriate chart.

Procedure

* Give each pair of children a couple of items from among those prepared for this Small Groups session (e.g., a set of name matching materials, and a set of the uppercase and lowercase matching materials).

* *EXTRA SUPPORT* Offer help, if children are having trouble finding matches for a name mounted on the background chart. You might say, *Jamal, the first letter in the name is* T, *so let's look at these name cards and find the one with the name that begins with* T. *This one starts with* B, *so that's not it.*

BOOK BROWSING

Exploring Books: Days 1, 2, 3 `Low support`

Purposes: Uses and shares books and other print in their play. Reads or pretends to read information books. Chooses independently to read or pretend to read books in the book area.

Materials: Add *Dandelion, Matthew and Tilly,* and *Hooray, a Piñata!* to the book collection from Unit 2, plus other books on Mexican celebrations.

Procedure

* Have children look at books in pairs or independently. Children can trade books, looking at three or four books during the period.

* Talk with children about books. For example, *Tilly is mad at Matthew because he broke her crayon. Have you ever been mad at someone because they broke something that belonged to you?*

* Book Browsing may be paired with other activities so that children remain engaged in small group work. Options are puzzles, writing, computers, or other activities of your choice.

Days 4, 5

Note to Teacher: If you plan a piñata party for Friday, the Day 5 activities below should move to Days 1 and 2 of the following week.

MATHEMATICS

Let's Share With the Hungry Monkeys: Days 4, 5 `High support`

Purposes: Helps child develop an understanding of division. Learns to use one-to-one correspondence to divide a set of concrete objects equally. Uses concrete objects to understand how whole objects can be divided into two halves.

Materials: Activity Aid 9: monkey cut-outs, Activity Aid 10: banana and cookie cut-outs, small bowl, 2 small plates, child-size scissors

Preparation: For each pair of children prepare 2 cut-out monkeys, a bowl, 2 small plates, 8 cut-out bananas, and 10 cut-out cookies

Suggested Vocabulary: same number, whole; one-half

Procedure

- Arrange monkeys, plates, and bowl so everyone can see them, and put four bananas in the bowl. You might say, *Today we are going to play a sharing game with two hungry monkeys.* Divide the set by simultaneously removing a banana with your left hand and one with your right hand. You might say, *We want to be fair and give each monkey the same number of bananas. Here's one banana for the girl monkey and one banana for the boy monkey,* and so on until the set is divided.

- Give a bowl of six bananas to one child in each team. You might say, *Share these bananas. Give each monkey the same number of bananas to eat.* After the first child has attempted to divide the set, ask if the monkeys have the same number of bananas. The second child can help by counting the bananas on each plate.

- Give a bowl of eight bananas to the second child in each team and repeat the activity above.

- *EXTRA SUPPORT* If a child makes an error or does not simultaneously remove two bananas from the bowl, provide extra support. Use the child's bananas to demonstrate again how to divide the set, and then have him or her try again.

- *EXTENDING THE ACTIVITY* Give a bowl of seven cookies to the first child in a team who correctly divided the sets. Repeat activity from above. When the child observes the remaining cookie,

you might say, *That is a whole cookie. How can the monkeys share it?* Then cut the cookie in half. You might say, *This is half a cookie.* Let children practice using the terms *whole* and *half.* Give a bowl of nine cookies to the second child in the team, and continue on as before.

Progress Monitoring

Note which sets (6 or 8 bananas, 7 or 9 cookies) the child correctly divided. Record types of errors the child made (putting all cookies on one plate; putting an unequal number on two plates) and whether the child had difficulty using one-to-one correspondence. Record the name of any child who was ready for you to extend the activity upward, and how he or she did on the extension problems.

GAMES

Picture Card Memory: Days 4, 5

Medium support

Purposes: Understands that pictures, print, and other symbols carry meaning. Interacts appropriately with other children by cooperating, helping, sharing, and expressing interest.

Materials: 3 sets of memory cards

Preparation: Make 3 sets of memory cards (each containing 4–5 matches) of pictures of items from the Unit 2 books (e.g., bowl, cash register, dandelion, envelope, hopscotch grid, pizza, pizza slicer)

Procedure

- Tell children they are going to play a game with pictures from stories they have seen before. Pair children and distribute one set of cards to each pair. Have children follow the same rules as they did for the Uppercase Alphabet Memory game in Week 1 (page 17). Remind children of the rules if necessary.

- *EXTRA SUPPORT* Look at the pictures with children who are unsure if they've made a match. You might say, *Both of these pictures are kinds of fruit. This one is red and and this one is orange. Do they match?*

- *ELL* As children turn over each card, have them name the picture. Repeat the word with them so they learn how to pronounce it and connect the sound of the word and the picture.

BOOK BROWSING

Exploring Books: Days 4, 5
Low support

Purposes: Uses and shares books and other print. Reads or pretends to read information books.

Procedure

- Add classroom Friendship Books made in class (photos and captions of classmates).

- Have children look at books in pairs or independently.

- Talk with children about books. You might say, *Who do you see in this photo? What are they doing?*

- *SOCIAL-EMOTIONAL SUPPORT* Compliment children who are careful with turning the pages.

- Allow children to pursue alternate activities like writing, using the computer, puzzles, playing games, or using materials from other Centers.

SUGGESTED RESOURCES

Books

Emberley, Rebecca. *Piñata.* New York: Little Brown and Company, 2004.

Estés, Kristyn Rehling (author) and Claire B. Cotts (illustrator). *Manuela's Gift.* San Francisco: Chronicle Books, 1999.

Developing Children's Language Through Conversation

Language enables people to build a sense of being part of a community by talking about things they have done together. Talking about past experiences stretches children's language skills. As the unit comes to a close, encourage children to reflect back on activities they enjoyed and books they read. Support them in accurately describing activities and in recalling experiences.

Building Language During Mealtimes

Sometimes children and teachers eat in noisy lunchrooms. Even in such a distracting setting, it is possible to converse with one or two children who are near you. Remember that you have very few opportunities to talk to individual children for such a long time; make the most of each occasion. Set up a schedule that ensures teachers sit next to different children and all children get to sit near a teacher each week.

Mealtime: Review the Unit to Reflect on Past Events

After the food has been distributed and children are eating, engage the children in a conversation about specific activities they did during the friendship unit. As children talk, listen very carefully to what they are saying. Position yourself at the level of the child who is speaking, look at him or her, and do not turn to another child who might try to interrupt you. Limit the time focused on one child so that you do not neglect the others.

A Model for Conversation

Mealtime: Reflecting on Experiences

Teacher: *We are ending our unit on friends today. We have done lots of things, haven't we? What activities do you remember?*

Juan: The store.

Teacher: *Right. We made a grocery store, and lots of people played in it.*

Desiree: Yeah, I liked to be the mommy shopping.

Willy: And I did the cash register.

Teacher: *Yes, I remember. Willy liked to be the cashier, and Desiree was a good customer. Juan, what did you like about the store?*

Juan: Umm . . . the food, the things.

Teacher: *That's right. You liked putting all the food on the shelves, right?*

Juan: Yes.

Teacher: *You did a nice job making sure all the boxes of food were where they belonged. What other things do you remember doing?*

Good Conversations

Try to use words that are being taught in connection with the storybooks. Listen for children's use of these words and comment when words are used. If possible, send a list of key words home, and encourage children to tell when they hear their new words at home.

Empathy and Helping Others

When you discuss feelings with children, do not assume that you know how a child is feeling. Ask simple open-ended questions, such as *How are you feeling?* When discussing events, use a similar approach: *Tell me about it.* Indicate interest in hearing more, but do not put words in a child's mouth, and do not press on when a child seems disinterested in talking.

▶ **Start-the-Day Centers** (see pages 130–132)
Two to three Centers are available as you greet children and their families.

▶ **Morning Meeting** (see page 130)
Orient children to center activities. As they choose Centers, create a turns list if necessary.

▶ **Center Time** (see pages 130–132)
Children spend time in Centers of their choice.

▶ **Story Time: 4th Reading**

Matthew and Tilly

Author: Rebecca C. Jones

Illustrator: Beth Peck

Read *Matthew and Tilly* Again

Assign girls Tilly's part and boys Matthew's part. Read the story, as usual. Together with children, act out riding bikes (hold hands out for handlebars); eating ice-cream (hold one hand as if with cone, and lick); chewing gum (move jaws and mouth for chewing). Help with dialogue by speaking it softly.

Taking On the Roles of Story Characters

Tilly: You broke my crayon – p. 15

No, it wasn't. It was a brand-new crayon, and you broke it. You always break everything. – p. 15

Well, you're so stupid. You're so stupid and stinky and mean. – p. 15

So am I – p. 25

Matthew: It was an old crayon. – p. 15

It was ready to break. p. – 15

Stop being so picky. – p. 15

You're always so picky and stinky and mean. – p. 15

I'm sorry – p. 25

Story Discussion

Prompt discussion with questions. For example, *We always see Matthew and Tilly playing where they live. Why don't we see them in school?* Guide children toward understanding that it's summertime. Point out summer clothes and open windows on the cover and on pages 24–25.

Other Book Suggestions

If you think children will not enjoy a fourth reading of *Matthew and Tilly,* read *It's Mine!* or another theme-related book (see page 7). *It's Mine!* is about three frogs who quarrel and bicker at first but become friends after a bad storm.

Making Connections: Ask children why they think the frogs became friends. This might be a difficult question for preschoolers. Accept their ideas, and add that perhaps they realized during the storm that they could help one another and share things.

▶ **Outdoor Play**
Call on children by clothing features. For example, say, *If you are wearing stripes . . . something with a front pocket . . . a long-sleeved shirt . . .* and so on. See pages 128–129 for suggested conversation topics during Outdoor Play.

▶ Songs, Word Play, Letters

Today children will be playing word games, singing songs, and reciting poems. Add your favorite game, song, or poem to this collection.

Songs

"Five Green and Speckled Frogs," Story-Character "Bingo" Song, "The More We Get Together"

Poem

"Five Little Owls in an Old Elm Tree"

Literacy Skills

We Can Change It and Rearrange It, Alphabet Letter Clue Game, Interesting-Sounding Words

Purposes

Separates words into syllables. Identifies the position of objects in a line, assigning the appropriate ordinal number to it. Segments the beginning sounds in words. Uses concrete objects to solve addition and subtraction problems.

Suggested Sequence for Today's Circle

1. "Five Green and Speckled Frogs"
2. Story-Character "Bingo" Song (and *Hooray, a Piñata!*)
3. We Can Change It and Rearrange It (and *Hooray, a Piñata!*)
4. "Five Little Owls in an Old Elm Tree"
5. "The More We Get Together"
6. Interesting-Sounding Words (and *Hooray, a Piñata!*)
7. Alphabet Letter Clue Game

Materials and Instructional Procedures

FIVE GREEN AND SPECKLED FROGS

Materials: CD Track 10, Song Lyrics page 163, flannel board and flannel pieces

Vocabulary: green, speckled, log, delicious, pool, cool

Procedure

- Tell children that you are going to start today with "Five Green and Speckled Frogs." Place two frogs on the log, and ask children how many there will be if you put two more frogs up. Put up the next two and count on . . . *3, 4.* You might say, *We have four frogs now. We need five. Here's the fifth frog, right here.* Add it to the flannel board.

- Perform the song as usual for the first three verses. Then remove two frogs in the next verse, leaving just one on the board.

STORY-CHARACTER "BINGO" SONG, WE CAN CHANGE IT AND REARRANGE IT (AND HOORAY, A PIÑATA!)

Materials: CD Track 2, Song Lyrics page 162 (for "Bingo"), book: *Hooray, a Piñata!,* card with "CLARA" printed in large letters, flannel board and flannel letters: C, L, A, R, A

Vocabulary: remove, replace, first, second, third, fourth, fifth

Procedure

- Show *Hooray, a Piñata!,* and tell children they are going to sing the "Bingo" song, but that they are going to sing about Clara, the little girl in the story, *Hooray, a Pinata!*

- Show children the card with "CLARA" printed on it. Point to the first letter in Clara's name and say something like, *The first letter in Clara's name is C, so C is the first letter I'll put on our flannel board. Here it is.* Point to the second letter, third, fourth, and fifth letters, and repeat, making sure to use ordinal number terms.

- Sing, *There was a girl who loved a dog and Clara was her name-o. C-L-A-R-A* (three times), *and Clara was her name-o.*

- Put the letters back up on the board, and tell children that you are going to make some new names using these letters. Remove *C* and ask children what they think the new name is. Say the sound /l/ to help out (LARA). Then, take away the final *R* and *A,* telling children you're going to rearrange the L and A, to make a new name. Sound out the *A* to provide an explicit prompt, if needed. *Yes, Al! We can change and rearrange letters to make new words.*

FIVE LITTLE OWLS IN AN OLD ELM TREE

Materials: *Big Book of Poetry:* Poem 7, CD Track 32

Vocabulary: owls, elm, tree, big, round

Procedure

- Show the page from the *Big Book of Poetry.* Point to the moon in the illustration, and ask children what they think this is. Children might say *sun,* but clarify that it is the *moon.*

- Ask if they know that owls stay awake at night, and sleep during the daytime.

Comment that some animals are like that, and we say they are nocturnal.

- Recite the poem, pointing to the moon this time, when you recite the last verse.

THE MORE WE GET TOGETHER

Materials: CD Track 13, Song Lyrics page 163, spiral or booklet type calendar

Vocabulary: together, happier, friends, calendar, week

Procedure

- Sing the song as usual. When finished, comment that the song seems to describe the children in the class. The more they get together, the more friends everyone is making, which makes everyone happy.

- Show a calendar to children, and say something like, *We started school in September. This is September. Each of these boxes in a row is a week, so we've been here* (point to and count each row in September). Do the same for October. *So, altogether, we've been in school for* [number] *of weeks, and we've made lots of friends.*

INTERESTING-SOUNDING WORDS (AND *HOORAY, A PIÑATA!*)

Materials: book: *Hooray, a Piñata!*

Vocabulary: piñata, smack, crack, cinnamon, whack, thwack, sound, letter

Procedure

- Tell children that you are going to talk about interesting-sounding words in the book *Hooray, a Piñata!*.

- Point out that *cinnamon* is an interesting-sounding word. Ask children to say it together. Start with /s/ by modeling and holding onto the sound. You might say, *Okay, let's say the whole thing.. cinn-a-mon. Do you like the part where your lips come together to make /m/?* Model by saying *cinnamon* again, holding onto /m/ this time. Have children say it with you.

- Show the *Hooray, a Piñata!* cover, and read the title, underlining the words. Ask children if there are any interesting words in the title. They might suggest *Hooray* or *Piñata.* Say, *Piñata is a Spanish word. Piñata starts with /p/ and it has other interesting sounds after /p/. Let's say the word a couple of times.* Treat *hooray* similarly.

- If there is time, go on to the rhyming words *whack, smack, crack,* and *thwack.* Comment that these are all noisy words. Say them as a series, and then repeat them with children chiming in with you.

- If time permits, ask children to stand up and sing "Shake My Sillies Out" as a way to get them moving before the next song.

ALPHABET LETTER CLUE GAME

Materials: clipboard with paper, or chart paper, marker with a thick tip

Vocabulary: letter, clue, guess, long, vertical, short, horizontal, next

Procedure

- Tell children that they are going to play a letter guessing game. Start with *E.* Draw the long vertical line first, and describe your actions. Ask if anyone wants to guess the letter. Accept all guesses, and say, *We'll see. I'll draw the next clue.*

- Add the first horizontal line, drawing it out from the top of the vertical line. Children might now guess *L* or *T.* Write an uppercase *L* and say something like, *I see what you are thinking, because the same lines are used in an* L. *But the short horizontal line is at the bottom of an* L, *not at the top. And, if I were making a* T, *I'd use one line across the top* (draw it).

- Draw the second horizontal line of *E.* Many children will shout out "F." You might say, *Yes, it is an* F, *but I have a different letter in my mind. If I add one more line down here* (point), *do you know what letter that would be?* Finish the letter and name it.

SUGGESTED RESOURCES

Book

Raffi. "Shake My Sillies Out." In *Raffi's Singable Songbook,* (New York: Crown Publishers Inc., 1980.)

CD

Raffi. "Shake My Sillies Out." *More Singable Songs.* Raffi. Rounder Records 1996

▶ Lunch/Quiet Time/Centers

This time is set aside for lunch, quiet time, and center activities. See pages 128–129 for suggested conversation topics during this time.

▶ Small Groups

For information about Small Groups, refer to pages 133–135.

▶ Let's Talk About It

Resolving Conflicts

Purposes

Shows empathy and understanding to others. Develops beginning understanding of using language to resolve conflicts.

Procedure

- Remind children that in two of the stories, children did things by accident that made their friends mad. Turn to the page in *A Letter to Amy* where Peter bumps into Amy. Say, *In this book, Peter accidentally bumped into Amy and knocked her down. Amy looked pretty upset about that.*

- Turn to the page where Matthew broke the crayon in *Matthew and Tilly.* Say, *In this story, Matthew broke Tilly's crayon by accident. Tilly was very upset and claimed that he did it on purpose.*

- Ask several children, *Did you ever hurt someone or break something that was theirs, by accident? What happened? Were you able to explain that it was an accident?* Prompt children further as they tell about these incidents. For example, ask, *Did your friend believe you right away, or did the friend think you did it on purpose? Were you able to be friends again on the day of the accident, or not until another day?* In case children have trouble thinking of ideas, be prepared to tell an appropriate short story of your own that children can understand. You can use this story to help them see that even adults need to solve problems.

▶ End-the-Day Centers

Children spend time in open Centers of their choice. As children leave for home, tell them that tomorrow more of them will have a turn to decorate a piñata. Tell them to talk with their parents and the stuffed animal or doll they plan to bring to the party this week about some of the things they are doing at school to get ready.

▶ **Start-the-Day Centers** (see pages 130–132)
Children spend time in open Centers as you greet morning arrivals.

▶ **Morning Meeting** (see page 130)
Teachers orient children to center activities.

▶ **Center Time** (see pages 130–132)
Children spend time in Centers of their choice.

▶ **Story Time: 3rd Reading**

Dandelion

Author: Don Freeman

Read the Story Again

In this reading, pause as you read, lingering over beginning sounds to invite children to chime in with short parts of the story. Prompt children's recall by pointing to the pictures of the *shampoo, cane,* and *cap.* If children do not chime in quickly on words or phrases, provide these yourself and continue reading.

Words and Phrases for Chiming In

(Vocabulary words appear in **dark** type.)

jumped out of bed – p. 1
fancy gold ink – p. 3
excited – p. 5
planned to get a haircut – p. 5
barbershop – p. 6
shampoo – p. 8
agreed – p. 12
curling his **mane** – p. 13
cap and a **cane** – p. 16
hostess – p. 19

bell – pp. 22, 38
surprised – p. 23
address – p. 25
mighty mistake – p. 27
shut – p. 27
paced – p. 28, 29
sweater – p. 33
awful **cloudburst** – p. 39
blushing – p. 43
stylish dandy – p. 44
me – p. 44

Story Discussion

Ask questions to prompt discussion. For example: *Jennifer Giraffe had her party on a Saturday. In* A Letter to Amy, *Peter's birthday party was on a Saturday, too. Can you guess why Saturday is a popular day for a party?* Support children's understanding that Saturday falls on a weekend, when most people don't go to school or work. Then hold up a calendar and name the days of the week as you point to them. Review quickly which are weekdays and which fall on the weekend.

> ### Extending the Book
> After reading about the barbershop, ask children who are ready for a challenge to read the sign for "Lou's Barber Shop" with you. Point to the words and sound out the letters.

> ### English Language Learners
> Repeat the words *cloudburst* on page 39, and *blushing* on page 43 to prompt children to chime in with you.

▶ **Outdoor Play**

Dismiss children by clothing items. For example, *If you brought a sweater to wear outside today . . . If you brought a cap or hat . . . If you wore a jacket . . .* and so on. See suggested topics for conversation during Outdoor Play on pages 128–129.

▶ Songs, Word Play, Letters

Today children will be playing word games, singing songs, and reciting poems. Add your favorite game, song, or poem to this collection.

Songs

"Clap Your Hands," "What Are You Wearing?," "Down by the Bay"

Predictable Book

Golden Bear

Literacy Skills

Chiming In With Rhyming Words, Guess What Word I'm Saying

Purposes

Recites songs, rhymes, chants, and poems, and engages in language and word play. Says words that complete rhymes. Blends phonemes together to form a word. Listens with increasing attention. Listens to/attends to a variety of genres read aloud.

Suggested Sequence for Today's Circle

1. "Clap Your Hands"
2. "What Are You Wearing?"
3. *Golden Bear* (and Chiming In With Rhyming Words)
4. "Down by the Bay"
5. Guess What Word I'm Saying (and *Hooray, a Piñata!*)

Materials and Instructional Procedures

CLAP YOUR HANDS

Materials: CD Track 12, Song Lyrics page 163

Vocabulary: clap, hands, turn, bow, jump

Procedure

- Tell children that you are going to sing "Clap Your Hands" next, but with some new verses. Start with "clap your hands," and then ask children to stand up.

- Continue with 2–3 new verses (e.g., "turn, turn, turn, like this; turn around together," "bow like this," "jump like this").

WHAT ARE YOU WEARING?

Materials: CD Track 14, Song Lyrics page 163

Vocabulary: wearing, day, long, shirt, pants

Procedure

- Tell children they are going to sing that song about the colors of the clothes they're wearing.

- Go around the circle using each child's name and sing about the color of an item of clothing he or she is wearing.

- Consider asking children to point to an item they want you to sing about when you reach them in the circle.

GOLDEN BEAR (AND CHIMING IN WITH RHYMING WORDS)

Materials: book: *Golden Bear*

Vocabulary: golden, bear, everywhere, dancing, stair, rocking

Procedure

- Read *Golden Bear* as you usually read it, keeping the natural rhythm of the verse.

- Linger on the first sound of the second word in a rhyming word pair. (Children should know the book well enough to chime in.) Some children might chime in on more of the text than just rhyming words.

DOWN BY THE BAY

Materials: CD Track 3, Song Lyrics page 162, flannel board and pieces for the song

Vocabulary: grow, go, snake, cake, frog, dog, mouse, house, goat, hen

Procedure

- Tell children that next, they're going to sing the song about those silly animals down by the bay.

- Add a new verse or two (e.g., "goat eating a coat"; "hen writing with a pen").

Guess What Word I'm Saying (and *Hooray, a Piñata!*)

Materials: book: *Hooray, a Piñata!*

Vocabulary: cake, store, dog, fur, leash, good, safe, mash

Procedure

- Show the cover of the book to children and tell them that you've picked some words from the story that you are going to say in a funny way. Tell children that they should listen to what you say and then say the words the right way.

- Say, *Here's the first word I'm going to say in a funny way:* /k/ (pause) *-ake. Yes,* cake! *That's the right way to say it, not* /k/ (pause) *-ake.*

- Say, *Here's another word:* /l/ (pause) *-eash.* Repeat, /l/ (pause) *-eash. Right,* leash. *That's what we put on a dog when we take it for a walk, so it doesn't run away.*

- Say, *You are good at this. We'll do one more:* /m/ (pause) *-ash.* Repeat /m/ (pause) *-ash. That's right,* mash, *which means to squish something.*

- Tell children they are good word detectives and that they'll play that game another day.

Progress Monitoring

Make copies of pages 158–159 to use as you observe children's progress. Notice which children engage quickly with known songs and which ones need prompting to remember words or motions. Note which children are chiming in with rhyming words, and with a lot of the text in a familiar, pre-dictable text story. Which children could blend the parts of the funny words to say them correctly?

▶ Lunch/Quiet Time/Centers

This time is set aside for lunch, quiet time, and center activities. See pages 128–129 for suggested conversation topics during this time.

▶ Small Groups

For information about Small Groups, refer to page 133–135.

▶ Let's Talk About It

Understanding Feelings

Purposes

Tells a personal narrative. Talks about understanding of relationships among objects and people.

Procedure

- Remind children that in the story *Dandelion,* Dandelion gets all dressed up for a special occasion—the tea and taffy party at Jennifer Giraffe's house. Ask several children, *Did you ever get dressed up for a special occasion? What was the occasion? Where were you going, and what were you going to do when you got there?*

- Prompt children who wish to talk to tell how they feel about dressing up by asking them further questions. For example, *What did you wear? Did you like getting dressed up, or not? How did you feel about it?*

- Encourage a few children to explain why they do or do not like getting dressed up, prompting as necessary. Some children might not like to get dressed up because they can't play and have been warned about getting dirty. Sometimes the events children dress up for also require behavior that is hard for children to maintain.

- Other children might like to get dressed up, especially for events like birthdays and weddings, because they like the fancy clothing, the treats given at the event, and the excitement of a celebration.

▶ End-the-Day Centers

Some children might like to sign the author pages at the Writing Center at this time. As children leave for home, say something that will help them look forward to the next day. For example, you might tell children that tomorrow more of them will get to make lemonade.

▶ **Start-the-Day Centers** (see pages 130–132)
Open two to three Centers as you greet families.

▶ **Morning Meeting** (see page 130)
Orient children to center activities, including turns lists.

▶ **Center Time** (see pages 130–132)
Children spend time in Centers of their choice.

▶ **Story Time: 3rd Reading**

Hooray, a Piñata!
Author: Elisa Kleven

Read the Story Again

In the third reading of *Hooray, a Piñata!*, linger over the beginning sounds of words as you read to invite children to chime in with short parts of the story. Don't be afraid to be dramatic where appropriate.

If there is time to read a second book, read a book from the list on page 7—perhaps *A Cake All for Me!*, or *Jamaica's Find*, about a girl who finds a stuffed dog at the playground.

Words and Phrases for Chiming In

(Vocabulary words appear in **dark** type.)

cake, balloons, piñata – p. 3
I love piñatas! – p. 3
. . . and **smack** them and **crack** them – p. 4
. . . and **smash** . . . – p. 5
and eat the candy! – p. 5
thundercloud monster – p. 7
Can I get him, Mama? – p. 7
. . . won't hold very much candy. p. 8
good little dog – pp. 8, 14

a **collar** and a **leash** and took him out for a walk – p. 10
Take care of that piñata. – p. 12
I will, Clara promised. – p. 12
Don't worry, Samson, he's safe! – p. 19
Hooray, a piñata! – p. 23
hugged the **thundercloud** – p. 23
they whacked it and cracked it and mashed it and bashed it – p. 25
THWACK! – p. 26
HOORAY! HOORAY! HOORAY! – p. 27

Story Discussion

Prompt discussion with comments and questions like these:

I was thinking about what might have happened if Samson hadn't thought of buying the thundercloud piñata for Clara as a present. What do you think would have happened at her party? Do you think Lucky would have been stuffed with candy, and whacked and smacked open? There is no right answer to these questions. Listen to children's ideas, and comment, based on what they say.

Extending the Book

Point out the words HAPPY BIRTHDAY, CLARA! opposite the title page and ask children to read them with you. Invite children during Start-the-Day Centers to make a nametag for their stuffed animal or toy, and to show it when introducing their toy at the end of Story Time.

English Language Learners

If children don't chime in the first time, say the words yourself slowly and clearly. Repeat the reading and again invite children to chime in.

▶ **Outdoor Play**

Transition to Outdoor Play by telling children that you are going to pretend that everyone's name starts with /p/ like *piñata*. Call names one by one, beginning each one with the /p/ sound. See suggested topics for conversation during Outdoor Play on pages 128–129.

▶ Songs, Word Play, Letters

Today children will be playing word games, singing songs, and reciting poems. Add your favorite game, song, or poem to this collection.

Songs

"If You're Happy," "Bingo," "Come On and Join In to the Game"

Poems

"Mix a Pancake"; "Five Juicy Apples"

Literacy Skills

We Can Change It and Rearrange It, I'm Thinking of ____ Clue Game, Interesting-Sounding Words

Purposes

Recites songs, rhymes, chants, and poems, and engages in language and word play. Follows multi-step directions. Separates words into syllables. Uses concrete objects to solve simple subtraction problems. Speaks clearly enough to be understood.

Suggested Sequence for Today's Circle

1. "If You're Happy"
2. "Bingo" (and We Can Change It and Rearrange It)
3. I'm Thinking of ____ Clue Game (and *Hooray, a Piñata!*)
4. "Mix a Pancake"
5. "Five Juicy Apples"
6. Interesting-Sounding Words (and *Dandelion*)
7. "Come On and Join In to the Game"

Materials and Instructional Procedures

IF YOU'RE HAPPY

Materials: CD Track 1, Song Lyrics page 162

Vocabulary: clap, hands, tap, toes, stomp, feet

Procedure

- Ask children if they remember the song that goes, *If you're happy . . .* (pause) *and you know it.* Invite children to sing it with you.

- Sing three verses using clapping hands, tapping toes, and stomping feet as motions.

BINGO (AND WE CAN CHANGE IT AND REARRANGE IT)

Materials: CD Track 2, Song Lyrics page 162, flannel board and flannel letters: B, I, N, G, O, T, R, S, W, P

Vocabulary: farmer, dog, clap, letter, name, replace

Procedure

- As you place the letters *B-I-N-G-O* on the board, let the children chime in with the names of each letter.

- Sing the song as usual, removing one letter for each verse and replacing the letter with a clap.

- Put the letters *B-I-N-G-O* back on the board. You might say, *This word says* Bingo, *as you know, but if I replace* B *with* T, *which says* /t/, *the word changes to* Tingo!

- Replace *T* with *R*, and let the children guess what the new word says (Ringo). Continue with other letters as long as they're interested.

- As you put the letters away, say something like, *We can make a lot of words with the same letters. We can change and rearrange letters to create a lot of different words.*

I'M THINKING OF ____ CLUE GAME (AND *HOORAY, A PIÑATA!*)

Materials: book: *Hooray, a Piñata!*, Picture Card: lightning bolt

Vocabulary: piñata, leash, dog biscuit, merry-go-round

Procedure

- Show the cover from *Hooray, a Piñata!* and tell children that you are going to play a guessing game about words from a book. Remind children to listen to the clues, think about them, and raise their hand if they have an idea for a word. Tell them not to shout out their answer because it might disturb others who are still thinking.

- For *piñata*, use these clues: *This is a toy that is hollow inside. People stuff it with candy or other little toys, and then break it open at a party to get the stuff inside. The name of this toy starts with* /p/.

- For *leash*, use these clues: *This is something that fits around a dog's neck when you take the dog for a walk. A person holds the other end. The name of this thing starts with* /l/.

- For *dog biscuit*, use these clues: *This is a snack for a dog that is something like a cookie. If we were offering one of these to a dog, we'd say, "Here, doggy. I have a dog* /b/ ___ *for you."*

- For *merry-go-round,* use these clues: *This is the name for a ride at a carnival or amusement park. Kids sit on horses that go up and down when they ride on it. The first word in the name of this ride starts with /m/.*

- For *lightning bolt,* use these clues: *Clara used the bottom part of the thundercloud piñata to make this. It has two words. The first word begins with /l/.* Show the picture card to reinforce the word meaning.

MIX A PANCAKE

Materials: *Big Book of Poetry:* Poem 8, CD Track 33

Vocabulary: mix, pancake, stir, pan, fry, toss

Procedure

- Show children the *Big Book of Poetry* illustration and read the title with children.

- Present the poem orally to children, at a pace that allows children to chime in on a few of the verses.

FIVE JUICY APPLES

Materials: *Big Book of Poetry:* Poem 5, CD Track 30

Vocabulary: juicy, apples, grocer, pair, store

Procedure

- Proceed as usual with the poem, using a different child's name each time. Hold up one hand with splayed fingers to count down from five to zero.

- Try to use every child's name, so no one feels left out.

INTERESTING-SOUNDING WORDS (AND *DANDELION*)

Materials: book: *Dandelion*

Vocabulary: dandelion, blinked, kangaroo, magnificent

Procedure

- Show children the cover of *Dandelion* and read the title. Say something like, *Let's see if we can find some interesting-sounding words in this book.*

- Encourage children to name words as you flip through the pages. Pronounce each word clearly, saying syllables slowly and varying intonation. Have children repeat each word after you. The focus should be on the interesting sound and how it feels to say it.

- Say, Blinked *is an interesting word to say. I like the way my lips and tongue feel when I say it. Let's say it together* . . . blinked.

- Say, Magnificent *is another interesting-sounding word. Magnificent is a long word that has many different sounds. Let's say it together* . . . magnificent.

- Say, Kangaroo *is a really fun word to say. Let's say it together* . . . kangaroo.

- Accept other words children offer and find something to say about the sounds in each one.

- If time permits, you could sing "Shake My Sillies Out." A source for this song is listed below.

COME ON AND JOIN IN TO THE GAME

Materials: CD Track 20, Song Lyrics page 163

Vocabulary: clap, come, join, game, sneeze, yawn, jump, laugh

Procedure

- Tell children they are going to sing "Come On and Join In to the Game" again. Sing the first four verses ("clapping", "sneezing", "yawning", "jumping") and model the motions as children follow.

- Sing the four verses again. Continue to model the motions as you sing.

SUGGESTED RESOURCES

Books

Raffi. "Shake My Sillies Out." In *Raffi's Singable Songbook,* (New York: Crown Publishers Inc., 1980).

CD

Raffi. "Shake My Sillies Out." *More Singable Songs.* Raffi. Rounder Records 1996.

▶ Lunch/Quiet Time/Centers

This time is set aside for lunch, quiet time, and center activities. See pages 128–129 for suggested conversation topics during this time.

▶ **Small Groups**

For information about Small Groups, see pages 133–135.

▶ **Let's Talk About It**

Social Skills Development: Why We Need Rules

Purposes

Contributes ideas for classroom rules. Thinks about events and experiences. Begins to recognize the needs, rights, and emotions of others. Talks about ways to prevent problems.

Procedure

- Tell children they will be opening piñatas at their piñata party. (The piñata party is scheduled two days from now, on Day 5.) Explain that rules are needed so everyone understands what they are to do (and not to do) when the contents of the piñatas spill to the floor.

- Ask, *How do you think you'll feel when the toys inside the piñata fall to the floor? What do you think you might do?* Give several children an opportunity to talk about how they think they will feel when the piñata breaks (excited, happy, concerned that they might not get some of the toys).

- Say, *We want the piñata party to be fun for everyone. Let's think about ways to make sure everyone has a good time and no one gets hurt.* Stress consideration for others, sharing, and the need to make sure the situation is safe (i.e., that children don't bump heads, or push one another).

- Tell children that some specific rules are needed for the piñata party, and that the next day—tomorrow—you will discuss these rules with them.

▶ **End-the-Day Centers**

Children spend time in Centers of their choice. As children leave for home, tell them that tomorrow they will sing the song "Willoughby, Wallaby, Woo," and more children will decorate piñatas for the party.

▶ **Start-the-Day Centers** (see pages 130–132)

Make two to three Centers available as usual.

▶ **Morning Meeting** (see page 130)

Orient children to center activities.

▶ **Center Time** (see pages 130–132)

Children spend time in Centers of their choice.

▶ **Story Time: 4th Reading**

Dandelion

Author: Don Freeman

Read *Dandelion* Again

Due to the length of this book, you may wish to repeat Reading 3 instead of attempting to assign children the part of Dandelion.

Story Discussion

Prompt discussion with questions. For example:

What if Dandelion had not tried again at Jennifer's house, but had given up and gone home? Then suppose he had met Jennifer the next day at the supermarket, and she had said, "Why didn't you come to my party?" What do you think Dandelion would have said? Help children identify the emotions that might prompt Dandelion's response.

Other Book Suggestions

If you think children will not enjoy a fourth reading of *Dandelion*, read *The Doorbell Rang* instead (see page 7). *The Doorbell Rang* is a story about two children, Victoria and Sam, who share a plate of cookies with many friends who come to visit all at the same time.

Making Connections: Comment that there was a houseful of guests at Victoria's and Sam's to eat cookies, just as there had been a houseful of animals at Jennifer Giraffe's to eat taffy at her party. Ask children whether they would or would not call the gathering at Victoria and Sam's house a party. Ask why or why not.

▶ **Outdoor Play**

To transition to Outdoor Play, call each child individually, explaining that you are going to say his of her name in a silly way. Say the children's names using /m/ as the first sound for all, or some other letter that works well. See suggested topics for conversation during Outdoor Play on pages 128–129.

▶ Songs, Word Play, Letters

Today children will be playing word games, singing songs, and reciting poems. Add your favorite game, song, or poem to this collection.

Songs

"Head and Shoulders, Knees and Toes," "The Wheels on the Bus," "The More We Get Together," "Clap Your Hands"

Poems

"Five Little Owls in an Old Elm Tree," "Ten Little Fingers"

Literacy Skills

First Sound Matching Story Characters' and Children's Names

Purposes

Finds words with the same beginning sound. Listens with increasing attention. Listens to and imitates songs.

Suggested Sequence for Today's Circle

1. "Head and Shoulders, Knees and Toes"
2. "Five Little Owls in an Old Elm Tree"
3. "The Wheels on the Bus"
4. First Sound Matching Story Characters' and Children's Names (and *A Letter to Amy, Matthew and Tilly, Hooray, a Pinata!*)
5. "The More We Get Together"
6. "Clap Your Hands"
7. "Ten Little Fingers"

Materials and Instructional Procedures

HEAD AND SHOULDERS, KNEES AND TOES

Materials: CD Track 4, Song Lyrics page 162

Vocabulary: head, shoulders, knees, toes, eyes, ears, mouth, nose

Procedure

- Sing the song as usual, touching the different parts of your body as you sing about them. Each time, leave out one more body part, until you do all the motions silently.

FIVE LITTLE OWLS IN AN OLD ELM TREE

Materials: *Big Book of Poetry:* Poem 7, CD Track 32

Vocabulary: owls, elm, tree, big, round

Procedure

- Ask children if they remember the poem called "Five Little Owls in an Old Elm Tree".
- Show the *Big Book of Poetry* illustration and talk about what's happening in the picture.
- Recite the poem, and tell children to listen for words that rhyme.
- Recite it again, but this time pause to give children a chance to chime in with rhyming words (e.g., *tree/be, fluffy/puffy, blinking/winking, eyes/skies*).

THE WHEELS ON THE BUS

Materials: CD Track 7, Song Lyrics page 163

Vocabulary: wheels, bus, round, town, up, down, horn, box, wiper, glass, driver, back

Procedure

- Sing the verses children already know, leading them in the appropriate motion for each verse.
- Introduce the remaining verses one at a time by singing each one once and modeling the motion. Invite children to join in as you sing it a second time, slowly enough for them to keep up.

FIRST SOUND MATCHING STORY CHARACTERS' AND CHILDREN'S NAMES (AND *A LETTER TO AMY, MATTHEW AND TILLY, HOORAY, A PIÑATA!*)

Materials: books: *A Letter to Amy, Matthew and Tilly, Hooray, a Piñata!*

Vocabulary: game, name

Procedure

- Show children the books, point to the titles, and read them. Say something like, *We've met lots of characters in these books, haven't we?*
- As you flip through the books, you might say, *In A Letter to Amy, there were Peter, Amy, and Eddie. In Matthew and Tilly, there were . . .* (pause to let children chime in) *Matthew and Tilly. And, in Hooray, a Piñata!, there were Clara and her friend Samson.*

- Tell children they will play a game with some of the names of the characters. Say something like, *I'll say a character's name. You think about the sound the name starts with. Then we'll go around the circle and say our own names to see if anyone else's name starts with the same sound.*

- Choose character names with initial letters that match at least one child's name in your class. Go around the circle and let each child say his or her name. For each one, let the group decide (with your help, if needed) whether the first sound matches the name you picked. Try to move the game along quickly, and continue as long as the children are interested.

- If time permits, you might want to sing "Willoughby, Wallaby, Woo." A source for this song is listed on this page.

THE MORE WE GET TOGETHER

Materials: CD Track 13, Song Lyrics page 163

Vocabulary: together, happier, friends

Procedure

- Tell children you're going to sing the song about friends.

- Sing the song as usual, pausing before the last word in each line to give children a chance to chime in.

- You might say, *It's a good idea to be friendly and nice to other people, even if they aren't your close friends. This is important at school where you are with lots of other people in a classroom. Everyone should feel welcome and comfortable.*

CLAP YOUR HANDS

Materials: CD Track 12, Song Lyrics page 163

Vocabulary: clap, hands, stamp, feet

Procedure

- Introduce the song. If children remember it, add more verses (e.g., "shake your hips", "bend your knees", "tap your toes", "blink your eyes").

- Make up verses of your own to add.

TEN LITTLE FINGERS

Materials: *Big Book of Poetry:* Poem 1; CD Track 26

Vocabulary: fingers, fold, high, low, open, shut, tight, together, wide

Procedure

- Show children the *Big Book of Poetry* illustration.

- Recite the poem, leading children in the finger movements.

Progress Monitoring

Note individual children's level of participation—no engagement, attentive but no participation, participating physically but not verbally, attempting verbal participation, or participating fully. Which children recognize the first sound of their names and which ones still need prompting? Which children recognize rhyming words? Use copies of pages 158–159 to keep a record of your observations.

SUGGESTED RESOURCES

Book

Raffi. "Willoughby, Wallaby, Woo." In *Raffi's Singable Songbook,* New York: Crown Publishers Inc., 1980.

CD

Raffi. "Willoughby, Wallaby, Woo." *Singable Songs for the Very Young.* Raffi. Rounder Records, 1996.

▶ Lunch/Quiet Time/Centers

This time is set aside for lunch, quiet time, and center activities. See pages 128–129 for suggested conversation topics during this time.

▶ **Small Groups**

For information about Small Groups, refer to pages 133–135.

▶ **Let's Find Out About It**

Discussing Rules for the Piñata Party

Purposes

Contributes ideas for classroom rules. Understands rules within the learning environment.

Materials

chart paper, marker, printed reminder notes for the piñata party

Suggested Vocabulary

Use new words in a way that makes their meaning clear during the discussion: fair, piñata, rules, safe, share

Procedure

- Based on yesterday's discussion, create a list of important things to consider when the piñatas are opened. Make items specific so that children will understand what they are to do. Read the list aloud.

- Consider the list of rules that are designed to keep things fair and safe. Go over each rule with children, and ask them if they think the rule is important or not, and why.

- Ask children, *Can you think of anything else that belongs on the rules list?* Invite them to offer ideas that should be added. Children might say, *If you get a lot of toys, and someone else doesn't, you must give some to the other person.*

Progress Monitoring

Which children listened carefully as you described the rules? Which children offered suggestions for the rules list? Which children seemed attentive, even though they didn't offer a suggestion? Record your observations on copies of pages 158–159.

Extending the Activity

Ask children if any of the rules apply in other settings. Discuss why any rule identified might be important in many settings.

English Language Learners

Point out certain words on the rules list, such as *push*, *bump*, and *grab*, for children to practice saying.

▶ **End-the-Day Centers**

Show children printed reminder notes about the party at the end of your discussion today (*Tomorrow is the piñata party*). Tell them these will be in the Writing Center for anyone who is interested in decorating a note to take to their stuffed animal or doll. As children leave for home, remind them that tomorrow is the piñata party and that you look forward to meeting their stuffed animal or doll friends.

▶ **Start-the-Day Centers** (see pages 130–132)
Two to three Centers are open to children.

▶ **Morning Meeting** (see page 130)
Orient children to Centers and reassure them that you are keeping a turns list.

▶ **Center Time** (see pages 130–132)
Children spend time in Centers of their choice.

▶ **Story Time: 4th Reading**

Hooray, a Pinata!
Author: Elisa Kleven

Read Hooray, a Pinata! Again
Due to the length of this book, we suggest that you repeat Reading 3 rather than attempting to assign children the part of Clara or Samson.

Story Discussion
After reading the story, ask questions to prompt discussion. For example:

Children usually play games at a birthday party, or do something like break a piñata to get the treats. Have you played games at a birthday party? What games did you play? If children do not mention Pin the Tail on the Donkey, you might explain how this traditional birthday party game works.

Other Book Suggestions
If you think children will not enjoy a fourth reading of *Hooray, a Pinata!*, read *Beady Bear* (see page 7) or another theme-related book. *Beady Bear* is a story about a boy who has a stuffed, wind-up bear who is his good friend. When left alone for a few days, Beady Bear has some adventures of his own.

Making Connections: Tell children that Thayer and Beady Bear remind you of Clara and Lucky in *Hooray, a Pinata!*, and of Lisa and Corduroy, in *Corduroy*. Ask children why they think you are reminded of these story characters. Ask children what they think Corduroy or Lucky might have done if left alone for a day or so. Remind them that these stories are just pretend. Stuffed animals are not really alive, but children often pretend they are, and treat them as friends.

▶ **Outdoor Play**
Dismiss children using first letters in their names. For example, say, *If your name starts with the letter B, you may go to your cubby.* When a first letter matches a story character's name, mention it. For example, *If your name starts with S, like Samson's, you may go to your cubby.* See pages 128–129 for suggested topics for conversation during Outdoor Play.

▶ Songs, Word Play, Letters

Today children will be playing word games, singing songs, and reciting poems. Add your favorite game, song, or poem to this collection.

Songs

"Head and Shoulders, Knees and Toes," "Five Little Ducks," "Five Green and Speckled Frogs"

Predictable Book

HUSH!

Literacy Skills

Can You Think of Words That Begin With the Same Sound as _____?, Alphabet Memory Pocket Chart Game, Guess What Word I'm Saying

Purposes

Recites songs, rhymes, chants, and poems, and engages in language and word play. Follows multi-step directions. Finds words with the same beginning sound. Identifies the position of objects in a line, pointing to each object and assigning an appropriate number to it. Counts up to ten objects in as set.

Suggested Sequence for Today's Circle

1. Can You Think of Words That Begin With the Same Sound as _____? (and HUSH!)

2. "Head and Shoulders, Knees and Toes"

3. Alphabet Memory Pocket Chart Game

4. "Five Little Ducks"

5. Guess What Word I'm Saying (and Hooray, a Piñata!)

6. "Five Green and Speckled Frogs"

Materials and Instructional Procedures

CAN YOU THINK OF WORDS THAT BEGIN WITH THE SAME SOUND AS _____? (AND HUSH!)

Materials: book: HUSH!

Vocabulary: weeping, wind, mosquito, sleeping, lizard, creeping

Procedure

- Show children the cover of HUSH! Point to the title and read it aloud.

- Read the book aloud, keeping the natural rhythm of the verse. Point to pictures to identify objects named.

- Tell children they're going to play a game with words from the story. Turn to the page with the lizard. Point to the word lizard and talk about the meaning of the word in the context of the story. You might say, The word lizard begins with /l/. So does the word leaf, like a leaf on a tree. How about the word mosquito? Does that have the same beginning sound as lizard? No, it doesn't, does it? How about ladybug? Does that have the same beginning sound as lizard? Yes, it does!

- You might say, Can you think of other words that begin with /l/? Go around the circle, letting each child offer one answer. If they suggest a word that does not begin with /l/, say I hear the /l/ sound in the word ball, but I don't hear it at the beginning like I do in lizard, leaf, and ladybug.

- Feel free to use another predictable text story of your choice, or reread Over in the Meadow, or Time for Bed, from Unit 1.

HEAD AND SHOULDERS, KNEES AND TOES

Materials: CD Track 4, Song Lyrics page 162

Vocabulary: head, shoulders, knees, toes, eyes, ears, mouth, nose

Procedure

- Sing the song as usual, touching the different parts of your body as you sing about them. Each time, leave out one more body part, until you are doing all the motions silently.

- When you're done, you might want to sing "Shake My Sillies Out." A source for this song is listed on page 155.

ALPHABET MEMORY POCKET CHART GAME

Materials: two sets of uppercase alphabet letter cards and poster board with one pocket for each child in the class. See Unit 2 (page 85).

Vocabulary: pocket, chart

Procedure

- Remind children of rules for playing the game. See Unit 2, Week 2 (page 85).

- Go around the circle, giving each child a turn to choose a pocket to see if it matches his or her letter. For example, *I choose pocket number seven. I think it will have the letter* B. If there is a match, give the matching card to the child. If there is not a match, put it back in the pocket.

- Continue the game until all the children have found their match.

FIVE LITTLE DUCKS

Materials: CD Track 11, Song Lyrics page 163

Vocabulary: out, over, far away, back

Procedure

- You might say, *Who remembers the song called "Five. . . Little . . .* (pause to let children chime in, make quacking sounds to give them a hint) *Ducks"?*

- Sing the song as usual, using hand motions to show the hill and the quacking. Encourage children to join in on the hand motions and the *quack, quack, quack* verse.

GUESS WHAT WORD I'M SAYING (AND *HOORAY, A PIÑATA!*)

Materials: book: *Hooray, a Piñata!*

Vocabulary: cake, store, dog, fur, leash, good, safe, mash

Procedure

- Hold up the book and say something like, *Hooray, a Piñata!* is a book we've been reading, and I'm going to say some words from it in a funny way, a way that is not quite right. I want you to say the words the right way. For example, *If I said* (pause) *-ollar, you would say "collar."*

- Say some words in the "funny way" and wait for children to say the word the right way. You might want to say *cr-* (pause) *ack, dr-* (pause) *-eams, fl-* (pause) *-apped,* and *m-* (pause) *-onster.* Repeat each of these twice.

- Go child by child around the circle to give turns, or just allow children to call out together, if they think they know the word. After children guess a word, use it in a sentence to convey its meaning. For example, *Yes,* crack *is the sound the piñata made when it was opened.*

- Do not pressure a child to respond. Provide added support to those children you expect will need it. For example, give hints about possible words.

FIVE GREEN AND SPECKLED FROGS

Materials: CD Track 10, Song Lyrics page 163, flannel board and flannel pieces

Vocabulary: green, speckled, log, delicious, pool, cool

Procedure

- As you place the pieces on the flannel board, ask children if they know what song you are about to sing. Let them count the frogs with you as you place each one on the board.

- Perform the song as usual, using the flannel pieces to show the motions in the song, and pausing to give the children a chance to chime in with the correct number of frogs remaining in the last few verses.

SUGGESTED RESOURCES

Book

Raffi. "Shake My Sillies Out." In *Raffi's Singable Songbook,* (New York: Crown Publishers Inc., 1980).

CD

Raffi. "Shake My Sillies Out." *More Singable Songs.* Raffi. Rounder Records 1996.

▶ Lunch/Quiet Time/Centers

This time is set aside for lunch, quiet time, and center activities. See pages 128–129 for suggested conversation topics during this time.

▶ Small Groups

For information about Small Groups, refer to pages 133–135.

▶ Let's Find Out About It

The Piñata Party

Purposes

Participates in the classroom community. Follows rules within the learning environment. Shows interest and curiosity in trying new activities and experiences. Interacts appropriately with other children by cooperating, helping, sharing, and expressing interest.

Materials

three piñatas, small paper bags, snack

Preparation

Prepare the piñatas ahead of time. Small toys and treasures are preferable to treats for stuffing the piñata. **Be sure you are aware of any food allergies when choosing treats.**

Suggested Vocabulary

Use new words in ways that help children grasp their meanings: decorations, guests, piñata, ribbons; bump, collect, push, scatter, share

Procedure

- The Let's Find Out About It and Small Groups time is devoted to the piñata party.

- Invite children to get their stuffed animals and dolls out of their cubbies and assemble for the breaking of the piñata.

- Organize three groups of children, one for each of the three piñatas. As the first group pulls ribbons and gathers goodies, have the other children wait for their turn and sit away from the area where the active participants gather. Remind children about not bumping or pushing. Provide small paper bags for the treats children will gather from the piñatas.

- After the piñatas have been opened and the goodies gathered, children have a special snack at tables. Treats should stay in the bag for taking home.

- For tips on managing the piñata party, see the Notes to Teachers on page 157.

Connect With Families

Encourage parents to listen to their child's reports about the party. Suggest that parents review the contents of their child's treat bag, and name the items with the child.

> **Extending the Activity**
>
> After the party, invite children to share how they felt about the party, and if they had fun with the piñatas.

> **English Language Learners**
>
> Slowly and clearly, say the names of the treats children gathered from the piñata. Invite children to say the words with you.

▶ End-the-Day Centers

Children spend time in open Centers of their choice. As children leave for home, you might say, *I won't see you for two days because it's the weekend again. I'll be glad to see you on Monday when our new week begins. Next week, we will read some brand new books and learn new songs. There will be lots of new activities in Center Time, too.*

Notes to Teachers

Here are some tips and suggestions that might be helpful.

Center Time

Blocks Area—Reluctant Children

- Notice if a child chooses not to play in the grocery store. Sometimes a child who is especially shy may stay away from such a busy, exciting area. Invite him or her to shop with you, saying, *I'm going to go buy a box of rice. It will be a short trip. Would you like to come with me?*

Art Area—Easel Sign Activity

- Given the size of these signs, suggest that two children work together on each one.

- Introduce the activity in this way at Morning Meeting. When calling this activity ask, *Are there two children who would like to paint this sign?*

Writing Center—Photo Album Author Page

- Encourage children to sign the author page of each photo album. Look for a good time to suggest that children sign the pages, like first thing in the morning during Start-the-Day Centers, as well as later in the morning, during Center Time.

- Stress that children may sign their name in any way they wish, and that scribble writing is okay. Help children who ask for it.

The Piñata Party

- Children will be very excited about the piñata party. Try to keep things as calm as possible. Be watchful of children's stuffed animals, and decide whether children can keep their stuffed animals with them during the whole day, or just for the party.

- It might be interesting for stuffed animals to "attend" Story Time and Songs, Word Play, Letters with children. Perhaps you can devise a game that includes the stuffed animals' names. For example, say, *Tell us your name, please.* [Child owner's name] *can help.*

- Be sure that each stuffed animal is in its owner's hands when the child goes home.

▲ Piñata Party

UNIT 2 Progress Monitoring Record

Child's Name _____

Observe each child as he or she engages in activities. Use this observation record to make notes of the child's accomplishments as he or she learns new skills and concepts. Include this in the child's assessment/portfolio folder along with work samples. Plan regularly for staff to discuss children's progress.

Story Time	Observation Notes
Shows interest in and enthusiasm for a new book; shows curiosity about the contents; reacts indifferently or negatively to the story	
Focuses on the story from beginning to end; loses interest	
Demonstrates understanding of the story by responding to events with smiles, frowns, giggles, shaking head, quizzical looks; demonstrates understanding with comments and answers to questions posed during reading	
Participates in story discussion	
Answers story questions: • What is happening here? • Who is this? • What happened next?	
Identifies characters' emotions; understands why story characters behave as they do	
Relates story events to personal experiences	
Predicts what will happen next in a story	
Songs, Word Play, Letters	
Engages quickly with known songs; needs prompting to remember words or motions; participates fully; participates physically, but not verbally; attempts verbally	
Anticipates and chimes in with rhyming words; distinguishes rhyming from non-rhyming words	

Chimes in with a lot of the text in a familiar, predictable story	
Recognizes first letters and sounds of their names; identifies letters in Story-Character "Bingo" Song; needs prompting to recall letters	
Shows interest in clue word game; figures out words when given meaning, number of syllables, sound, and rhyme clues	
Blends onsets and rimes to form words (/l/ [pause] -eash; leash)	

Let's Find Out About It

Understands characteristics of musical instruments; makes comparisons of various instruments	
Follows directions for making a bowl drum	
Shows interest in various supermarket jobs; understands what each worker does	
Uses new words related to grocery store jobs: *stocker, cashier, bagger*	
Shows interest in learning about invitations; begins using new vocabulary such as *invitations, date, day, time, place*	
Understands that the list of rules helps to keep things fair and safe; offers suggestions for the rules list	
Shows interest in creating personal stationery and a monogram; writes for a purpose using stationery	

Small Groups: Mathematics

Counts objects in a set	
Solves addition and subtraction story problems with objects: constructs the initial set, performs the operation; gives the sum or remainder	
Shows understanding of ordinal number names	
Uses one-to-one correspondence to equally divide a set of objects; shows difficulty in dividing a set of objects; shows difficulty in using one-to-one correspondence	

Unit 2 Extending the Unit

Activities in Extending the Unit are designed to help you create a fifth or sixth week of programming. The activities reinforce budding skills and emerging concepts, and provide opportunities for children to continue activities they enjoy. Add your own favorite activities as well.

Week 5

 Story Time

You can choose to read books that were suggested earlier in the unit or the one suggested here. Or, you might prefer instead to read a favorite of your own.

Book Suggestion
- Waddell, Martin (author) and Barbara Firth (illustrator). *Hi, Harry!* Cambridge, MA: Candlewick Press, 2003.

▶ Songs, Word Play, Letters

Songs and Poems

Enjoy singing and reciting your own favorites with children. Several sources of familiar songs and poems are listed on pages 101 and 109.

Rhyme

Continue to develop children's sensitivity to rhyme, using Unit 2 games. (See "Those Words Rhyme!" on page 108, "Chiming In With Rhyming Words" on page 142, and "Can You Think of Words That Rhyme With ____?" on page 124.) You can create a new game called Rhyming Words "Bingo" Song using pairs of rhyming words from *HUSH!* and *Golden Bear*.

Beginning Sounds

Continue to build children's sensitivity to beginning sounds in words using literacy skill activities from Unit 2. (For example, "First Sound Matching Story Characters' and Children's Names" on pages 150–151 and "Can You Think of Words That Begin With the Same Sound as ____?" on page 154.)

More Predictable Book Suggestions
- Hindley, Judy (author) and Brita Granstrom (illustrator). *Eyes, Nose, Fingers, and Toes.* Cambridge, MA: Candlewick Press, 1999.
- Root, Phyllis (author) and Jane Chapman (illustrator). *One Duck Stuck.* Cambridge, MA: Candlewick Press, 1998.

▶ Let's Find Out About It

Pet Care

In *A Letter to Amy*, Amy had a pet parrot. A lady in *Matthew and Tilly* had a pet kitten. The little girl in *Hooray, a Piñata!* pretended that the paper dog was a pet. Introduce the idea of pets and explain that pets are animals that are a kind of friend. Tell children that people must be good friends to their animal pets by taking care of them. Share simple books borrowed from the library that provide information about animals, such as puppies, kittens, gerbils, and birds, and how to care for them. Read aloud parts of books and have children share their experiences in caring for their own pets.

Book Suggestion
- Stein, Sarah B. (author) and Edward Judice (photographer). *Great Pets! An Extraordinary Guide to More Than 60 Usual and Unusual Family Pets.* North Adams, MA: Storey Kids, 2003.

▶ Center Time

Draw and Label Pictures of Pets

Using colored chalk or pencils, children can draw pictures of family pets, a pet they'd like to have, or a classroom pet, and write the names with your help. For children who are ready for a challenge, you might encourage them to write or dictate a story about their pet or a pet they wish they had.

Week 6

 **Story Time**

Read a suggested book from Unit 2 or a theme-related book of your own.

Book Suggestions

- Alborough, Jez. *Duck in the Truck.* New York: HarperCollins Publishers, 2000.
- Galdone, Paul. *The Little Red Hen.* New York: Clarion Books, 1973.

▶ Songs, Word Play, Letters

Songs and Poems

Continue to sing familiar songs and recite poems. Add your favorites to the collection. See pages 125 and 155 for suggested sources.

Alphabet Letter Knowledge

Continue to develop children's ability to name uppercase letters. Sing the "BINGO" song. Then show children how you can make new words with the same letters using the flannel board letters. Put G and O on the flannel board and read "GO" to the children. Then substitute N for G and read "NO." Replace other letters to make new words (bin, win, tin, sing, ring). See Story-Character "Bingo" Song on page 115 for another innovation on "Bingo."

Story Words

Choose several new words from the story *Duck in the Truck* or another choice. As you read, provide brief explanations of the words or point to the illustrations to clarify meaning. Reinforce new words by playing the "I'm Thinking of ___ Clue Game." You can provide meaning, sound, and picture clues to help children guess the words.

▶ Let's Find Out About It

Be a Builder

Tell children that they know about road construction vehicles, and that big equipment is also needed to build a house. Carpenters and roofers are also needed, and so on. Introduce house building by reading *Builder* or another book on this topic of your own choice. Ask children what job they would like to have for building a house. If possible, visit a place in the neighborhood where a house or other kind of building is under construction.

Book Suggestion

- *Builder for a Day.* New York: Dorling Kindersley Limited, 2003.
- Gibbons, Gail. *How a House Is Built.* New York: Holiday House, 1990.
- Llewellyn, Claire. *Trucks.* Danbury, CT: Scholastic Library Publishing, 1996.

▶ Center Time

Book Browsing

Add information books on building a house to the Book Area.

Dramatic Play

Add a construction hardhat and overalls to this center, if possible. Provide tools safe for children, such as a tape measure, socket wrench, level, and empty paint cans with brushes.

▶ Small Groups

How Food Tastes

Children enjoy talking about food and how it tastes. Begin by showing pictures of food and/or actual samples of food for children to taste. (Check on allergies first!) Remind them of foods they may have had for snack or lunch, of the lemonade they made recently, and of the treats in the piñata. Ask children to describe how specific foods taste, and help them remember the words *sweet, sour, salty,* and *spicy.* Start a chart that looks like the one below and have children add ideas for foods for each taste.

How Food Tastes

Sweet	Sour	Salty	Spicy
jam	lemon	pickles	pepperoni
honey			anchovies

IF YOU'RE HAPPY

1. If you're happy and you know it, clap your hands. *(clap, clap)*
   If you're happy and you know it, clap your hands. *(clap, clap)*
   If you're happy and you know it, then your face will surely show it.
   If you're happy and you know it, clap your hands. *(clap, clap)*
2. . . . stomp your feet. *(stomp, stomp)* . . .
3. . . . shout, "Hurray!" *(Hurray!)* . . .
4. . . . do all three. *(clap, clap, stomp, stomp, Hurray!)* . . .

BINGO

1. There was a farmer had a dog,
   And Bingo was his name-o.
   B – I – N – G – O,
   B – I – N – G – O,
   B – I – N – G – O,
   And Bingo was his name-o.
2. . . . *(clap)* – I – N – G – O! . . .
3. . . . *(clap)* – *(clap)* – N – G – O! . . .
4. . . . *(clap)* – *(clap)* – *(clap)* – G – O! . . .
5. . . . *(clap)* – *(clap)* – *(clap)* – *(clap)* – O! . . .
6. . . . *(clap)* – *(clap)* – *(clap)* – *(clap)* – *(clap)* . . .

DOWN BY THE BAY

1. Down by the bay *(echo)*
   Where the watermelons grow, *(echo)*
   Back to my home, *(echo)*
   I dare not go. *(echo)*
   For if I do, *(echo)*
   My mother will say, *(echo)*
   "Did you ever see a snake baking a cake?"
   Down by the bay.
2. . . . "Did you ever see a frog walking a dog?" . . .
3. . . . "Did you ever see a mouse painting a house?" . . .

Suggestion:
Make up new rhyming verses (*a pig dancing a jig, a cow taking a bow, a hen counting to ten . . .*).

HEAD AND SHOULDERS, KNEES AND TOES

Head and shoulders, knees and toes, knees and toes,
Head and shoulders, knees and toes, knees and toes,
Eyes and ears and mouth and nose,
Head and shoulders, knees and toes, knees and toes.

Motion:
Touch each part of the body named as you sing.

Suggestion:
Sing the song four more times. The first time, leave out the word *head* and just do the action. Continue to drop body part words till you are just performing the actions.

EENTSY, WEENTSY SPIDER

The eentsy, weentsy spider went up the water spout.
Down came the rain and washed the spider out.
Out came the sun and dried up all the rain,
And the eentsy, weentsy spider went up the spout again.

Motions:
A. Make circles with thumbs and index fingers of both hands, close circles and twist upward.
B. Wiggle fingers and bring hands down.
C. Push hands out toward sides.
D. Make a circle with arms above your head.
E. Wiggle fingers and move hands up.

OLD MACDONALD HAD A FARM

1. Old MacDonald had a farm, E – I – E – I – O!
   And on his farm he had some chicks, E – I – E – I – O!
   With a chick, chick here, and a chick, chick there,
   Here a chick, there a chick, ev'rywhere a chick, chick,
   Old MacDonald had a farm, E – I – E – I – O!
2. And on his farm he had some ducks, E – I – E – I – O!
   With a quack, quack here, and a quack, quack there,
   Here a quack, there a quack, ev'rywhere a quack, quack,
   Chick, chick here, and a chick, chick there,
   Here a chick, there a chick, ev'rywhere a chick, chick,
   Old MacDonald had a farm, E – I – E – I – O!
3. . . . cow . . . a moo, moo here . . . *(Repeat duck and chick sounds.)*
4. . . . turkey . . . a gobble, gobble here . . . *(Repeat cow, duck, and chick sounds.)*

Motions:
A. Move head up and down.
B. Put thumbs under arms and flap elbows.
C. Close fists and motion as if milking a cow.
D. Hook thumbs together and wiggle fingers.

Add more animals to continue the song. (Horse, *neigh, neigh* while lifting feet like a high-stepping steed; rooster, *cock-a-doodle-doo* while flapping hands against sides; goat, *baaa-baaa* while tossing head, index fingers held up for horns)

THE WHEELS ON THE BUS

1. The wheels on the bus go round and round,
   Round and round, round and round,
   The wheels on the bus go round and round,
   All through the town.
2. The people on the bus go up and down,
   Up and down, up and down,
   The people on the bus go up and down,
   All through the town.
3. The horn on the bus goes toot, toot, toot . . .
4. The money in the box goes ching, ching, ching . . .
5. The wiper on the glass goes swish, swish, swish . . .
6. The driver on the bus says, "Move on back" . . .

Motions:

A. Circle fists in a forward, round and round motion for a wheel.
B. Bounce up and down in seat.
C. Push palm outward as if pressing the horn.
D. Pretend to drop coin in a box.
E. Move forearms left to right like windshield wipers.
F. Gesture with thumb over shoulder.

OPEN, SHUT THEM

Open, shut them.
Open, shut them.
Give a little clap, clap, clap. *(clap, clap, clap)*
Open, shut them.
Open, shut them.
Put them in your lap, lap, lap.
Creep them, creep them *(walk fingers up chest to chin)*
Slowly creep them
Right up to your chin.
Open up your mouth *(open mouth)*
But do not let them in.

FIVE GREEN AND SPECKLED FROGS

Five green and speckled frogs
Sat on a speckled log,
Eating some most delicious bugs.
YUM! YUM! (spoken)

One jumped into the pool
Where it was nice and cool.
Then there were four green and speckled frogs.
GLUB! GLUB! (spoken)
(Repeat in descending order until there are no frogs left on the log.)

FIVE LITTLE DUCKS

Five little ducks went out one day,
Over the hill and far away.
Mother duck said, "Quack, quack, quack, quack."
But only four little ducks came back.
(Repeat, losing one more duck each time until you are left with one duck. For the last verse, have mother duck say "Quack, quack, quack, quack," and then end with "And all five little ducks came back.")

CLAP YOUR HANDS

1. Clap, clap, clap your hands,
   Clap your hands together.
   Clap, clap, clap your hands,
   Clap your hands together.
2. Stamp, stamp, stamp your feet . . .
3. Shake, shake, shake your hips . . .
4. Bend, bend, bend your knees . . .

THE MORE WE GET TOGETHER

Oh, the more we get together,
Together, together,
Oh, the more we get together,
The happier we'll be.

For your friends are my friends,
And my friends are your friends,
Oh, the more we get together,
The happier we'll be.

WHAT ARE YOU WEARING?

1. Mary's wearing a red dress, red dress, red dress.
   Mary's wearing a red dress all day long.
2. Pedro's wearing a white shirt . . .
3. Keisha's wearing a blue coat . . .
4. Tony's wearing a yellow hat . . .

COME ON AND JOIN IN TO THE GAME

1. Let everyone clap hands like me. *(clap, clap)*
   Let everyone clap hands like me. *(clap, clap)*
   Come on and join in to the game,
   You'll find that it's always the same.
   (clap, clap)
2. Let everyone sneeze like me. *(ah-choo!)*
   Let everyone sneeze like me. *(ah-choo!)*
   Come on and join in to the game,
   You'll find that it's always the same.
   (ah-choo!)
3. Let everyone yawn like me. *(yawn, yawn)*
4. Let everyone jump up like me. *(jump)*
5. Let everyone sit down like me. *(sit)*
6. Let everyone laugh like me. *(ha-ha)*

SIX LITTLE DUCKS

Six little ducks,
That I once knew—
Fat ones, skinny ones,
Fair ones, too.

(Chorus)
But the one little duck
With the feather on his back,
He led the others
With a quack, quack, quack.
Quack, quack, quack,
Quack, quack, quack.

Down to the river—
They would go,
Wibble, wobble, wibble, wobble,
To and fro.

(Chorus)
Back from the river—
They would come,
Wibble, wobble, wibble, wobble,
Ho, hum, hum.

Glossary

alphabetic principle the concept that letters and letter combinations are used to represent phonemes

alphabet letter knowledge the knowledge of the names and shapes of letters

cardinal numbers numbers that tell how many

comprehension Listening comprehension refers to the ability to understand spoken language. Reading comprehension refers to the ability to understand what one reads.

comprehensive curriculum a curriculum that provides content reflective of standards across all domains: language and literacy, mathematics, science, social studies, social and emotional development, physical development, and the arts

concepts of print the growing understanding of how print functions and how books are used; concepts include the distinction between pictures and print, knowing that English is read left to right and top to bottom, and understanding that print is always read the same

consonant a speech sound or phoneme that is not a vowel and is formed with obstruction of the flow of air with the teeth, lips, or tongue

decoding the use of relationships between printed letters and the sounds they represent to translate print into words

early reading the initial phase of reading during which children develop a basic understanding of how to read. This phase includes children's early interactions with books and other print, pretend reading, growing familiarity with print, and initial ability to read selected words.

early writing the initial phase of writing during which children gain familiarity with and control of the elements of print. This phase includes scribble-writing, creation of letter-like forms, inventive spelling, playful uses of written forms, and writing of names and selected words.

expository text nonfiction; any text that is not fiction, such as an information book, map, chart, schedule, and game instructions

integrated curriculum a curriculum that addresses several domains of learning together and provides a broad range of experiences. An integrated curriculum is often organized around units of study.

literacy the term used to refer to reading, writing, and the creative and analytical acts involved in producing and comprehending texts

nonstandard measurement measurement done with objects, such as craft sticks or string, rather than with standard tools, such as a ruler or tape measure

observational assessment the gathering of information about children by watching them, usually in the context of typical, on-going classroom activities

one-to-one correspondence the pairing of items from one set with the items in a second set

onset the consonant(s) at the start of a syllable. The remainder of the syllable is called its rime. In *pail*, *p* is the onset and *ail* is the rime.

ordinal numbers numbers that designate the place of an item in a series, such as *first, second, third*

patterns regularities that occur systematically, such as two red blocks, three blue blocks; two red blocks, three blue blocks, two red blocks, three blue blocks

phonemes the smallest units of sound that combine to form syllables and words. For example, *pond* has four phonemes: /p/ /o/ /n/ /d/.

phonemic awareness the conscious awareness that words are made up of segments of speech that are represented with letters and the ability to focus on and manipulate individual phonemes; for example, *Brad* without /b/ is *rad*. This competence requires attending to sounds, rather than to their meaning.

phonological awareness the awareness of the sounds of speech apart from meaning. It includes attending to syllables, onsets and rimes, and phonemes. This is a more encompassing term than *phonemic awareness*.

print awareness growing recognition of the conventions and characteristics of written language, such as print carries meaning, a book is held upright, and pages are turned from front to back. It also includes understanding the concept of a letter and the concept of a word.

predictable text book books that use rhyme, alliteration, repetition of a sentence pattern, and other devices that make a text relatively easy for children to recall

rational counting matching a number word in order to each item in a set; understanding that the last number word tells how many items are in the set

retelling process of recounting, or telling what happened; a personal narrative or story heard from a book

rime the portion of a syllable that follows the onset. In *pail*, *p* is the onset and *ail* is the rime.

rote counting recitation of the number words used for the counting sequence; done from memory, without enumerating anything

rubrics sets of descriptive behaviors that are used to describe the abilities individuals are developing in selected areas. Teachers use rubrics to help determine a child's developmental status and plan instruction.

scaffolding instructional support that teachers provide to enable a child to complete a task. That support is carefully reduced over time as the child is more able to work independently.

self-regulation the ability to control one's behavior in ways that enable one to engage in social interactions in an acceptable manner

social skills behaviors used for initiating and sustaining interactions with others

standard measurement measurement done with standard tools, such as a ruler, tape measure, or scale

standard units of measurement conventionally recognized units, such as inches, feet, pounds, ounces, and miles

syllable a unit of pronunciation that is organized around a vowel. It may or may not have consonants before or after the vowel. For example, the word *baby* has two syllables: *ba* and *by*.

vocabulary words a person understands and can use

vowel an open phoneme that is the nucleus of every syllable (*a, e, i, o, u,* and sometimes *y*)

Index